BEHIND
the PIT WALL

BEHIND the PIT WALL

My life in Formula One and beyond

Bob McMurray

with Eric Thompson

HarperSports

An imprint of HarperCollinsPublishers

Wherever possible, the authors and publishers have made every attempt to determine the ownership of photographic material used in this book. However, it has not been possible to establish the origin and ownership of some photographs given to Bob McMurray. If anyone has information about the source of these photographs, please contact the publishers in the first instance.

HarperCollins*Publishers*

Harper*Sports*
An imprint of HarperCollins*Publishers*

First published in 2010
by HarperCollins*Publishers* (New Zealand) Limited
PO Box 1, Shortland Street, Auckland 1140

HarperCollins*Publishers*
31 View Road, Glenfield, Auckland 0627, New Zealand
25 Ryde Road, Pymble, Sydney, NSW 2073, Australia
A 53, Sector 57, Noida, UP, India
77–85 Fulham Palace Road, London W6 8JB, United Kingdom
2 Bloor Street East, 20th floor, Toronto, Ontario M4W 1A8, Canada
10 East 53rd Street, New York, NY 10022, USA

National Library of New Zealand Cataloguing-in-Publication Data

McMurray, Bob.
Behind the pit wall : my life in Formula One and beyond /
Bob McMurray with Eric Thompson.
ISBN 978-1-86950-854-8
1. McMurray, Bob—Career in automobile racing. 2. Automobile racing.
I. Thompson, Eric, 1958- II. Title.
796.72092—dc 22

Cover design by Carolyn Lewis
Cover images of TRS supplied by Bruce Jenkins
Typesetting by Springfield West

Printed by Printlink, Wellington

Special thanks to
TOYOTA I *Believe*

Foreword by Mika Hakkinen

Finn Mika Hakkinen raced for only two teams, Lotus and McLaren, in his Formula One years from 1991 to 2001. He joined McLaren in 1993 and won two Formula One world championships in 1998 and 1999. He had 165 race starts, won 20 times, was on the podium 51 times and sat on pole 26 times. In many circles he's regarded as one of the best F1 drivers of the modern era.

It came as a surprise, albeit a pleasant one, when Bob asked me to contribute the Foreword to his book. Over his years at McLaren he got to know many great drivers and world champions, and so I welcome the opportunity to write something.

I was with Team Lotus in 1991 and 1992 and Bob was with Ron Dennis then. I believe the McLaren people had been keeping an eye on me, and when they saw I was doing a good job at Lotus they decided to take me to the McLaren team.

Bob was very, very close to Ron, and it was automatic that when I was contracted to the team Bob came into the picture immediately. He gave me great, great support from day one.

When I first met Bob I sometimes struggled to understand his New Zealand sense of humour. It gradually got through to me, though, and after a while I came to realize he was a very big-hearted man and a positive person. He was a hard-working member of the team and would stop at nothing to help people out. Bob was a lot like Ron himself in that they were always working hard on the small details to make sure the big things worked really well in the team.

Bob and his wife, Shaune, helped me settle into the team but it's hard to single out any one person for their contribution. Racing is a team sport; everyone has to do their bit to make the big picture work, and everybody supports everyone else because it's a tough business.

It's no easy life travelling all around the world and handling the disappointments that racing in Formula One can throw at you. It's not always about winning, but it *is* all about teamwork. And as I mentioned earlier, Bob was very close to Ron and so naturally I got very close to Bob.

I had some incredible times, and not always the best, in my early racing at McLaren in 1993. It wasn't that fantastic a start for me there, even though I out-qualified Ayrton Senna that year. But I was young and when going flat out made a mistake and flew off the track. That was really disappointing; I thought it was the end of the world and I'd lost everything. But Bob and everyone else at McLaren were incredibly supportive. They said, 'Hey Mika, there's another race coming up so think positive and put your foot down, man.'

At the same time, McLaren were very demanding when it came to performing — as they should have been — and Bob was a tough guy. I found him to be *really* hard, actually, until I steadily got to know him better and began to realize he only had the best for all of us at heart.

I even visited him in New Zealand once; I went to his and Shaune's house where we had a great barbecue. It is when you see this couple at home, away from the tough environment and heavy responsibilities of working in Formula One, that you truly realize what fantastic people they are.

Bob and Shaune are absolutely brilliant people. I have always found it a pleasure to know them and work with them, and even after so many years it is good to talk about them — and heart-warming to remember just how much support they gave me.

Mika Hakkinen

Contents

Introduction

Over the following pages I'll be taking a ramble through my life, both on and off the track, with the intention of recreating some of the colour, interesting characters and strange and humorous stories I remember from my wonderful years as a mechanic and head of hospitality with the McLaren Formula One team.

This is by no means a chronological account of my years in motor racing. If you're after a lap-by-lap commentary on every race I attended while working for McLaren, this is not the book for you. Who set the fastest time at Monaco on lap 32 in 1987 and in what car on what tyres, what coloured overalls he was wearing and whose logo was on his helmet can be found on the Internet, not here.

Within these covers is a tale of how a great motor-racing team was started by New Zealander Bruce McLaren. This enterprise became one of the leading lights of Formula One, which it still is today. In terms of what it has achieved on the track, McLaren is second only to Ferrari.

I have interwoven my stories from both the pit paddock and away from the racetrack. I explain how every time I tried to leave, somehow I was enticed to stay. There are stories of adventures we had on the high passes of European mountain ranges, dicing with death in a helicopter being flown by an ex-combat pilot, and getting out of more scrapes than you can poke a stick at.

Since retiring from globetrotting as part of McLaren International Racing I've been asked the same question a thousand times: 'When was the best era in Formula One?' My standard answer is, 'Best for whom?'

It depends on your perspective. For the drivers it was the time they were at their peak, racing competitively and on a good day winning a Grand Prix, or the ultimate, a world championship. For the mechanics it was when they were building and maintaining a championship-winning car.

For the rest of us, and probably for fans at large, it was when we were all aged between 18 and 45. That's when you could work hard, play even harder and still manage to get up in the morning and make it to work on time to do a bloody brilliant job. Along the way, if you were lucky enough or you just happened to be in the right place at the right time, you got to experience the full wonder of travel and the excitement of being part of the glamorous sport of Formula One, which is raced in some of the most exotic places in the world.

I was fortunate to have been introduced to the world of F1 at about the age of 20 and after an on-off relationship, soon became completely immersed in the sport and remained so until I turned 55. With hand on heart, I'd have to say not a single day was all bad, except of course, when news came through of a tragedy, and I don't just mean one involving a driver.

Part of the attraction and fulfilment I got from the job was because Ron Dennis was my boss for virtually the entire journey. But the icing on the cake was being able to work with my wife Shaune for around 20 of those years. There are not many couples who can say they worked together for that long, touring the world and meeting some of the most interesting characters you'd find anywhere.

I arrived in Formula One when the sport was going to either implode or make the great leap into an uncertain future, embracing the concept that to survive, it had to become a profitable business. A key part of that strategy would be to establish itself as a global player in television markets and ratings. Who would have thought back in the late 1970s that F1 would be racing in China, the Middle East and Singapore (the latter under lights)?

There were battles both on and off the track. Political interests and personal egos were clashing with such ferocity that — to borrow a quote from British politician Enoch Powell from around the same time — the streets (of pit lane) could easily have run with rivers of blood. Talk about birthing pains! As the world of motorsport morphed into the financial behemoth we now recognize, the paddock became littered with destroyed (or severely battered and bruised) egos and careers.

All of which were fun and games to watch from inside the tent, rather than from outside as most of the world did. It was a time when global corporations had so much money sloshing about that they had to chuck it at something — so why not Formula One? Man and his racing machines had come of age and the characters were just as exciting as their highly tuned race-cars. Mind you, we will not see the likes of James Hunt, Niki Lauda, Keke Rosberg, Jackie Stewart, Gilles Villeneuve and Ayrton Senna again.

Many of today's drivers have had a personality bypass and are programmed to be their sponsor's mouthpiece or puppet. Not to worry — things change and move on for better or worse, but it would be great to again see some of the personal battles that made F1 as fiery off the track as it was on it. Some of the world's largest corporations were flooding the paddock with more cash than had ever been invested in a single sport. There were a few millionaires involved with the Formula One teams in the early days, but that was to change over the coming decades until F1 boasted more cash per square metre of paddock space than any other sport. I saw paddock revolution, driver tantrums, industrial espionage, intrigue and more scandal than an American soap could ever dish up. I also enjoyed more friendships, fun, camaraderie and the closest bonding between team members than is possible to convey in words.

This book is not about just the racing side of Formula One. What I want to share is 'Bob's Big Adventure' — one that was inspired by being part of a motor-racing travelling circus — and to try to give an accurate and entertaining account of my years with McLaren.

I have not set out to malign anyone, or to seek revenge in print, as almost without exception everyone with an active role in F1 got there because they were driven to succeed. Be they a truck driver, garage floor painter, race strategist, team owner, F1 driver, chef or mechanic, each had a burning desire to be part of Formula One. You do not stay in F1 for long if you are not competitive and determined to excel in your own field. Therefore, all those people in the paddock, whether I liked them or not, had their own characters and strengths.

There's a saying in Formula One that you make thousands of acquaintances and very few friends. Yet many of the people I met during my years of involvement in the sport have become lifelong friends and many are mentioned in this book — although a few of the names may have been changed to protect the innocent, if you get my drift.

I was lucky enough to have met royalty from at least a dozen countries, stars from the big and small screen — some of whom, like David Niven, are no longer around — pop stars, world-famous political figures, and people who were just stars in their own eyes.

As most of us eventually realize, the older we get, the more people from various walks of life we meet. It can sometimes be said that the ordinary folk are actually the most interesting. Those anonymous people, who simply wanted to see what the inner paddock of Formula One was like, gave me some of my most rewarding moments.

For example, there was this young lad named Stuart Hullah who was confined to a wheelchair; he looked really ill and I wondered how long he might live. It had been his lifelong wish to get behind the scenes and have a peek at what it was like being part of a successful Formula One team. The visit was duly arranged, Stuart got his wish and the McLaren boys rallied around and raised enough cash to buy him a new wheelchair. The paint shop gave it a going over and re-sprayed it in the McLaren racing Day-Glo red. Ron Dennis presented him with Ayrton Senna's gear lever as his joystick to operate the chair.

Stuart eventually moved on to the big paddock in the sky, but the smile on his face when he was presented with the chair and Ayrton's gear lever, and on the faces of his parents and sister when they visited the paddock on occasion, outshone any superstar visit for us.

I hope after reading this book you'll be able to understand just how much pleasure it was for me to spend most of a working life being part of a sport I love. There are so many people I should mention and thank that it's simply not possible to do so without making it a separate chapter. Suffice to say, 'They know who they are.'

My special thanks go to Eric Thompson for listening to me go on for hours reciting my various stories and then crafting them into something we both hope you'll enjoy. There are three other people I owe a huge debt of gratitude to. I want to thank my wife Shaune for allowing me to live my dream for so long, and my parents Ernie and Maisie for pointing me in the right direction.

Finally, I'd also like to thank the people at McLaren for allowing me to be part of the greatest team in Formula One. Of course this includes the many drivers I've had the pleasure of meeting, socializing with and at times getting close to. I owe a special debt of gratitude to Ron Dennis, who generously gave me some 35 years of patronage and friendship. On many occasions when my overly excited temper should have resulted in my getting the proverbial black flag, RD simply listened and gave me another chance. I cannot thank him enough, but I hope this book will give him and you a sense of what I experienced during my years with his team.

Bob McMurray

McLaren's quick-fire stats

I don't intend going into any great statistical depth about the McLaren Formula One team but I think the book deserves a quick summary of what was achieved over its long and illustrious career. Other sources can provide a year-by-year, race-by-race and even a lap-by-lap breakdown of McLaren's history, so I'll just paint the big picture here.

The McLaren F1 team is the second most successful F1 team behind Ferrari, but the Italians had a head start, beginning racing in 1950, while Bruce set up his team in 1963. Back then the team was called Bruce McLaren Motor Racing Limited and three years later they made their debut at the 1966 Monaco Grand Prix. McLaren scored their first F1 Grand Prix win in 1968, when Bruce piloted a McLaren Ford to victory. Tragically, though, the New Zealander lost his life in a Can-Am testing accident at the Goodwood Circuit in England in 1970, but the team continued his legacy, winning races in Formula One and expanding into Indy after dominating Can-Am racing since 1967.

In 1974 the team celebrated its first Formula One drivers' and constructors' championship win, with Emerson Fittipaldi in the McLaren Ford M23. The next drivers' championship came courtesy of English driver James Hunt, behind the wheel of the McLaren Ford M23 in 1976.

To date the team has achieved the highest number of double race wins of any pair of Formula One drivers with team-mates Ayrton Senna and Alain Prost notching up 14 wins between them in the 1988/89 season. The Senna/Prost partnership also holds the accolade for the most Grand Prix wins in a season. In 1988 the pair won 15 out of the 16 races on the calendar.

The team has won four consecutive drivers' and constructors' championships (1988–1991) and secured eight constructors' world championship titles, the first of which was in 1974. By early 2010 the team had a record 12 drivers' world championship titles and eight constructors' world championships.

FORMULA ONE STATISTICS

Number of races: 664

Grand Prix victories: 164

Formula One Drivers' World Championships: 12

Formula One Constructors' World Championships: 8

Pole Positions: 145

Podiums: 436

Double Wins (1-2s): 44

Fastest Laps: 136

12 Formula One Drivers' World Championships

Driver	Wins*	Championships*
Lewis Hamilton	11	1 — 2008
Heikki Kovalainen	1	0
Fernando Alonso	4	0
Kimi Raikkonen	9	0
Juan Pablo Montoya	3	0
David Coulthard	12	0
Mika Hakkinen	20	2 — 1998,1999
Ayrton Senna	35	3 — 1988, 1990, 1991
Gerhard Berger	3	0
Alain Prost	30	3 — 1985, 1986, 1989
Niki Lauda	8	1 — 1984
John Watson	4	0

James Hunt	9	1 — 1976
Jochen Mass	1	0
Emerson Fittipaldi	5	1 — 1974
Denny Hulme	6	0
Peter Revson	2	0
Bruce McLaren	1	0
Total	**164**	**12**

*Whilst driving for McLaren

8 Formula One Constructors' World Championships

Constructor	Season
McLaren Ford	1974
McLaren TAG Porsche Turbo	1984, 1985
McLaren Honda Turbo	1988
McLaren Honda	1989, 1990, 1991
Team McLaren Mercedes	1998

Chapter 1

Rookie years

Some people will always remember the 2001 Monaco Grand Prix for the miserable sight of David Coulthard getting it horribly wrong on the grid when the lights went out. As the rest of the field streamed away, the Scotsman sat forlorn, all on his tod, having stalled the car after making pole the previous day. Needless to say, Michael Schumacher serenely went about his business, collecting his fifth trophy on the streets of the principality.

That incident sprang to mind as I was about to embark on my next big adventure after leaving McLaren. Although I was no longer physically at the races in 2002, I was now going to be Television New Zealand's expert commentator for the various rounds of the F1 championship. A long bow to draw in comparing an F1 race and my first live-in-front-of-the-camera-in-a-TV-studio-in-New Zealand gig you might think, but as with the Coulthard incident at Monaco, I knew it didn't matter how much pre-race preparation you did; if you didn't get it right on the day, it all came to nothing.

Media-wise I wasn't quite the blushing bride, as I'd been doing phone-ins from Grand Prix to TVNZ about the weather just before events. I was also doing race reports from most GPs for Pete Montgomery at Radio Sport every Sunday morning direct from the track. My first F1 commentary for TVNZ brought home to me how different this experience was going to be compared with being involved as a team member at the track. Moving on to another phase of my life, I would be a key link between Formula One and the New Zealand motorsports fan. Although I had never anticipated this kind of career-change during my McLaren years, my travels, contacts, experiences and 'total immersion' in the sport had set me up beautifully for this exciting new challenge.

While the drivers were going through their pre-race preparations, getting a well-balanced and nutritious meal inside them along with the correct hydration and having last-minute chats with engineers, mechanics, team principals, wives and girlfriends before suiting up, I too was getting my act together and dealing with my nerves.

Both camps were worried about making a mistake. In the drivers' case their error could result in a lengthy stay in hospital. Mine, on the other hand, would only make me look like a complete prat who didn't know his arse from his elbow.

The date was 26 May 2002 and this was my first big gig on New Zealand television. I was sitting in the control room watching other commentators and feeling very pensive indeed. I was praying to every god I could remember from Greek history at school, hoping the link to ITV in the UK would hold for the entire race. If the link broke, I'd have to pick up the dead air and fill in for the race commentary.

For 25 years I'd been at all the races working; now I had to comment on exactly what was going on during a race. To describe myself as scared would not be accurate, but there was certainly quite a sense of trepidation floating around inside me. I was fortunate my colleague for this venture — a half-hour build-up to the Grand Prix — was the vastly experienced Geoff Bryan. He's been a leading television sports presenter for more years than you can remember, and has all the necessary skills to comment on everything from archery to water polo and probably pigeon racing as well, although he had no in-depth knowledge of Formula One.

Aside from worrying about getting a driver's name wrong, or placing him with the wrong team, I was also concerned Geoff might not appreciate my occasional unasked-for intrusion, but he quickly put that to rest. He told me I was there to provide the kind of insight you can only get from working on the Formula One scene for a very long time. Thirty minutes before the red lights went out in Monaco, the green light came on in our TVNZ studio and we went live with our preview of the race.

I didn't just leave F1, jump on a plane and rock up to TVNZ telling them they needed me as an expert comments man because I knew F1. That sort of thing just doesn't happen — you have to have done some media work already, know your specialty better than most of your viewers and be able to explain things clearly and in an uncomplicated manner. It's not like the pretty young things who read from an autocue and smile sweetly. Doing expert commentary means you have to be able to think on your feet, answer all sorts of unexpected questions and interpret what's going on at any one time during the race. You have to try to second-guess team bosses and make sense of some bizarre decisions by pit bosses and drivers. Hard to get it right, easy to get it wrong.

I moved into commentary with some uncertainty but with my eyes wide open. I'd actually dabbled in the dark arts of media for a number of years. And it was at Monaco where it all began for me. The Monaco Grand Prix is regarded as one-third of the triple crown of motor racing, along with the 24 Hours of Le Mans and the Indianapolis 500, and is one of the most popular events on the F1 calendar.

Graham Hill is the only driver able to lay claim to a triple crown, having won the Monaco Grand Prix in 1963, '64, '65, '68 and '69, the Indy 500 in 1966 and Le Mans in 1972. There are a number of reasons the fans flock to the Monaco weekend, chief among them being that it's the place to be seen, and to see the beautiful people. Fans can also get up close to the racing. Monaco remains the only circuit where Formula One cars go through a tunnel, as the series hasn't raced at Detroit since 1988.

In 1991 I was working for McLaren as their hospitality manager, a position I'd held for several years. We had a number of guests at that year's Monaco race sitting in the grandstand at Casino Square. From there they had a fantastic view of the cars hurtling past at 200-plus kilometres an hour. All well and good as a spectator sport if no one actually wanted to know what was going on. At the revs the cars were pulling, to the uninitiated they must have sounded like a pack of wailing banshees. At such speed things are a bit of a blur, so it would have been a miracle if any of the guests could have picked Senna from Prost. It didn't help that they were in similar-coloured McLaren cars.

After much head-scratching and thought, someone at McLaren came up with the bright idea of providing our guests with headsets and feeding them a live personal commentary throughout the race. We contracted professional race commentator Ian Titchmarsh to do the job for the day. The plan was for him to sit in front of a TV screen and provide a continuous, expert commentary on the race as it progressed. Of course we'd never attempted anything like this before, although the technology had been around for a while.

Just to be safe we all agreed it would be wise to test the system during the practice sessions. On Thursday's free practice before race weekend there was a TV, a booth, a microphone, some headsets and all the paraphernalia, but no one to do the live voice-over. I must have been thinking about something else or making a few notes, because when I looked up, the place had been abandoned. Everyone else must have suddenly remembered there were a hell of a lot of very urgent jobs to be done. You get the picture.

Some smartarse also offered their opinion that it should be the hospitality manager's job to entertain our guests during the race. Not being able to come up with a decent enough excuse to get out of it, I duly picked up yet another hat and set about to trying to do my best rendition of Murray Walker.

Not being the most outgoing person in the world, I wasn't overly keen on doing race commentary to a bunch of people I didn't know, but I consoled myself with the thought that it couldn't be too hard. Wrong. Trying to keep track of 22 F1 cars flying across a tiny 14-inch TV screen verged on the impossible. By the time I managed to retrieve a driver's name from my brain, get it to my tongue and then out via my mouth, another three had blazed past. My first attempt may have been commentary but it sure as hell wasn't coherent.

By the time I finished my mangled effort my admiration for Murray Walker and John Watson, his co-commentator of the time, had grown enormously. So much had my respect grown for the pair that I went and apologized to them shortly afterwards. Like so many other people, I'd taken the mickey out of them about their cushy job. I was much relieved Ian Titchmarsh was going to do the real thing — as no doubt our guests would be, too.

Although my first foray into the world of media wasn't exactly a raging success, strangely enough that didn't deter the good folk at McLaren. We ran an exclusive Paddock Club for specially invited guests and corporate personnel that was expertly handled by Caroline Sayers. McLaren had to keep its profile high, so it was best to invite celebrities like Michael Douglas and Catherine Zeta-Jones, George Harrison and Boris Becker, to name but a few.

The corporate people who were there also wanted to get up close and personal with the team and the cars, as their companies had forked out a lot of money so Ron Dennis could take us all racing and, more than a few times, winning. Naturally, we wanted these people to have the most fantastic time when they arrived at a Grand Prix, so we provided them with all sorts of extras in an effort to enhance the overall experience. To add extra spice to the weekend, we installed a camera in the pit garage and a television in the Paddock Club. This allowed the guests to watch the inner workings of an F1 team and what the mechanics got up to without getting in the way of a crew member.

What we were doing was something of a new concept in the corporate entertaining field at a Grand Prix. A marketing person was conscripted to chat to our guests, explaining what the mechanics were doing and what various parts of the car did and how.

It started off with a 'live' mic as well, but too much colourful language was being picked up so we resorted to my having a personal mic. Selling a concept is all well and good, but when a specific question is asked about racecraft, mechanics, engineering or tactics, you need someone who has lived and breathed the sport. Therefore it was a natural progression to put an experienced motor-racing person in the garage to chat live to the assembled guests in the Paddock Club. A marketing person would have been well out of their depth, and since somebody had remembered that in an earlier life I had occasionally worked on race-cars alongside Bruce McLaren, it was decided I should be the one to do the garage reports.

'Great,' I thought, but there was no point in trying to argue when a decree has come down from on high. Accepting the *fait accompli* of my new role as a commentator, I decided I may as well try to enjoy it, as there would be only a few listening to me, rather than a global audience of a billion-odd people. The big plus for me was that I knew the sport, having spent so much time immersed in it.

Having made the leap of faith to convince myself I could do the job, I thought all would be plain sailing from there on. However, that proved a false expectation. I knew my audience was a select few who had been invited as guests of McLaren. Some would have absolutely no idea about Formula One, while others would be the trainspotters of the sport and would probably know the inside-leg measurements of all the mechanics. So trying to pitch a middle ground was always going to be hard.

The engineers and mechanics didn't help matters much in the garage when I had to interview them on camera. Although I knew my way around their precinct, the car, race tactics — to a certain degree — and a lot of other details, the audience back in the Paddock Club weren't there to listen to me bang on. They wanted to hear it from the people actually doing the business.

To begin with I had the upper hand, as I had the microphone and most people quite like the idea of being interviewed on television. Once I got into the swing of things I found I actually enjoyed this interviewing and commentating lark, and as I knew all the team it wasn't that onerous. At least that was the case until the novelty wore off with the mechanics and other team members and the pranks started.

At the start I had to sneak up on a member of the pit crew and grab a fistful of shirt to stop them running in the opposite direction. As my confidence grew in the job so did theirs, and before long we were old hands at it, which caused a few problems for me. The technicians (they were no longer called mechanics) had begun to gang up on me during an interview. While I'd be in the middle of a serious interview with one technician about downforce, the importance of the correct tyre pressure or how fuel load affects the balance of the car, his mate would be on his hands and knees out of line of sight of the camera.

In his hand he would have an aerosol can of brake cleaner, which he'd shove up my trouser leg and spray extremely cold stuff all up my leg. Meanwhile I had to keep a straight face, as the interview was being shown live back in the hospitality area. And it wasn't just the mechanics who liked to play the joker. Mika Hakkinen was McLaren's driver at the time and his favourite trick was to tie my shoelaces together while I was busy doing something else.

This reminds me of an occasion when a very intense journalist-turned-TV pundit called Mike Doodson was interviewing Swedish McLaren driver Stefan Johannson. Out of Doodson's sight, four motorhome crews including Shaune and me started doing a little jig and dancing about as well as doing impressions of John Cleese's Ministry of Silly Walks. After 10 minutes the cameraman had to stop filming because Stefan was laughing so much. When Doodson realized what had happened he went berserk. That's when it sunk in just how much effort it takes to set up a TV interview and get camera angles right. But it seemed amusing to us at the time.

As with many jobs, one thing can lead to another. My roving reporter act in the garage meant I was often asked to escort visitors around McLaren's Woking factory. A lot of New Zealanders came visiting including members of the Bruce McLaren Trust and previous team personnel. On one occasion former team mechanic Jim Murdoch turned up at the factory with his children, one of whom, Andrew, is now part of the New Zealand Olympic sailing team. The first thing he noticed was Denny Hulme's M7 Formula One car hanging from the ceiling in the reception area.

'Look,' he said to his kids, 'you can still see the elbow rests outside the cockpit. I made those in 1970.' Jim then went on to explain they'd been fitted to the car so that Denny could lever himself out after he'd burned his hands at Indianapolis. That piece of news was a revelation, as until Jim's visit, most people at McLaren had not been able to figure out what they were for.

In mid-October 1999 I hosted a guest who would turn out to play an important role in my future. TVNZ producer David Turner was in England covering the Rugby World Cup and being a keen motorsport fan, he took the opportunity to make the trip to Woking to see the McLaren operation. His timing was perfect: the team had just returned from a Grand Prix the previous day so there was plenty happening, and as he was the only visitor I had to look after, he got the full works on a very thorough tour. We got on well and in the usual manner made murmurings about keeping in touch. People often say things like that then never see each other again. We did, but I never got any Rugby World Cup tickets.

I met up with David in New Zealand later that year and twice more the following year, when he came to the Melbourne GP with TVNZ and interviewed me for his TV show — as he did again in 2001. I was at the Pukekohe race circuit south of Auckland in March 2001 and we met up again. The matter of televised motorsport coverage came up and I tried to delicately suggest I thought it could be improved. David was responsible for bringing free-to-air motorsport coverage to the country, and he agreed. When we met a few weeks later in Melbourne, I could hardly refuse when he asked me to take part in an Australian Grand Prix preview show.

It was almost an extension of the closed-circuit TV work I'd done in the past. I talked to David about the logistics involved in getting the McLaren crew to Australia and introduced a few of the team personnel, who talked about their roles in the team. It was brief, relatively painless and I thought little more of it. Clearly, though, it left David with the germ of an idea.

I'd told him I was planning to retire from my role with McLaren and return to New Zealand in the near future. Several months later that's exactly what I did. Before I had even finished arranging the office in the house the phone rang and it was David asking if I'd make a guest appearance on a television preview show for the 2001 Monaco Grand Prix with Wayne Munro in the lead role.

Snatches of our previous conversations flashed through my mind . . . TVNZ is mad paying so much for race rights without adding a decent preview programme . . . motorsport coverage here could definitely be improved, just look at the way ITV build the excitement with their pre-race show. With these utterances I'd managed to paint myself into a corner and that's how part two of my motor-racing career began and is what I'm still doing as I write this.

I'd love to be able to say I was born from motor-racing stock, with maybe Alberto Ascari as a godparent, Stirling Moss as an uncle and Piers Courage as a cousin. I can't even claim I came into the world in the back seat of a taxi as it raced to the hospital. My arrival actually took place at Hillingdon Hospital in Middlesex in 1947. My mother, Mary Kirkpatrick, came from Carrickfergus in Northern Ireland and was known as Maisie to her friends and — nobody knows why — as Midge by my father. His name was Ernest and he claimed to be one-third Irish as well, though I know of no evidence to support this. This is where it gets a bit odd in my family. His friends called him Ernie but my mother calls him Jim — that's the Irish for you.

I can't remember much about my early childhood years, but whatever I did wasn't enough to put my parents off children, because my sister Joanne arrived when I was five. We lived in a typical three-bedroom semi-detached house just like millions of others in England. Between them, Mum and Dad provided everything that Joanne and I needed — love, food, shelter, warmth, bikes and holidays. Although these were the post-war years in England, I never had a sense of being deprived of anything. At the same time, we weren't mollycoddled.

My father, who had a chrome-plating business, was a tall, strong, vigorous man — as he still is today in his early 90s. These days he works two jobs: mowing lawns for 'old people' and doing security work, believe it or not. Protecting what from whom I'm not too sure. He has always been determined to stay young, a tendency in him I discovered when I was 12.

On this occasion my friends and I had ridden our bikes home from school entirely on the footpath. Technically this was illegal, as I believe it still is today. In the late 1950s, though, policemen actually had the resources to take action against such villainous activity. We were followed the whole way by a copper puttering along on his Velocette motorbike. As we reached our house I could see my father standing on the doorstep with a look of thunder on his face. My heart took a nose-dive towards my feet and instantly I knew whatever trouble I'd ever been in before, a whole world of new hurt was about to be visited on me. 'Uh-oh guys, I'm in real trouble. There's my old man standing at the door,' I yelled to my friends.

My mates scarpered as I pulled up to the house. My father marched over to the policeman and told him he'd deal with me. I slunk inside, trembling. As soon as the door closed my dad grabbed the front of my shirt and hauled me up off the floor with one hand. 'If I ever hear you call me "the old man" again, I'll give you a cuff behind the ears,' he hissed through clenched teeth.

He dropped me onto the floor and marched off seething. I can't remember ever using that terminology again. Generally, though, we got on as well as any father and son could. I was always keen to spend time at Dad's work and after I'd turned eight he'd let me come down to the workshop and help him on Saturday mornings. I was so excited because I was allowed to use the metal-polishing machine — a perk of being the boss's son. I wanted to be just like all the men there, so

I tried to do everything they did. I even washed my hands like they did and that was a mistake.

Working in a chrome-plating factory gives you tough skin because there's a lot of acid splashing around and invariably some lands on exposed skin. So these guys used to clean their hands in a vat of weak sulphuric acid to really get all the dirt and grime off, as well as the odd layer of skin to toughen up the hands. Copying what the workmen were doing, I dipped my soft, lily-white, eight-year-old hands into the same solution and quickly pulled out a pair of bright red ones. The shock of immersing both hands in a vat of diluted sulphuric acid remains vivid in the recesses of my memory.

My dad and mum remain the people I admire the most. They are the best parents anyone could have had, and along with Ron Dennis, would be the biggest role models in my life.

I went to the all-boys Featherstone County Secondary Modern Boys School. Classes were streamed according to academic ability and I was always in the alpha stream, the top class, which meant I attracted more than the average amount of abuse from those in the lower streams. When I was made a senior prefect I was able to exact my revenge, although not necessarily on the right people. Senior prefects were allowed to stand at the school gates and question any boy who was late. Technically we were supposed to take their name and report them to the headmaster, but practically we took it on ourselves to reduce his workload and simply gave latecomers a hiding instead. It was the school tradition.

My favourite subject was English and I did pretty well at that. It helped somewhat that I really connected with the teacher, Ben Faure. He was the epitome of an English teacher, right down to his leather elbow patches, pipe and dandruff-dusted shoulders. He had an absolute passion for writing and he enthused his pupils so much that we all enjoyed practising our writing skills. Once I wrote a long story about two criminals who escaped from jail and became reformed citizens. It so impressed Mr Faure he entered it in a Middlesex schools' writing competition, where, to my surprise, it won. I was delighted and so was Mr Faure, though he was still a bit dubious about my future.

'If only you liked maths and physics too,' he said, 'that would give you a much better chance in life. Still, I expect you'll end up in a job writing or talking about cars.' It's spooky how teachers cotton on to these things so early.

I stayed at school until I was 16 and by that stage I'd sat my O-levels, matriculating in English, English Literature, Geography, Religious Instruction, Art, Metalwork and Physics — the latter only just. I also had a car at that stage, despite the legal age for driving in England at the time being 17. My father decided to help me buy one so I wouldn't get a motorcycle. My mother was dead set against the idea of a motorbike as she'd already had to patch me up after I'd fallen off the back of a friend's Velocette Four Square and ended up in the Western Road Bakers shop doorway.

I would have been able to buy a car myself from the savings I had, thanks to working for my dad, but it wasn't enough to get the sort of car my parents had in mind. They decided to loan me a few hundred pounds so I could buy something decent. I became the proud owner of a near-new, red Mini Cooper, registration number BMH272A. BMH soon came to stand for Bobby Mc's Hack, but I didn't care. As far as I was concerned it was a very cool car and I set about making it even cooler by adding fat wheels, a fat exhaust and all the other go-faster accessories I could get my hands on. There were no fluffy dice though.

Running a car in the early 1960s was no less expensive, relatively, than it is today and since I'd left school I really needed to get a job.

Given my success in English, I thought the advertising industry might appreciate my talents. I'd seen an advertisement in the paper seeking a writer to work on the Ford account at the J. Walter Thompson agency. What better job could there be, I thought? Getting paid to write about cars was about as good as it could get. Sadly, few 16-year-olds just walk into their dream job and I was no exception. There were dues to be paid.

To get to the heady heights of the advertising industry you had to start at the bottom of the heap, which meant being a lowly messenger. In today's hyperlinked world it's hard to imagine, or remember in my case, what life was like before email and the associated electronic revolution. In the early 1960s life ran at a much more sedate pace. In the world of advertising this meant copy — actual ink on real paper — was couriered from agency to client to printer, back to agency or any number of people and places, by the person employed as the messenger.

Fortunately, at about the same time I was looking for a job, an advertising agency called Notley's was looking for a messenger. I had all the qualities they were looking for — two legs, a couple of arms and a brain that mostly functioned, allowing me to catch the right bus to correct location and back again. On the other hand, Notley's had all the things I was looking for, like a job with wages, variety and prospects.

The offices were located just off Berkeley Square in Hill Street, Mayfair, which could be described as central London. It wasn't long before I was spending all day, every day walking around the area or catching a bus, or taxi, to where I had to go. I got to know London exceptionally well. I would have breezed The Knowledge exam London black cab drivers have to take before they can operate in the city of London.

The novelty of spending all day wandering around the city

delivering and picking up packages soon wore off and I started looking for other ways of making money that would involve cars. One of my messenger-mates at the time was a bloke called David Parkinson and together we decided to set up a weekend business. David's family lived in a massive house on the very up-market Wentworth Estate at Virginia Water. That was all very nice but it was the neighbours who interested us. Nearby lived game show host and presenter Bruce Forsyth, pop singer Engelbert Humperdinck, and others. As you would expect, these people had the most beautiful and expensive cars you could imagine — Rolls-Royces, Bentleys, Mercedes, Porsches, BMWs, Ferraris and other marques.

Dave and I figured the rich and famous were far too busy making money and being seen to worry about washing their cars. A niche market, we thought. Using his father's water and washing liquid, we spent part of the weekend removing dirt from cars and money from wallets. Being true entrepreneurs, we employed someone to clean the interiors and her name was Shaune Johnson, at the time my neighbour and later my wife. Sadly, several months into this venture, David's father discovered he was underwriting our scheme and promptly turned off the taps, hid the washing liquid and instructed us to take our sponges elsewhere. The car-wash business dried up overnight.

I wasn't too upset about the fledgling weekend business coming to a premature end, as I was enjoying life at Notley's. Things were moving along there quite nicely, and once I'd been there a year I even got involved in some of the actual advertising side of the business. One of the accounts I was involved in was Carven, the French perfume manufacturer. It may not seem a big deal now, but I'm proud to say my creative contribution to the company was the stripes on the side of the box for their Ma Griffe perfume. Those stripes are still there today.

Though I was having an increasing input into some of the creative

31

advertising decisions, this still didn't negate the daily grind of having to commute into London on the tube. Any readers who have had to wrestle with the London Underground will know what I mean. It's fine if you're a tourist visiting for a short while but using the city's transport system for six months during winter is soul-destroying. It tends to sap any enthusiasm you have for the job before you even set foot inside the office door.

My trip from Hounslow to Green Park was the best part of an hour each way and at 18 years of age I didn't feel like I should be living the same life as all the other lemmings on the tube. I made it to 18 months at Notley's before I threw in the towel and left to become a car salesman. It wasn't a spontaneous decision. I'd always been keen on cars and figured that I could make some real money by dealing in them.

Returning home, I joined the Mamos Group at Hillingdon Motors where I sold E-Type Jaguars and AC Cobras and other exotic beasts as well as Austin Allegros, 1800s and all sorts of bog-standard BMC cars. I then went to the Harrow showroom after a year to sell Rovers and other posh stuff, then six months later to Stanmore. Better yet, I had a company car, even though it was only a Morris 1100. I'd been at Hillingdon for only a year when I was transferred to the Stanmore branch in Middlesex and it was there that I really hit my stride.

On the lot was a used Mercedes no one had been able to sell. A local Jewish businessman was interested in it and he'd been haggling with the dealers for months over the price. When I came on the scene he became my customer and the negotiations began afresh. I decided to up the ante and offer to put a £10 set of mudflaps on the car to see if that would hook him. It did, the papers were signed and the car left the dealership with its new owner.

A few hours later the same guy who'd spent so much time haggling over the cost of the car invited the entire sales team out for lunch. I couldn't understand it and thought he must be barking mad. 'This lunch is costing you far more than you saved on the car,' I said to him over lunch. 'How come you're doing this?'

'When it's business, it's business,' he replied. 'But when it's pleasure, it's my own money that I've saved doing business and I can do whatever I want with it.'

In a roundabout way, that deal and customer sent me on my way to fame and fortune — well, sort of. The sale got me noticed at head office and I moved up the chain of command to become the youngest sales manager in the group. I had six people working for me and I received commission on each of their sales. I was making a fortune. At a time when £1000 a year would have been considered a good salary, I was raking in £8000 and here I was, still only 21.

The only thing that could have made things better was to get Shaune to marry me. After I plucked up the courage to pop the question, much to my surprise and relief she said yes. It was one of the best days of my life.

Shaune and I were virtually destined to be together. We'd first met when we were just five years old, as our parents were friends and we lived in the same neighbourhood. Her father worked for BOAC (forerunner of British Airways). Subsequently, the family moved about with his various postings, but the house near ours was their UK base.

Shaune was born in Bermuda and educated in Tokyo, Tehran, Bangkok and Zurich, and to a young 10-year-old lad she appeared to lead a very glamorous life. To be honest, I think I was in love with her from about 12, as she was great fun to be with and we got on really well — and still do 50 years later.

After nine years of on-and-off courtship, only because Shaune was often living somewhere else, we decided to get married at 21.

We planned to have a small wedding that was big on style. Shaune's sister Lynne and her husband Ian 'Griff' Griffiths, who was also my best man, had rented a lovely house with a pretty garden near Sunbury-on-Thames, which we thought would make a great place for the reception. The bonus was the local church, which was one of those idyllic, steepled affairs dating from the early 1800s.

Venue sorted, church organized, reception found and a honeymoon in Wales planned. Easy . . . or so you'd think. On the day, the best man and some of my other mates pointed out that it was important for the groom to visit the local pub for a few quiet ones before the ceremony. During the course of this intended quick visit, Griff lost count of how many 'a few' were and we all proceeded to get somewhat legless. Somehow we still managed to get to the church on time, but when we arrived we found the venue too was a little the worse for wear.

A couple of days earlier it had been closed for renovations. The builders had been in and started to pull a few things apart, leaving the place temporarily unsuitable for hosting weddings. Nobody had told us anything about this. Scratch idyllic church building and substitute Portakabins in the carpark. It wasn't quite the style Shaune and I had had in mind but we were there for each other, not the scenery, so we made the most of it. Our family and friends thought it was a hoot. They laughed so much during the ceremony the vicar had to stop and remind them about the sanctity of marriage.

Griff spent half the service leaning against me to stop himself collapsing, and of course he couldn't find the ring at the right time. To cap it off, during the final hymns he pulled his wallet out to pay the vicar. Well, at least we had the reception to look forward to.

About 35 people came back to Lynne and Griff's lovely cottage. At some point in the afternoon we started to notice a rather unpleasant smell in the air and thought their baby son Rhodri had left a small package in his nappy. He was duly changed and the soiled nappy flushed down the toilet. However, the smell remained. A little later someone noticed that the lid on the drain in the back garden had lifted with sewage seeping out. It turned out that the disposable nappies weren't actually that disposable and had blocked some of the drainpipes that were the main sewer line for the street. All the extra people using the toilet had overloaded the system and the nappy had been the final straw.

Shaune and I decided at that point it would be a good time to make an early exit. The last memory I have of the reception is of my father, my crazy Uncle Gus and another man using a bucket to ladle raw sewage out of the drain, still kitted up in all their wedding gear. Safely inside my Austin-Healey Sprite, we fled the scene, knowing that things could only get better but the smell would remain. Friends had played the prank where you place a fish in the heater intake vent, so we spent most of the trip with the windows open. It was only a six-hour drive to Caswell Bay in Wales where we were going to spend our honeymoon.

At 10 p.m. we arrived at the hotel and opened the bottle of champagne we had brought with us. The guesthouse didn't have any glasses close at hand so we settled for some very stylish tin cups to drink from before heading out for a romantic dinner. After everything that had happened so far on our wedding day, we should have known even the simple task of trying to find somewhere to eat in the local village of Mumbles in 1970 wasn't going to end as we hoped. Sure enough, everything was closed bar the fish-and-chip shop.

So we ordered today's dinner wrapped in yesterday's newspaper and sat on the end of the bed to enjoy our first meal as a married couple.

Chapter 2

Getting started

Every newly-wed couple would like to move into their own house and we were no exception. But despite our long courtship, Shaune and I hadn't arranged to rent a place once we got married. Instead, we moved in with Shaune's sister Lynne, her Kiwi husband Griff and their baby Rhodri.

Being keen on motorsport, I viewed the prospect of shifting in with Griff as a pretty good move. As a member of Bruce McLaren Motor Racing, Griff had considerable value to me as a brother-in-law. In the late 1960s and early 70s, motor racing was still very much an enthusiast's pursuit. If you were in the right place, knew the right people and had the right stuff, it wasn't too difficult to get involved with a team. So there was nothing all that unusual about my tagging along with Griff when he went to McLaren's Colnbrook workshop to work on race-car gearboxes.

It wasn't long before I also found myself up to my elbows in grease, fixing various things. Not being one to make much of a noise, I kept to myself at first and soon earned the nickname 'Nameless Mate'.

Becoming part of McLaren usually meant having a nickname bestowed on you. Some of the team were given nicknames without apparent rhyme or reason. Joint managing director Teddy Mayer was known as 'The Wiener' (after the Mayer sausage company in the US). Teddy was no relation to the American Mayer family but the name was a big deal in the US. The other joint managing director,

Phil Kerr, became 'Sunny Tours' because he arranged travel and accommodation. General manager Harry Pearce became 'Harry the Box' because he was responsible for packing equipment sent to the US.

Racing manager Alastair Caldwell was 'Garth', simply because he was square-jawed like the comic strip cartoon character. Welder Geoff Close became 'JC' because he wore a straggly beard and sandals even through the English winter. My brother-in-law Griff became 'Sinbad' because he'd worked for a while as a ship's engineer. Workshop manager Don Beresford was known as 'Mother', presumably because he oversaw the production of every car.

Mechanic Leo Wybrott, who came over from Lotus, was known as 'Squeak'. Jim Murdoch was called 'Sponge' because he had a massive Afro hairdo that looked like a sponge. Dennis Davis loved working at Indianapolis and was called 'Double D' not just for the obvious reason, but because Double D was a heavily advertised beer brand in England at that time. Mechanic David Luff became 'Mrs Muff' and another mechanic, Howard Moore, was 'H' for obvious reasons.

Howard was the number one mechanic on Emerson Fittipaldi's car in 1974 when he became world champion. Howard distinguished himself by owning a left-hand-drive Ferrari-engineered Fiat Dino that had been brought to England by a former McLaren mechanic who'd gone to work in Novarra, Italy for a year. Howard hadn't bothered to register the car in England either, so whenever he was stopped for speeding he would simply produce an Italian library card and pretend to speak their lingo.

I was with him the day when his scheme for getting off fines came unstuck. Howard was pulled up on the M4 motorway near Windsor by a cop who just happened to speak Italian fluently. The officer was not impressed by Howard's library card, nor by his fake Italian. He was lucky to get away with just a speeding ticket, and I remember the cop telling him in no uncertain terms in English to get the car registered and stop pretending to speak Italian.

Even though I'd been keen on cars all my life, I'd never really contemplated making a living out of working in the racing scene. However, all that changed at a BOAC 1000-kilometre world championship event held at Brands Hatch on 12 April 1970. That race, that day, heralded a change in my way of thinking about motorsport.

I stood in the pouring rain on the outside of Paddock Bend watching Mexican Pedro Rodriguez outclass the field. Lap after lap his 4.5-litre Porsche 917K swept over the brow of the hill and flew down the off-camber track as if the surface were dry. He never spun. He never backed off. And no one came remotely near him in speed or finesse. From seven laps down and in twelfth place, Rodriguez finished five laps ahead of second place. Watching him drive got me completely hooked on motorsport.

At the end of an evening's work at McLaren HQ, we would all head across the road to the Golden Cross pub for a few beers. Three or four sessions like that and you were pretty much one of the team.

I'd met Bruce McLaren at the workshop during one of my early visits there. He was very pleasant to me then, as he was on all the other occasions we met. He certainly never indicated that having untrained volunteers hanging around the place was a problem. What came across was his tremendous enthusiasm for racing, and the fact that he was way ahead of his time in his thoroughly modern approach to all things motor racing.

He was quietly spoken, but you got the idea he knew exactly what he had to do. I think his determination and passion for his sport inspired those who worked for him. He was certainly the leader of the team and had no difficulty getting people to help him — even amateur volunteers like me. I think part of his success stemmed from the fact he was an engineer and a driver and was intimately knowledgeable with most aspects of the team's work. You felt you were working for a person, not just a corporation. As Formula One got bigger, the line between working for someone, as opposed to something, has become increasingly blurred.

There were about 30 people employed at Bruce McLaren Motor Racing in the late 1960s whereas there are about 800-plus at Vodafone McLaren Mercedes, or whatever it's called these days. Even with a mere 30 crew, McLaren Racing back then was regarded as a large outfit. For example, in 1973 they fielded an entry in the Indianapolis 500, two Formula One cars, two Can-Am cars and a Formula Two car. By that stage there were about 45 people working for the company, but I still can't get my head around how they managed to keep all those balls in the air when it now takes 800 to get two F1 cars onto the grid in the 2000s.

I was now passionate about motor racing, so when another Kiwi, John Nicholson, turned up to live with the five of us I had no objection. John had arrived in England to work for the McLaren team as their Formula One engine builder. A competent driver himself, he competed in the Formula Atlantic series, which had replaced Formula 5000 in many countries due to the fact the cars had become so expensive. Even Formula Atlantic drivers need a crew so I pitched in and became part of his team, making it a crew of two with the occasional help from some other mates.

It was a great way to learn about all aspects of motor racing and I picked up a lot of mechanical knowledge during the three years we spent helping out. In 1971 we decided to shift to a large house in Englefield Green, near Wentworth in Surrey. Naturally, John came along. Like many New Zealanders in England, he acted as a magnet for new arrivals. There always seemed to be someone extra living in the house. I stopped being surprised at finding some complete stranger in the kitchen when I came down to breakfast. The person at the breakfast table would always turn out to be a friend of John's or Griff's or somebody's or a mate of a mate or one of John's ladies who'd just arrived in the country and was heading for a job at McLaren.

About this time, 1971, John was racing in Formula Atlantic in the UK in a March 702 race car. The car was housed and prepared in the garage-cum-shed that was part of the semi-detached house we were living in. Work on the car was done under the cover of darkness in a secret squirrel sort of way, as we didn't want to violate the lease on this very expensive and posh house. We overcame the problem of having a race trailer near the house by secreting it on a piece of lawn behind the hedge so passing folk wouldn't realize we were 'motor-racing' people.

Englefield Green was a very up-market area, and the neighbours in our no-exit street were a tight-knit lot. They included, among others, the Egham town clerk, the general manager of a large banking chain, the captain of the nearby Wentworth golf club, and the managing director of the huge sports store on London's Piccadilly Circus, Lillywhites. They had one thing in common: all were somewhat standoffish, in keeping with the general understanding of the English upper class.

The house, coincidentally, also backed on to a great little pub, and there was only a small fence between our garden and the pub. It didn't take long for us to fashion a small doorway to ease clandestine visits there and back to the establishment in various states of inebriation.

Despite being quite a useful driver, John didn't have any sponsorship, so everything was done on a shoestring. This meant John and his trusty mechanic (me) usually had to overnight at race meetings sleeping in the car. John often used to sleep with his Nomex underwear on underneath his racing overalls underneath his pyjamas. Oulton Park and Croft could get bloody freezing at night, especially when you're trying to hunker down in an unheated car in the middle of a paddock.

Late one night we were preparing the car in the by now rather cramped garage to leave early the next morning to get to Silverstone. John had to fire up the engine to do some work on adjusting the jets, or something, and we were trying to do this on the quiet.

The traditional way of muffling the sound was to hold a box containing damp rags over the exhaust. This all went according to plan and just after midnight we decided to call it a night and went inside the house to have a couple of beers. We were dog tired and soon headed off to bed. A couple of hours later Shaune woke up and decided to get herself a cup of tea. As she waited for the kettle to boil in the kitchen, she became aware of a burning smell. After a while, Shaune realized the smell was coming from outside. She opened the back door and the smell got stronger and by now really smelt like burning rubber. Smoke was starting to billow out from under the garage door and, with a sinking feeling, Shaune realized there were about 50 gallons of race fuel stored in there.

By this stage I had arrived outside the garage door as well and, without thinking, opened the side door, thankfully not to be confronted by a wall of flames but instead by clouds of thick black tyre smoke. Since there were no flames, I threw open the front garage doors to try to get rid of the smoke.

I realized what had happened. The rags used to muffle the sound of the exhaust had got very hot and been left on the right rear tyre, which had started to smoulder as well. Having worked out I wasn't about to enter a raging inferno, I quickly got the car out into the open and proceeded to get things under control — without waking up the neighbourhood at 2 a.m.

Just as I started to think we might get away with it, I heard the faint noise of sirens somewhere in the distance. To start with, I thought they were headed somewhere else, but soon the noise was getting louder and headed in our direction. Unbeknown to me, John's girlfriend had woken him up and then called the fire brigade.

Before long, four bloody great fire trucks were roaring up our street making enough noise to wake the dead. Talk about lights, noise and action — the place was lit up like a movie set and the neighbours' windows were lighting up like Christmas trees.

It must have been a quiet night for the emergency services because right behind the fire tenders came two ambulances, also sounding like a bunch of wailing banshees. If that wasn't enough, just to make sure everyone was awake in the area, three police cars joined the fray, adding their own particular noise. No place to hide now — our cover was well and truly blown.

By now the entire street was lining the pavement in various dressing gowns and over-garments, gawping at a smoke-filled garage owned by one of their friends who was on a two-year overseas business assignment, and it was clear that the precious family home had been rented to a bunch of itinerant gypsies with racing cars and an untold number of vagrants dossing down in various rooms.

The fire guys did their thing, the ambulance people realized they were not needed, and the cops, after looking at the race car and inviting the firemen to take photos of it, decided the fun was over and they all prepared to go back to their doughnuts at the station.

Just when we thought it couldn't get much worse, another car pulled up. The local press guy had heard about the commotion and decided it was newsworthy. Oh shit — this was all we needed. Any chance of keeping a lid on things was now well and truly impossible.

He did his interviews, and after a couple of hours the street eventually settled back into normal suburbia. While things around us got back to normal, we all realized our little game was up and the lease was sure to be revoked.

A couple of hours later, we decided we might as well still go racing and started to load the car onto the trailer. As we were tying it down, the town clerk walked over and we thought we were in for a bit of a rocket. He started, 'You can't have that race car in that garage any more.' Oh boy, I thought, here we go. But then he said, 'It'll be far too smoky in there for you to work on it, so why don't you put it in my garage when you come back from the weekend? It's twice the size and clean.'

While trying to get our heads around that offer of help, the Lillywhites guy also came over and offered us a large tarpaulin with which to cover the car while it was on the open trailer.

The bank manager followed and asked if he could help with the car and if we needed anything doing. A chap from two doors away came down and said he had some specialized tools we could use. The whole damn street adopted us as 'their' race team!

More was to come, though.

The local paper ran an article along the lines of 'local racers with no sponsorship suffer fire damage'. A West London paper then took up the story, which was seen by some people from Yellow Pages, who rang us and asked if we wanted to be sponsored by them.

'Of course we did!' we exclaimed, punching the air.

From the very next race, the car proudly carried their name and colours. It just goes to show that some clouds do have a silver lining.

Despite all the euphoria about the help and sponsorship deal, we still had a smoky garage to clean up. After we had spent hours, and a decent chunk of money, cleaning up the garage, when the lease finally expired, the owner made us forfeit our bond due to 'the damage'. There was none but apparently he'd somehow seen the newspaper article. Luckily, he didn't inspect the house because then he might have had some grounds to complain.

I was still out working in the real world and only playing at being race crew. An altercation with an inflexible bank manager forced me to chuck in my job as a very successful car salesman and look for a proper job. The then severely restrictive mortgage criteria held by British banks had forced my hand. Although I was earning a small fortune in commission, my base salary retainer was considered inadequate as income security for any mortgage lender. Never mind that my commission far outstripped the salaries of most people. Rules were rules and they weren't there to be broken for the likes of me.

So I gave up my high-paying job with the Mamos Group and started working for British European Airways (BEA) as a load controller. This was a reasonably responsible job, since I was the one who signed the piece of paper declaring the aircraft was safe to take off. I had to balance the weight of the passengers, freight and fuel to ensure there was a prescribed margin of safety. It wasn't adrenaline-pumping work as such, but if I got it wrong, instead of gracefully climbing towards the heavens, an aircraft could just as easily plough through the fence at the end of the runway with all the grace of an overweight pig with wings. And I would be in a hell of a lot of trouble.

It was rewarding in its own way, and I guess it exposed me to the science of logistics, which would come in useful later in life. Meanwhile, Griff was living the life of a racing team member, which meant a good deal of time away from home, including stints in the United States to work on the McLaren Can-Am cars. Even then it was demanding, perhaps more so than today because travelling times were longer, and Griff had made up his mind that he wasn't going to stay in motor racing forever but would return home to New Zealand. In 1972, this idea moved a step closer. When Griff went off to America for the Can-Am series, Lynne flew to New Zealand to have a look around at possible places to settle.

With neither of them home, the house at Wentworth seemed far too large, so we moved to Shepperton briefly and then Shaune and I finally became homeowners, buying a property in Stanwell. Our family still consisted of three because John moved with us. When Griff and Lynne came back from their respective travels they rented a cottage at Foxhills, partly, I think, because there was a garage attached to the house. A while later, Bruce McLaren's M6GT road car was stored in it.

The lack of space at the Colnbrook factory meant anything not immediately connected with the racing side of the team had to find a new home and the McLaren road car was one of those items. It had been stored at the garage for nearly a year and once a week Griff would wheel out this most beautiful of mechanical creations, feed himself inside it, flick a few switches, prime a few pumps and hit the button. Within seconds the mechanical gods would raise themselves from slumber and roar in unison. The sound of that car, when it settled down from a cold start, was truly music to the ears of anyone with an appreciation for a finely tuned and well-balanced engine. If there was such a thing as the nectar of the gods for the ears, this was it. And to top it all off, the car was sex on wheels — it looked amazing and it was fully road legal. Imagine a Can-Am car with plates — you couldn't get much better than that.

Around this time, Denny Hulme was still driving for the McLaren team and eventually he and one of the former team directors, Phil Kerr, shipped the car back to New Zealand. It was displayed at Auckland's Museum of Transport and Technology for a while, and then it went down to the Queenstown Motor Museum. In the mid-1980s, a Kiwi living in America bought the car and shipped it to the States. Today that epitome of engineering excellence is owned by Harry Mathews and is part of a collection of McLaren cars in Denver, Colorado.

This now brings me to one of the saddest days of my motor-racing career, 2 June 1970, the day Bruce McLaren died while testing at Goodwood. I was helping out down at the factory, working with a couple of mechanics getting things ready to drive down to Goodwood.

One of the crew came running into the workshop shouting there'd been an accident at the track and Bruce had been severely injured. Unfortunately it proved to be worse than that. While the new M8D Can-Am car was being put through its paces, the rear body shell flew off. The resultant loss of downforce threw the car off the track and straight into a concrete marshal's stand at 270 kph, killing Bruce.

In a sort of epitaph that can only happen in motor racing, 12 days later Dan Gurney won the opening Can-Am race of 1970 at Mosport for McLaren. The M8D won nine of the ten races that year and Denny Hulme won the championship. The following year Peter Revson, also driving a McLaren, dealt to the 1969 world champion Jackie Stewart, winning eight races and taking the title.

It's quite ironic, in an odd sort of way, what Bruce had said about the death of a team-mate of his earlier in the year.

'We sat on top of the pits in the sun at Longford waiting for the first practice session to start — Timmy Mayer, his wife Garrill, the mechanics — our team. We had a view of the picturesque countryside and immediately below was the paddock area.

'It was colourful, with polished sports and racing-cars and trade tents in the background.

'We were all happy. This was the last event of our tour. For two months we had worked, raced and relaxed together and, perhaps more than anyone else, Timmy was enjoying himself. He told me he really liked Australia.

'Intelligent and charming, he had made dozens of friends. As often occurs, to look at him you wouldn't take him for a racing-driver. You had to know him, to realize his desire to compete, to do things better than the next man, be it swimming, water-skiing or racing. So when, during the second practice session, he crashed at high speed and we knew immediately that it was bad, in our hearts we felt that he had been enjoying himself, and "having a go".

'The news that he died instantly was a terrible shock to all of us. But who is to say that he had not seen more, done more and learned more in his 26 years than many people do in a lifetime? It is tragic, particularly for those left. Plans half-made must now be forgotten, and the hopes must be rekindled. Without men like Tim, plans and hopes mean nothing.

'To do something well is so worthwhile that to die trying to do it better cannot be foolhardy. I can't say these things well, but I know this is what I feel to be true. It would be a waste of life to do nothing with one's ability; life is measured in terms of achievement, not in years alone.

'To those who have shown Garrill, his wife, Teddy, his brother, indeed all of our team, so much kindness and consideration, I want to say "thank you". Telegrams that arrived from all over the world bore testimony to Timmy's wide circle of friends and the loss they felt. Timmy was a true friend and a fine team-mate.'

(Bruce's eulogy for Timmy is courtesy of the Bruce McLaren Trust.)

It's almost as if Bruce had been writing his own eulogy. When the news of his death was confirmed, everyone in the workshop looked ashen-faced. We all drifted down to the Golden Cross pub that night so we could at least all be together. Everyone stood around wondering what on earth they were going to do, or worse, trying to decide if it had been an error on their part that had caused Bruce's car to go off the track. A heavy thought, I can tell you.

I remember thinking this must be what it feels like to lose your mother or father. The impact on people was so enormous I honestly thought the team would fold, and that Bruce's dream would die with him. It was the middle of the racing season and the next race on the calendar was Spa, where the team withdrew from competition as a mark of respect for Bruce.

The directors were not prone to knee-jerk reactions and made the decision to see out the rest of the season, reasoning they all loved motor racing, so why stop? That year they came fourth-equal in the constructors' championship, which justified their decision. It is to their great credit that Teddy Mayer, Phil Kerr, Tyler Alexander and Denny Hulme took the courageous option by choosing to continue. Of course, there was no way the team culture could ever be the same as it had been with Bruce at the helm. Teddy, who took over as managing director, was a lawyer and very much a corporate operator who was bound to leave a different mark on the place. Everyone agreed things would change and a new phase of McLaren Racing would begin. The most important aspect was that the team would continue.

Two people who also figured prominently for us in that late 1960s era were Bruce's wife Patty and their daughter Amanda. Shaune and I got on well with Patty when we saw her later in the 1970s when we were running the Marlboro hospitality unit. She was friendly with everybody including the mechanics, though she never helped make tea or sandwiches. Clearly she didn't want that kind of involvement. I'm not surprised because I remember Patty as very glamorous, one of the famous drivers' wives who used to sit on the pit wall timing the cars with stopwatches. In the days before electronic timing, drivers' wives were regarded as reliable and accurate timekeepers.

With Graham Hill's wife Bette, Patty became a leading light in the Doghouse Club, an informal group of leading racing-drivers' wives. Shaune and I remember Patty McLaren as a very nice lady and still enjoy her company when we meet occasionally.

In 1973 McLaren introduced the M23 at the South African Grand Prix with Denny Hulme making an immediate impression by putting the car straight on pole. Not being a bona fide signed-up team member, I wasn't at Kyalami to see it happen.

The world was at that moment hurtling towards an historic economic downturn brought on by the oil crisis. Every cloud has a silver lining, as they say, and in my case I stumbled upon a timely idea, one that offered me an opportunity to go out on my own. I had noticed that the price of plastics had rocketed up along with the price of oil, the latter being one of the raw materials. So with two willing partners, neither of whom had any money, I set up a dedicated plastics recycling company. I can confidently say we were way ahead of the tree-huggers and their dreamy ideas of trying to save the world. We saw a niche market and a chance to make some money and we went for it.

Initially I kept my job with BEA, but this was becoming more difficult as the recycling business gathered momentum, so I quit my day job and became a full-time entrepreneur.

The three of us scoured the city for waste material that could be turned into profit. The East End, Broadmoor Mental Hospital, rubbish tips — no place was too dirty, difficult or horrible for our scrounging escapades. I didn't always feel 100 per cent comfortable about some of the places we visited. I have to admit Broadmoor, with its criminally insane inhabitants, was a particularly disturbing place.

Initially we used a subcontractor to process the plastic, but as business grew we decided to set up our own factory. We rented our second premises in High Wycombe after leaving the Chertsey area and purchased a huge machine for crushing and granulating the waste plastic, so it could be reused to make plastic bags. It was so effective you couldn't retrieve anything that fell into it accidentally. One day I learned the hard way just how effective the machine was in recycling, when the strap on my very expensive Baume and Mercier gold watch broke after I caught it on the edge of the intake chute. It fell in and we spent hours practically dismantling the machine down to its last nut and bolt but all I could find of the watch were tiny specks of leather and few bits of metal that may have once belonged on my wrist.

It wasn't long before we outgrew that site and had to move. We thought we'd organized everything perfectly; however, on moving day, we found the crane we'd hired to shift our new granulating machine couldn't get through the doors of our new factory. Nothing for it, then, but to put the granulator on rollers and pull it into place. The wheels fell off this good plan when my hand, for some god-awful strange reason, ended up underneath a roller with 10 tonnes of machinery on it. When the roller moved on enough for me to pull my hand out, it wasn't a pretty sight. My normally sausage-like fingers had been turned into pancakes, each about four centimetres wide.

When the pain hit I could barely see and in some sort of weird partisan logic brought on by the excruciating agony, I decided to wrap my hand in a handkerchief and carry on helping the others. I managed to direct operations for only a few more minutes before someone noticed a torrent of blood pouring down my arm and persuaded me I really did need to get to the hospital smartly. The plus side of trying to turn my hand into a spade is at least I did it in High Wycombe, the centre of England's furniture industry. The local hospital was well used to seeing all manner of crush injuries, mutilated limbs and missing body parts.

When the hospital staff realized it was an emergency, I was rushed into a cubicle and put on the bed where I began to feel decidedly queasy. John, one of my business partners, stood at the side of the bed patting my shoulder and making reassuring noises. A young nurse came in and asked to have a look at my hand. Gingerly I unwrapped the handkerchief to show her the bloody mess.

Suddenly there was a loud crash and the bed lurched sideways. The nurse and I turned as one and couldn't see John. There was a groan from somewhere under the bed and when we looked down, there was John in a crumpled heap. The sight of my mangled hand had been too much for him and he'd fainted. I was sitting there nursing my injury and puzzling over his reaction when the nurse told me to wrap up my hand again and go and wait outside.

'I'm sorry,' she said, 'But because your friend is unconscious we'll have to attend to him first.'

Oh, great. I was the one in agony and John couldn't feel a thing. I wasn't having a bit of that and made enough fuss for the nurse to change her mind about who should be attended to first. First they injected local anaesthetic all over the hand and fingers and for the first time in what seemed an eternity, the raging pain settled down to a manageable throb. The most mangled parts of my fingers were trimmed away and the bits they could save were tidied up and stitched back together. Given the potential damage a 10-tonne rolling mass could have done to my hand, it could have been worse and a surgeon might have had to amputate. I still consider myself lucky to have lost only the tops of two fingers.

Being self-employed has its pros and cons and one of the cons is that if you're not working, you're not earning. Therefore, I felt I had to go back to work the next day, even though one hand was swathed in bandages. Having just the one functioning arm, I wasn't particularly useful. Ah, I thought, I'm sure I could cut up some plastic sheet. How hard could that be?

Holding the cutting blade in a half-arsed manner in my bandaged hand, I began to slice through the plastic. Because of my lack of grip, the blade skipped across the plastic and I impaled my good left hand. We piled into the car again and headed across town to High Wycombe Hospital where the same nurses were on duty again. Two hands, two days and two trips to hospital. The nurses could scarcely believe it was possible and because the blade in my hand looked just like the sort of thing you can buy in a $2 shop, they thought it was some kind of a hoax.

We'd already unscrewed the knife handle from the blade easily enough but were switched on enough to remember to leave the blade in the wound to staunch the blood flow. Laughing, one of the nurses wiggled the blade, thinking it would just fall off my hand. Instead I let out a howl of pain, which made them realize I wasn't playing games, so off we went to the emergency ward again.

For the second day in a row Shaune received a call from the hospital to tell her I had been admitted again and to come and get me. She told them they'd made a mistake, as I'd been there the day before. 'Oh no,' came the reply, 'your husband made the mistake and stabbed himself in the hand earlier today. And this time please keep him in the house for at least ten days. We do have other patients we have to attend to.'

I had no choice but to follow the hospital's instruction, as my arms were strapped across my body as if in a straitjacket. I put up with that state of affairs for four days before begging Shaune to unwrap me and let me get back to work. She didn't take much convincing. By that stage she'd seen more of me than she ever wanted to. You really know who your friends are when you have both arms strapped to your shoulders — try doing that and going to the loo.

The recycling business trundled along nicely for nearly a year and then, just as suddenly as it started, the oil crisis was over. Overnight, new plastic was cheaper than used and our recycling scheme was no longer the money-making venture it had been. With our business rapidly heading towards the wall, and the bank even more rapidly closing on our mortgage, it was time to look around for something more lucrative to do.

It seemed the time could be right for me to get into motor racing properly rather than being a volunteer on the periphery. I was 27, I'd sold cars, worked in the advertising and airline industries, started my own business, lost all of my money and half of two fingers. Motor racing seemed the logical next step.

Working on the principle that it's not what you know, it's who you know, I asked the McLaren team for a paid position. Unbeknown to me in the intervening years since I had last worked with the team, they had changed their philosophy and now required relevant qualifications. This change in employment criteria had also filtered down through the Formula One teams, so I set about finding another avenue into motor racing.

At that time, a company called International Race Tyre Service (IRTS), run by none other than that supreme entrepreneur Bernie Ecclestone, supplied tyres for race-cars in Europe. IRTS stocked Goodyear rubber and shipped them out to races for all the teams.

Not only that, they also employed specialist tyre-fitters to go to the various races and look after the tyre needs of all the teams.

The only qualification needed for that job was a truck driver's licence, which at the time I didn't have. They could be had for £50, which I also didn't have. Like the Good Samaritan, my father came to my rescue and loaned me the money, which rather put the pressure on me to pass the test. If I failed, not only would I have no job and still no money, I'd have to face 'the old man'.

Fortunately I passed, and that £50 turned out to be a wonderful investment, especially as I don't recall ever repaying the loan. The truck driver's licence was my ticket into the world of motorsport and for the next two years I worked full time for IRTS, going to Formula Two meetings all over Europe.

It wasn't long before I set off on my first trip to Europe with my trusty co-driver Maurice. Being an Aussie, he had absolutely no idea about the geography of the Continent, which compounded our predicament as we had no maps in the truck's cab. All we knew was our instruction to head for the Paul Ricard circuit in the South of France.

I drove the massive tyre truck off the ferry at Le Havre and turned to Maurice for directions. 'Left, then head for a place that starts with L,' he said confidently. We trundled out and saw a sign for Lille. 'That's it,' he exclaimed happily. It was a sign, but not the right one. I had a nagging feeling that we were heading north and after 30 kilometres I pulled into a service station to take a look at a map. A very good move on my behalf I'd have to say, as the L we should have been heading towards was Lyon, which was in the exact opposite direction to the way we were travelling.

I swung the truck around and off we went again, only to get lost on the infamous Boulevard Périphérique in Paris some time later. We'd not thought to buy a map at the service station because being typical men, we had an enormous amount of confidence in our own sense of direction. Wrong again and lost again.

We parked — illegally of course — by the Eiffel Tower then rapidly made our way to the top, visually traced out the route south, climbed back down and set off in that direction. Eventually we somehow made it all the way to Paul Ricard without any further drama.

One of my first customers at Paul Ricard was Ron Dennis. I'd seen him around the motor-racing scene frequently and had met him socially when I'd been out with the McLaren boys and at the Four Horseshoes pub in Chobham Common. He was always a good man to have a chat with and we'd become quite friendly over the years. Ron had started his motor-racing career as an apprentice racing mechanic and by 18 he'd been to his first Grand Prix meeting, where he worked on Jochen Rindt's Cooper-Climax.

Ron and Jochen must have got on, because when Rindt moved to Brabham in 1968, Ron went with him. Three years later Ron and chief mechanic Neil Trundle launched their own Formula Two team, Rondel Racing. Later, Ron would refer to that team as Project One.

He quickly made friends with all the tyre-fitters, which meant he usually got his tyres fitted before anyone else. Not only was Ron a good guy to do work for, he often showed his appreciation for our efforts by sending over a crate of beer after a meeting.

Soon after these encounters I started working for Ron full time when he bought a huge former furniture-removal truck from the French driver Bob Wollek, who was using it as a transporter. He'd had his eye on it and had finally managed to buy it. He had nobody to drive it, however, and that's when my long working relationship started with Ron.

Now that the money had begun to roll in again, Shaune and I

could afford a trip to New Zealand again to see her sister Lynne and her mum, Mrs J, who had moved there permanently. We liked the place so much we decided to join them. Within months of our second visit in early 1976, Shaune and I applied for citizenship. We became naturalized Kiwis in 1977 and throughout our McLaren careers we travelled on New Zealand passports.

Some folk may think spending all your life travelling, and a fair amount of time in airports, would be a curse rather than a pleasure. For me it has always been exciting and I loved flying to other countries. For example, in 1988 I flew from London to New York to pick up a bag tank because the manufacturer had supplied one that didn't fit the new McLaren MP4/4 Formula One car.

My travel schedule allowed for an overnight stop, but as the flight from London had arrived early, I decided to see if I could get back the same day after the messenger had delivered the bag tank to me at the airport. Sure enough, British Airways had a seat on a flight leaving in less than three hours. The booking clerk reserving a seat for me was aghast I didn't want to spend some time seeing her city. 'But sir, you've just arrived in Noo York,' she said in a broad Bronx accent.

'Yes, I know,' I replied. 'But I simply don't like the place and I want to go back.' My refusal to budge from the airport brought a visit from a representative of the New York Tourist Authority, who was terribly disappointed that I didn't want to see his city. However, on this occasion the object of the exercise was to get back to McLaren headquarters with the required part as quickly as possible.

In 1973 Ron Dennis embarked on what would become known as Project Two, a pair of Ray Jessup-designed Formula Two Motul-Rondels that were driven by Tom Pryce and Chris Meek. At Paul Ricard in 1974, Ron was running two Surtees Formula Two cars for a pair of Ecuadorian hopefuls. The team, financed by tobacco company

Philip Morris, had its mechanical base in Germany and logistical centre in England.

Despite Ron's organizational skills, the logistics proved too difficult and the team was uncompetitive. To the astute observer, however, it was clear the team had potential. It just needed to overcome some of the constraints it was operating under. Never was this more obvious than at Thruxton in 1974. I turned up in my IRTS role and was impressed to find that Ron had attracted the Swedish Formula One Grand Prix winner Ronnie Peterson as a substitute driver for one of the Ecuadorians. There was no way a driver of Peterson's standing would start a race unless the car he was driving had a chance of winning.

My two years working for IRTS fulfilling the tyre needs of Formula Two cars were good fun, but I didn't exactly feel like I'd made it to the top of the motorsport mountain. In 1975 Ron phoned me to ask if I was interested in working for him as part of a Formula Two team for the following season. I jumped at the chance. I was hired as the team's tyre-fitter, but was also expected to drive the transporter that carried the cars, parts and assorted personnel to the series races. Some of these events took place in England, while others were held on European tracks. If we had a couple of distant races one after the other, we didn't bother driving all the way back to the UK after the first. We'd just stay somewhere handy and do any work on the cars on the road. Literally.

By the time the team arrived at Hockenheim in 1976 and the trouble with Schnitzer had been sorted out (see Chapter 5), I now had considerable responsibility within the team. Along with Scotsman Jimmy Tully, I was essentially acting as team manager, with duties including setting up before races and collecting prize money afterwards if Ron had to rush back to the UK.

Delegating these tasks to us freed up Ron to look after the sponsorship and financial side of the business and it added a great deal of satisfaction to my job. Unfortunately, a few things came to a head in my personal life and it looked like it was all going to come to an end.

I had been married for six years but was seldom at home with Shaune. I had agreed to follow her to New Zealand once the Formula Two season had finished. Working for Ron had been great fun, but it was seasonal, and I was looking forward to resuming a normal married relationship again. So when the season was over, I got on a plane and headed for my new life in Auckland.

Chapter 3

Early days at McLaren

There has been more than enough Brazilian rainforest cut down to feed the books written about how Bruce McLaren's original Formula One team morphed into the Ron Dennis juggernaut it became. Suffice to say, just in case anyone reading this book may have missed something, Bruce McLaren Motor Racing and Ron's Project Four merged at the behest of Philip Morris.

This came about because the Marlboro McLaren cars had delivered little in the way of results since James Hunt had won the world championship in 1976. To get things rolling, former Bruce McLaren Motor Racing car designer John Barnard was persuaded to join the newly named McLaren International with the promise of a free hand to design a new Formula One car. John was associated with Ron when he had Project Four Racing before McLaren International was formed.

Ron and P4 had no money but lots of ambition and McLaren had lots of money but seemed to have lost the ambition. John Barnard was hired by Ron with the promise that whatever he needed to build a winning car would be made available.

John had been in America during the mid- to late 1970s and had designed a new Chaparral in which the four-time Indianapolis 500 winner Al Unser led the 1978 race. The Chaparral was a big step away from conventional American open-wheelers of the day, but John's new McLaren car would set Formula One design on its head. Visually it was not a great departure from the cars of the time (unlike the Tyrrell P34 raced by Jody Scheckter in the 1976 German Grand Prix with its six wheels); it was the construction of the MP4/1 that broke the existing mould.

For the first time in nearly 20 years, a designer had junked the idea of using sheet aluminium to construct the chassis and instead worked with a revolutionary product called carbon fibre. Ron called me over to the workshop one day in early 1980 for a preview of a quarter-size mock-up of the new car with its carbon-fibre tub. It was an eye-opener, as I'd not seen that material used in F1 car construction before. But it was a typical Ron leap of faith, which had worked well in the past for him, and would turn McLaren into the world championship-winning team once again. John and Ron had been working with the Hercules Corporation in the USA, which made composite structures for aerospace use.

It was all well and good making a great technological leap forward, but it came at a cost. The amount of extra money needed to construct a car out of the new compound was horrendous and the mind boggles to think what would have happened if the grand scheme had tanked. If that had happened, instead of enjoying many years being part of a great championship-winning team, more likely I'd have gone back to New Zealand and become a market gardener.

However, as William Jennings Bryan once stated, 'Destiny is no matter of chance. It is a matter of choice: It is not a thing to be waited for, it is a thing to be achieved.' Ron's motto really, whether he knew it or not. In fact he was able to get the money to build the car and the rest, as they say, is history.

The quarter-scale model that had been built of the concept car was intended to get sponsors Marlboro to buy into this brave new world. For some odd reason I ended up with the original scale model, which had been displayed in Ron's personal office for many years until he gave it to me in 2000, and it's now on more-or-less permanent loan to the Bruce McLaren Trust in Auckland.

Although the promise of funding for the carbon-fibre car was in the air, Ron hadn't got his hands on the cold hard cash yet. Not long after seeing the scale model, Shaune and I flew to America for the United States Grand Prix at Watkins Glen, to run the Marlboro McLaren team hospitality. What we were about to learn was that Ron was also at the track. With him was another Project Four director at that time, Creighton Brown.

I can only guess that the two of them must have had a cunning plan up their sleeves to get their new toy up and running as a real race-car. It can't have been a coincidence that the Philip Morris head office was in New York — just a five-hour drive from the circuit — and all the executives who counted would be at the race. It was the perfect opportunity for Ron and his colleagues to get ink on paper so they could start building the new carbon-fibre F1 car and begin to revolutionize the sport.

I had no idea what they were trying to hatch, but soon I found myself sitting in the back seat of Ron and Creighton's car feeling more than a little surreptitious, as if we were negotiating a drug deal. The two of them spent a fair amount of time grilling me on what I knew about the McLaren/Project Four merger and wanted to know what I'd heard in the motorhome. They thought as I spent a lot of time in and around the motorhome, and was responsible for all those who utilized it, I may have overhead some juicy piece of gossip that might give them an inside edge with the negotiations.

To explain things more fully, at this point in the 1980s I was actually employed by Charles Stewart of Marlboro and not by Ron Dennis. Marlboro had been sponsoring Ron's Formula Two and

Three teams, and they (Marlboro) wanted to get more involved in F1. Ron's very successful teams were just the ticket Marlboro needed to move up and play with the big boys.

Hence Ron and Creighton suspecting I might know what Marlboro was thinking, since I'd spent time hobnobbing with the decision-makers. Anything I'd overheard in the motorhome might be a good indicator of Marlboro's intentions. Although I'd learnt a long time ago to keep my mouth shut about pit gossip and not give secrets away, this time I decided to tell the truth and let these two know what my impression was. I told them I had the feeling the deal was as good as done and Marlboro sponsorship would finance the new company and the new car.

For several years Ron enjoyed a good relationship with John Hogan, the marketing director for the Marlboro brand, and it was no secret that John wanted to see Ron involved with the Formula One team. It's all water under the bridge now, but a year later McLaren International was formed with Teddy Mayer and Ron Dennis at the helm.

Most people assume the first race-car's designation, MP4/1, launched on 6 March 1981, was a combination of McLaren and Project Four, but I have a different view. The Marlboro influence was so powerful at that time, I believe MP4/1 stood for Marlboro Project Four and as the tobacco company's participation diminished, the M may have come to stand for McLaren, especially when the team became sponsored by West cigarettes in 1997.

It was fairly clear early on that Ron wanted to divorce McLaren International from the Bruce McLaren Motor Racing team as quickly as he could. When the two organizations merged, around 45 per cent of the original Bruce McLaren people left, while only 10 per cent of Project Four people moved on.

At the beginning it wasn't a seamless merger of the two and for a while there was an underlying them-and-us feeling. My impression was that the former Bruce McLaren people were under the illusion they were better than us. It wasn't long before that thinking was kicked into touch when the old school realized the new school had a better car, a better paint scheme, a bigger and better workshop and even a new tea lady.

By the time John Watson won the 1981 British Grand Prix in the new car, everyone was singing from the same hymn sheet at McLaren International. The Dennis/Mayer marriage, however, failed to grow with the rest of the team and it wasn't long before cracks appeared in that relationship. The chasm grew wider until the two parted company in early 1982.

Mayer, along with another old Bruce McLaren stager, Tyler Alexander, joined up with some of the other former team members and headed to the Force Formula One team launched by IndyCar stalwart Carl Haas. Teddy and Tyler first went to CART in the US and started Mayer Motor Racing in 1984 (which was quite successful), and then at the end of 1984 they were hired by Carl Haas to run the Haas/Force Formula One Race Car Engineering team with huge backing from the Beatrice Group. Their designers included Neil Oatley, Adrian Newey and Ross Brawn and the cars were badged as Lolas.

In the meantime, during 1981 we had all moved to the new premises at Boundary Road, Woking, which within a year proved to be too small. The size wasn't the only problem. Getting the big race transporters in and out of the place was a nightmare. 'Tats' (you can guess where he got his moniker) Cook was one of the senior drivers — in fact, if my memory serves me correctly, he was the chief truckie — and he soon found out just what a pain in the arse the place could be.

Whenever the trucks departed for a race it became a spectator event, with most of the employees wandering outside to watch them leave. Ron would occasionally view the proceedings from his upstairs office as the trucks moved out, and I believe he did so with a sense of pride. Once the truck unit had reached the road, it had to make an immediate hard right turn and then accelerate to avoid taking out half the side of one of the buildings.

On one occasion, Tats accomplished the first part rather well, but shortly afterwards the wheels literally fell off. As he accelerated, the full-size 30-tonne trailer unit carrying the exorbitantly expensive F1 race-cars let out a screech of tortured metal and the whole front of the damn thing collapsed onto the ground. The lever securing the fifth wheel coupling of the truck to the trailer pin had not been locked in, so the trailer just slid off the tractor unit. Tats' face in the rear-vision side mirror would have made an albino look well tanned. Gasping like a fish out of water, he leapt down from the cab and legged it to the back of the truck unit to see the damage.

Ron appeared so fast we thought he'd beamed himself down from his office. He asked Tats, who was now looking like a stunned mullet, what he was going to do about it. 'Uuummm, pick it up?' Tats offered hopefully.

'Yes,' Ron agreed. 'A bloody good idea, but how are you going to do it?'

Luckily there was less damage to the trailer unit than we expected and with the help of some of us, the odd hydraulic jack and some fiddling, the trailer was eventually hooked back up to the truck, securely this time, and away went Tats, to everyone's relief.

Before long at the new premises, Ron and John Barnard had greatly increased the level of professionalism, which in turn changed the business from being a race shop into a manufacturing facility. They integrated new design and management systems that at the time were unpopular, but these measures helped return the team to success on the track.

It may astound you now, but back in those days the phrase 'quality control' meant you had one or two mates count how many screws were left over. And if it was in single figures everything was good to go. Things had improved a lot since Ron had taken control but even then it wasn't unknown that something as simple as a rollbar might not be interchangeable between chassis no. 1 and chassis no. 2.

Things took another big leap forward when then two-time world champion Niki Lauda was enticed out of retirement in 1982 to drive McLaren forward. It wasn't long before he'd earned the respect of all the mechanics. At the start there was some scepticism, despite there already being two world F1 championship trophies on his shelf, that he would be able to cut the mustard after two years out of the game. Those doubts were soon put to rest, in emphatic style.

Unfortunately, much to my regret, I wasn't at Silverstone on his first day of testing in a McLaren Formula One car, when Niki proved to one and all he still had it. He turned up at the circuit with his usual understated confidence, eventually climbed into the car and proceeded to do a couple of laps to bed everything in. He then turned up the wick and pulled a couple of very quick laps before rolling into the pits. On leaping out of the car he turned to the assembled mechanics and quietly told them how the car was understeering and a wheel weight was missing from the left rear.

Despite a few raised eyebrows, the crew removed the rear wheel and found that Niki was correct: the wheel weight was indeed missing. He garnered instant respect from everyone who was there that day. Not only did Niki know how cars worked, he also had a damn good idea how to get an F1 team to work together and get the best out of everyone involved.

At the same time, Niki was no humble wallflower. He expected to be treated like the superstar he was but he came without a lot of the trappings. He was very direct, did not mince his words and showed this when he wrote some uncomplimentary things about Ron Dennis in his 1985 autobiography *To Hell and Back*.

Direct or not, in paddock politics he was one of the shrewdest drivers around. At McLaren he had no problem outmanoeuvring John Watson, who generally let his driving performances speak for themselves. But it was a different matter altogether when Alain Prost replaced Watson.

If there's something the French are good at it's internal politics and Prost took to it like a duck to water. Alain 'The Professor' Prost was one of the friendliest and most personable drivers around and great company to boot. However, if there was something he wanted to achieve politically, he had a very close band of French journos around him who hung on his every word. Always speaking in French to them, much to Ron's annoyance, he was able to 'plant' stories and watch them grow. He was also on very good terms with Mansour Ojjeh, and I thought he was very politically aware.

When Niki joined McLaren he introduced a new era in physical fitness. He placed a great deal of faith in the ability of fellow Austrian Willi Dungl to get him fit and keep him fit for racing. He credited Willi with preparing him mentally and physically for his return to racing only six weeks after the 1976 Nurburgring crash that almost cost him his life. Like many people, Willi had neglected his fitness as a youngster but had later discovered the benefits of taking care of it, through a structured regime of diet and exercise.

When he came to McLaren with Niki, it wasn't long before many of the crew recognized the benefits of Willi's programme and he virtually became the McLaren team doctor, treating all kinds of minor injuries and ailments. Wili would insist on Niki's having a slice of black German bread and little else pre-race. Niki would wait until Willi had disappeared then throw it away and have Shaune make a strong coffee and a ham sandwich.

Willi's daughter Andrea Dungl later took on the same role when he returned to Austria to build up the clientele at his clinic. Because she too ate natural and high-fibre foods, she could fart and burp with the best of them at any time of day and in any company. She saw no reason for embarrassment, merely commenting that it was perfectly natural.

When Andrea left, Josef Leberer took over the reins, looking after Ayrton Senna until he left McLaren at the end of 1993. Josef stayed on for several years until the job of caring for a racing-driver's health became a seven-day-a-week vocation. He was reluctant to leave his home in Salzburg for the entire Grand Prix season, so at the instigation of Ron Dennis, the newly acquired Mika Hakkinen found other trainers. Josef was still with Formula One in early 2010, working with BMW Sauber and their drivers. It was from about Willi's time that personal trainers, head shrinks, nutritionists, dietitians, physiologists, psychologists and all manner of other 'ologists' came into their own in motor racing.

On a lighter note, though, one of the benefits of working for McLaren and having all these motor-racing superstars parade through the garage was the succession of very lovely young women who presented themselves at the motorhomes. James Hunt, Niki Lauda, Jochen Mass, to name but a few, all had a lively interest in admiring their admirers and there was no shortage of companionship if a single-seat driver wanted some company.

One of the prominent schmoozers was Paddy McNally (known as 'Toad' in the camp) whose girlfriend Sarah Ferguson was a genuinely nice person with a warm, outgoing personality. She was also probably the best female joke-teller I have ever met, especially the one about the bald eagle . . . but never mind. I felt very sorry for her during all her trials and tribulations with the Royal Family after she had married Prince Andrew and become the Duchess of York. I can imagine she would have had great difficulty fitting in with their stuffy protocols. From what I knew of her, and both Shaune and I got to know Sarah quite well, it just wouldn't have been her style.

Around this time we headed to Monaco for the 1983 Grand Prix and one of McLaren's darkest F1 weekends. Niki Lauda and John Watson failed to qualify for race day and to my knowledge it's the only time both McLarens failed to qualify for a Grand Prix. Stephen South was substituting for Alain Prost at the Long Beach Grand Prix in 1980 and failed to qualify the M29.

Like several other leading teams' cars, McLaren's were powered by Ford DFV engines that had been good enough to claim first and second in the United States (West) Grand Prix at Long Beach a month earlier. John Watson also failed to qualify in 1980 at Monaco in the M29. Both cars were pre-Ron and John designs.

How this hugely embarrassing situation came about is no mystery. The set-up for both cars in Thursday's first practice simply wasn't right and they languished at the back of the field. But this was not considered a problem as Niki and John had qualified 22nd and 23rd at Long Beach and gone on to end up on the podium.

The Michelin tyres being used were designed mainly for the turbo cars and the DFV McLarens could not get heat into them. New tyres were produced, arriving on Friday (a non-track day) and these were to be tested during Saturday's free practice. They were good and would have got the cars mid-field at least. Various adjustments were made for the second practice on Saturday and the team had high hopes as at the time Monaco also had a 20-car grid limit.

Come Saturday, though, it rained and when it rains at Monaco it makes so much difference to lap times it practically adds a day. No matter how many laps Niki and John flogged around the circuit, they were not going to qualify. Mighty McLaren was left in the same situation as Osella, RAM, Theodore and other also-ran teams, having to pack up before race day.

We wondered why this indignity couldn't have happened at Zolder or Imola, anywhere the media spotlight wasn't quite so bright. Shaune and I began packing up the motorhome until Ron Dennis wandered over and put a halt to that. 'No, you can't go,' he said cheerfully. 'We have lots of guests coming tomorrow and someone has to be here to entertain them.' We had some Philip Morris board members in the motorhome as well as some Italian sponsors and their guests.

It turned out to be an embarrassing afternoon, having to explain to various high-powered Marlboro folk why it was an interesting race, even though there were no McLaren cars competing. Although it was a weekend for the team to forget, non-qualification meant Shaune and I, outside of race day, had some spare time to play with. On Saturday night we had nothing to do for the mechanics as they had all disappeared. Some had gone home, and as hotel rooms were already paid for, some stayed in situ to enjoy the rare luxury of having a Saturday night off in Monaco.

Unfortunately every man and his dog travelling through Europe wants to spend some time in the principality and the place wasn't designed to handle that much waste. Although the sparkling Mediterranean looks beautiful when you are standing on the promenade, what lurks beneath is a completely different story.

Since no racing was happening over the weekend, I decided to have a tiki tour around the marina in one of the little tourist boats that plied its trade on the harbour waters. I was a little behind schedule so I decided to leap over the sea wall, as it was next to the paddock wall, onto the pontoon where the rest of the sightseers were waiting for our water ride. Having vaulted the wall, I landed a bit heavily on the pontoon and my wallet flew out of my pocket, arching gracefully into the sparkling waters of Port Hercule.

The wallet itself was of no great concern. The contents, on the other hand, included receipts for thousands of francs and other currencies for motorhome expenses. Back in those days it was a case of 'no receipts — no payment' and if you think Monaco these days is an expensive place to take a breath, let alone buy anything, it was no different back then.

When one door shuts, another one opens and purely by chance there was a race mechanic who had brought his scuba gear along to the racetrack. He was one of the Essex balloon erectors who travelled the globe doing all the Essex petroleum promos for the Lotus team sponsor. In the other harbour he had an old hippy type of boat he used for cruising the Nile. He had a small rubber ducky and at times rushed around from the other harbour with a blue light attached and made wailing, police-type noises with his mouth.

There's nothing like a £100 bribe to motivate a man to get suited up and head into the depths of a Monaco harbour. Half an hour after the wallet had swan-dived into the murky waters, my man was ready to have a shot at retrieving it. I was beginning to worry 40 minutes later, as I knew he had only 35 minutes of air, when a sea of bubbles broke the surface, quickly followed by a hand rising out of the Mediterranean like Excalibur from the lake. It had taken that long to find the wallet, as the bottom of the harbour was a rubbish dump littered with the detritus of modern man from shopping trolleys to bicycles to bottles and plastic bags full of rubbish. Mix this in with all the silt and water run-off from the town and I'm surprised the diver didn't rush himself off to the nearest hospital for a tetanus jab. On a Monday morning after a Grand Prix you can almost walk over the water on the rubbish and toilet effluent from all the boats in the harbour.

During that same Grand Prix weekend, former Alfa Romeo driver Bruno Giacomelli asked Shaune and me if we'd like to go for a ride in his powerboat. We'd known Bruno from the days when we ran the Marlboro motorhome and catered for all the Alfa people. Shaune must have had a premonition because she gently declined the offer on the pretence of having something more pressing to do.

In a moment of bravado I accepted the invitation to go for what he called a 'spin'. I should have guessed, but his boat wasn't what you'd call a pleasure cruiser — more like an aquatic F1 car minus the wheels. Apparently they're known as 'cigarette' boats, probably because they're long and thin and will burn you if you're not careful. The real reason is they were used to smuggle cigarettes.

I should have guessed all was not as it should be. Bruno told me the handles on either side of the seat were for holding on to and there were no belts, because if we tipped over we'd be thrown out of the boat to avoid being trapped underneath it. Charming.

My sense of impending doom wasn't allayed when the twin-V 1000 horsepower engines in the back of the boat roared into life, no doubt causing the little old ladies and small dogs ambling about to clutch their respective chests in terror. As we nosed our way out of the harbour I looked around for somewhere to sit down but realized there were no seats and I just had to hang on for dear life for the next 20 minutes.

Once clear of the relative safety of the marina, Bruno planted his foot on the accelerator and the boat took off across the water like a scalded cat. Up to that point I had been unaware an engine could shove quite a large boat along that quickly. I can now say with some authority, I know what a moving part in a pneumatic drill must feel like. If you think being thrown around in a race-car is dancing with the devil — try it in three dimensions. I had no idea boats could fly, but if fish can, why not a powerboat? I still don't understand how Bruno could see where he was going, as the ride was bone-jarringly vicious. By the time my eyeballs had stopped pinging around like a ball-bearing in a paint tin, we were way down the harbour. It's easy to see why there are hardly any gauges or knobs to fiddle with on the dash, as everyone's hanging on for dear life — including the driver.

Unbeknown to Bruno and me, Brabham F1 driver at the time, Riccardo Patrese, had noticed us leaving the harbour and decided to join us in his own cigarette boat. Within minutes the two F1 duellists were going at it hammer and tongs on the water at speeds that defied common sense. They had simply taken a tarmac racetrack fight and transferred it to a different medium.

As the speeds increased, so did the wake produced by the boats and it wasn't long before each hull was leaping in the air over the other's wake. By about this time I had resigned myself to the fact that I may not be setting foot on dry land any time soon. The two drivers were having so much fun trying to catch each other out that the 20-minute ride turned into a nerve-wracking two-and-a-half hour visit to Dante's Inferno. Eventually we all made it back to the dock but it was on very wobbly legs that I clambered back to the safety of terra firma. Taking inspiration from the Pope, I knelt down and gave the ground a big kiss, much to the amusement of Bruno and Riccardo.

I wasn't the only one having an adventure that year. McLaren's chief mechanic Gary Anderson, along with all the other McLaren chief mechanics of the past, had disappeared at Monaco. Not into the harbour, though. Gary vanished for an entire day at the 1978 Grand Prix after being arrested for the usual reasons, normally to do with antics at the famous Tip Top bar at Monaco. This was the mechanics' favourite evening bar, just 50 metres or so from the casino and right on the track between turn four (Casino) and turn five (Mirabeau Haute). Marlboro's John Hogan pulled a few strings and Gary was released on bail the next morning.

While some of us were trying to get Gary out of clink, McLaren's managing director Teddy Mayer had spent the previous 24 hours asking where Gary was, to which he received various replies along the lines of, 'He's in the pits', 'He's up at the garage', 'He's getting some spares.' When Gary finally reappeared, he marched straight up to Teddy and asked, 'Where the hell have you been? I've been looking everywhere for you.'

I nearly landed in the Monaco jail myself in 1978. I was in town on a mini-bike, quite lost I'd have to admit, hoping to find my way back down to the paddock and the team. After pissing about for ages I decided to ask a local Monegasque policeman, as they're easy to spot with their long black boots and baggy riding breeches. Almost immediately I saw one at an intersection, raced over and asked him how to get to the Formula One paddock. Instead of a friendly smile he gave me a thunderous look and began bellowing at me in French.

It was a while before I realized the front wheel of the little monkey bike I was riding was resting against his foot. He reached down, turned off the engine, kicked the front wheel viciously then reached for his handcuffs. I didn't hang around to apologize. Leaping back on the bike, I fired it into life and roared away down the hill, surely faster than the bike had ever gone before. Luckily I didn't see that cop again all weekend but on subsequent visits to the Monaco Grand

Prix I've seen him many times. He always recognizes me, smiles and makes a motion with his hand akin to revving a motor.

They really were exciting times back then because McLaren was big enough to be regarded as a serious racing team, yet still remained small enough to allow everyone to rely on one another. Perhaps it was a bit different for Shaune and me in the motorhome, it being the hub of the team when on the road, as we were privy to everything that was going on. Well, nearly everything. We never got to see or hear Ron negotiating money with the drivers, as that was definitely a closed-door scene.

Some days, though, we were aware when Ron and a driver weren't seeing eye-to-eye. If the car wasn't right it was Ron's fault because he was the boss. If a driver had an off day and bent a car, Ron would be in his ear. So unless everything was going according to plan, there was always a hint of tension in the air. This whole on-edge situation between Ron and drivers continued until Mika Hakkinen arrived at the team and over a period of time the two built a strong relationship.

There's no doubt the design and engineering talent of John Barnard propelled McLaren right to the front of the grid of Formula One constructors. Ron and John had what I'd call a scratchy relationship, which at times was downright explosive but generally worked well. The two of them knew what they wanted and respected each other for their personal and technical skill-sets, and in an odd sort of way each complemented the other.

I firmly believe John would never have become the highly regarded, legendary designer he is today if Ron had not financed his early designs. Conversely, it's quite possible McLaren may have disappeared if, as a team, it had not produced a winning car in 1981 as Ron had promised Marlboro. I think it's a shame John didn't stay with McLaren, but that's life, I suppose.

Perhaps the glue that kept the Dennis/Barnard relationship together and stopped it from breaking down was McLaren International board member Creighton Brown. He is often seen as little more than a ship that passed McLaren in the night, but Creighton and Ron got along very well and he played a big part in building up McLaren in the early years between 1979 and 1984. He quit the board only when well-connected and wealthy businessman Mansour Ojjeh arrived to finance development of the new Porsche Formula One engine in 1984.

Creighton had run a very successful Formula Two team with considerable ICI backing and was a successful racer and car constructor in his own right. He merged his interests with Project Four in 1979, becoming a director of the company, and from then on played an invaluable role in sponsorship because he could, and would, talk anybody into anything. As he had a lot of business savvy, he had considerable involvement in McLaren's road car project.

Although I would describe Creighton as an English gentleman, he was unafraid of getting his hands dirty, as he was also a pig farmer. Shaune and I went to his farm one night for dinner and were shown the piggery. On our walkabout, we were somewhat taken aback to see our smartly dressed host bound over a piggery wall, land smack-bang in the middle of a god-awful slop of muck and crap, to rescue a distressed piglet and its mother. Not just a gentleman farmer then, but a real farmer, one who also had an eye for investments. He even convinced Ron to part with some of his own money for a joint venture in pig farming in Brazil, where Creighton eventually settled.

In the meantime, Creighton was schmoozing sponsors for McLaren where he entertained, did presentations, wrote releases — you could almost describe him as a one-man PR department. This was years before the rest of the F1 teams realized PR was such a big help in getting funding for mechanics, designers, drivers and team principals to go and play with their very expensive toys. Unfortunately Creighton died of cancer in 2006.

The sponsorship deal with Marlboro, and the money it brought, allowed Ron to develop and build John Barnard's revolutionary carbon-fibre chassis but it also came with a rider — Ron had to hire Italian Formula Two driver Andrea de Cesaris as number two in the team. Andrea's dad was Italy's biggest importer and distributor of Marlboro cigarettes.

While Andrea was certainly a personable young man, in my view he was probably out of his depth in Formula One at that stage. Without doubt his main contribution to McLaren during 1981 was the rigorous crash-test programme to which he subjected the carbon-fibre chassis. Not that this programme was intentional, but Andrea was uninjured in a season-long series of spins and crashes. In 14 races he crashed or spun off six times and retired in two others. While his performances did little for team morale, at least John was able to thumb his nose at critics who claimed the impact-resistant properties of carbon fibre were inferior to those of conventional monocoque construction materials.

Andrea had a couple of physical disabilities that I found disconcerting in a racing-driver. First, his jaw would drop open for no reason at all and second, he had what you could call a nervous tic that caused his eyes to roll upwards. He claimed this never affected his driving, but I found this hard to believe. There is a famous photograph of him on a starting grid in which his eyes appear to be white because his eyeballs rolled so far upward his pupils disappeared. Did it make a difference to his driving? Believe what you like, but I'm sure it must have. After yet another practice crash, this time at Zandvoort, and with only three races left in the season, McLaren management decided Marlboro money or not, Andrea de Cesaris was a luxury the team could not afford, so he had to go at the end of the season.

With Marlboro backing, Andrea continued his crash test programme for several other Formula One teams during several subsequent seasons. The other driver at the time was John Watson, who was very fast when everything was going right for him. Not that very much was going right for him in 1979 and 1980 when he had to wrestle the awful McLaren M28 and M29 around various circuits. However, I could never see Wattie getting to the top of the tree in Formula One because I think he was too soft. He was just too nice a person. For a while he was known as John Whatswrong, but remembering the M28 and M29, who could blame him?

It was quite an eye-opener at times to observe who would turn up in the pits on any given race weekend, a great number of them proclaiming to be 'very good friends' of the Ojjehs. Margaret Thatcher was the British Prime Minister at the time and often her son Mark would show up, eliciting a collective groan from the team. Not to be too harsh, though, he did have a genuine interest in racing and competed in club races with a limited amount of success. He hung on to his mother's coat-tails a little too much for my liking. He was always going on about 'Mother thinks this' and 'Mother thinks that' or 'the Prime Minister thinks' and dropping into the conversation who he was.

An example of his over-inflated sense of self-importance was an entry in the visitor's book we kept in the motorhome. Just about anyone with a claim to fame had signed the book, from F1 drivers, film stars and ministers of state to the fabulously wealthy and royalty. All of them wrote just a short note and signed on the dotted line. But not Mark — he took up a whole page and in large writing at the bottom added his address: 10 Downing St., London. Just in case you didn't know where the Prime Minister of the United Kingdom lived. I thought he was a complete prat. I understand he was a successful businessman, but I can only imagine his success stemmed from the fact his mother was Prime Minister for so long. Margaret Thatcher never showed up, but we met her husband Denis, who popped in for a visit at the British Grand Prix one year. I was reminded of Mark's visits to McLaren a few years later when he hit the headlines as a result of a foolish escapade in Africa. In 2004 he was implicated in a plot to overthrow the government of Equatorial Guinea. He subsequently agreed a plea bargain while denying any knowledge of the plot and was fined approximately US$500,000, and copped a four-year suspended jail sentence in South Africa, where he was living at the time.

As sports sponsorship became more professional, so did Marlboro's marketing efforts to widen the brand's awareness. As a result, Marlboro, through Tony Thomas and John Hogan, who ran the English company Charles Stewart & Co — the marketing arm of Philip Morris — decided there would be work for us during the northern hemisphere winters of 1978/79 and 1979/80, which Shaune and I were happy about as it meant we wouldn't have to wait until the next F1 season to start earning money again.

Since Marlboro was sponsoring the World Cup ski races and the European rounds were primarily held in Germany, Austria, France, Switzerland and Italy, it was easy for us to drive across the Continent and attend each meet. By easy, I mean on the map. Driving a bloody great truck and trailer unit in the snow and ice is not only impractical, but verges on the impossible. Trying to manoeuvre the vehicle on a small, slippery mountaintop carpark was fraught with grief and it was a pig of a thing to dig out after an overnight snowfall.

After a couple of painful meetings we parked the motorhome, a small American one was contracted with a driver to take it around, and we switched to transporting the Marlboro Hot-Dog ski team to some of the swankiest ski resorts in Europe in Range Rovers. Ski racing was, and still is, huge in Europe and I can remember back in 1975, when Niki Lauda won his world championship driving a Ferrari, his fellow countryman, skiing great Franz Klammer, received more fan mail than Niki after he won eight of nine downhill races.

Needless to say the Hot-Dog team, a mixture of American and Canadian free spirits, livened things up at each round of the World Cup with a variety of freestyle, aerial and mogul tricks. You could almost say these guys were the forerunners of the Winter X Games. The only drawback was that back in the 1970s, training techniques and safety gear didn't hold a patch on the stuff today and hence a few of the aerial ski pioneers ended up in hospital with various cases of paralysis.

On our first day at Val-d'Isère, each of us in the support crew was equipped with everything necessary for skiing — goggles, gloves, thermal underwear, a sort of muddy brown ski suit, boots and at the time the very latest, French-made K2 skis.

I was very proud of mine, despite the fact they were extra-long skis, fine for downhill racing, not so good for learning, but I didn't know that. There were eight of us similarly equipped: Shaune, me, a couple of junior Marlboro executives and four others who made Marlboro's motor-racing films. The film crew had another Range Rover so they could follow us around and make a documentary about the Hot-Dog team.

Having all decided to try our new ski gear, we sensibly headed for the beginners' slopes. In hindsight, that was probably the only sensible thing we did all day. Instructors? We reckoned we didn't need them. Ahh, the cockiness of youth. Moving forward on our racing planks proved to be easy, turning and stopping a little more trying. Most of us worked out learning an instant means of stopping was preferable to mastering the art of turning two planks of glass fibre, fastened to a pair of rigid boots attached to two legs getting information from a brain that hadn't a clue what the hell to do.

At the slightest sight of impending danger, we either promptly sat down and used the skis as a sort of snowplough or dived left or right and did a starfish impression in an effort to arrest any forward momentum. However, as always, there's someone who doesn't deem it necessary to learn the fundamental art of coming to a halt in the advent of danger and one of the film crew was to be our entertainment.

Building up a bit of speed, the aforementioned cameraman found himself heading straight towards a small train operating on a cog railway. Thankfully, the train driver had spotted the out-of-control skier and hauled on the brakes, slowing the train just enough to allow the paralysed-with-fear film-crew guy to fly across the front of the engine as various ski passengers flew out of the carriages. Some injured themselves enough to warrant an ambulance being called.

During the resultant brouhaha, the rest of us took off our skis and scurried away to a small bar, trying to look inconspicuous — not easy in Range Rovers with Marlboro markings plastered all over them.

Not being content with causing chaos on the slopes, Shaune, me and our intrepid skiing companions, all dressed up like an Olympic downhill ski team, thought we'd wreak havoc on the ski lift a couple of days later. We decided after a day or two we'd sort of mastered the art of skiing, without spending most of the time on our backsides, and so off to the T-bar we went in anticipation of getting higher up the mountain and a longer run back down again.

Shaune was first up to the T-bar, as they were single-pull; she grabbed hold of it but unfortunately didn't get it quite right.

Before she knew it, she was being dragged half-cocked up the hill trying desperately to get organized with the seat between her legs. Unfortunately, the lift operator saw her flapping in the breeze and instantly hit the stop button, bringing the entire 500-metre-long lift operation, with 300 people on it, to an immediate halt. This was much to the chagrin of a number of other skiers, who were unceremoniously thrown off their perches to end up face down in the snow.

We made a tactical withdrawal and went in search of a proper ski lift where you could sit down on a rudimentary seat and hang on to a bar. After a few runs we decided to follow Marlboro executives Paddy McNally and Tony Thomas to the top of the mountain and try these so-called black runs. We had no idea what a black run meant and Paddy and Tony didn't say much either. We looked at a map of the runs and decided that red meant danger and black meant safe for five-year-olds. Exactly the opposite of reality. We soon found out these runs weren't just black in name, but black in nature.

A black run is often described as steep. Bollocks. It's a sheer drop off the side of a mountain. Discretion is the better part of valour, so Shaune and I gingerly made our way down, side-stepping and gently sliding to areas where we could ski without having a cardiac arrest, then back to side-stepping until we reached the lower slopes.

One of our ski party, a camera operator, wasn't so lucky and careened out of control into a tree. It was more like he straddled the tree at speed doing God knows what damage to his family jewels. He retired hurt from any more skiing that season. There was also reportedly some hesitation in his amorous attempts at convincing any number of chalet girls to inspect his etchings.

As much fun as swanning around Europe and skiing at the best snow resorts is, it's also hellishly expensive so we decided to put an end to those antics and find something else to do to amuse ourselves.

It wasn't long before I discovered that a Range Rover is as good on snow as under it.

We soon discovered the snow-blowers hauled along by the various road-cleaning trucks created huge drifts of very light snow on the side of the road. When the drifts got to a certain height, I would flick the steering hard right and race into the ploughed snowdrift, completely submerging the car. The best distance I got under a blanket of snow while still moving was 45 metres before the car re-emerged into the daylight.

Of course, not everyone in the ski resort had access to a four-wheel-drive vehicle and the daughter of the owner of the hotel we were staying at in Val-d'Isère had to abandon her elderly Citroën 2CV in a snowdrift one night. Worried about what would become of her old but much-loved car, she asked us if we could help her retrieve it with our 4WD.

Not being ones to leave a damsel in distress, we agreed to drive her to where she left the car in the morning. Arriving at the place where the car had been parked the night before, we found there wasn't even an indent in the snow to suggest a 2CV had been there.

We all got out and began to search for any signs the car had been stolen, towed away or moved in any manner. As I clambered halfway up the snow-covered bank to get a better view of the surrounding area, I caught a glimpse of the 2CV's wheels poking out of the snow further along the bank. It took only a few minutes to work out how the car had migrated up the bank, ending on its roof. During the night a rather large snowplough or snow-blower must have driven along the road and turfed the lightweight car to the spot where we found it.

Before long we had righted the car and other than a collapsed canvas roof and slightly wonky front wheels, it was ready to go. The old 2CV may look light but it's made of pretty sturdy stuff. The following year when we returned to Val-d'Isère, apart from some missing paint and a few dents, the little car was still going strong.

Around about this time Leo de Graffenried had arrived as part of the Marlboro executive team. His father Toulo had been the first Swiss driver to win a post-World War Two Grand Prix when he triumphed at the 1949 British Grand Prix at Silverstone.

Leo decided the Range Rovers needed to be spotlessly clean for some special event he had arranged. If you've ever tried to clean a car in temperatures hovering just above freezing you'll understand what happens when you rinse the dirt off. The thin film of water left freezes over and only thaws at speed due to the friction of the air over the body panels. This makes the car wet again, and all the road grime sticks to the clean car once more.

I came up with a plan. After washing the car yet again, I let the water freeze on the bodywork, but before driving off, I found a brush and turning it over, started to knock the ice off. By doing it this way I knew I could drive off with an ice-free exterior and, as a result, the dirt couldn't stick. As always, though, the best-laid plans of mice and men are bound to come unstuck.

Not realizing Range Rovers were skinned in aluminium, my bashing the bodywork left the entire car looking like a golf ball on wheels. It had small dents all over it and was subsequently relegated to ferrying ski journalists up and down the mountain rather than transporting dignitaries to posh functions.

The Range Rover really impressed me, especially with the hiding I gave it, and it let me down only once. I accepted a challenge from a guy driving a snow-groomer truck that he could get up a hill faster than me. I lost. To tell the truth I got stuck halfway up the slope so he won by default — or maybe his vehicle was better equipped for the circumstances than mine.

When Leo finally found time to inspect the Range Rover a day or two later, he was unimpressed as to its, how could I say, slightly shabby dimpled condition. Of course I pleaded innocent as to any knowledge of what could have happened and mumbled something about snowploughs, grit, drunken guests and a few other handy excuses. Eventually I told him about my de-icing system, which went down like a lead balloon and Marlboro had to pay for a complete new Range Rover body shell.

While the ski resort life was pleasant, it could also be physically and financially taxing. Ski racing always came to a halt when the sun dropped behind the mountains as the piste turned to ice, making downhill racing impossible. Being stuck up a mountain in winter doesn't leave many options open but there's always the bar. But even that became tedious after a few days. A walk in the snow was always a good alternative but the low temperatures outside meant it was always necessary to dress very warmly — and that took a lot of time and effort.

The second winter we spent in Europe we took McLaren Formula One show cars to various exhibitions, motor shows and other similar promotional events in northern Europe. In Sweden and Finland the winter temperature is seriously bad for your health, sometimes getting as low as minus 30 or 40°C. When Shaune and I checked into a hotel we'd put our little plastic ice-cube maker outside on the balcony while we poured ourselves a gin. It took about three minutes for the water to freeze and be ready to drop into our waiting glasses. Unfortunately, or probably more likely stupidly, I learned just how cold it gets outside in a Scandinavian country.

After an exhibition at Malmö in Sweden, I was packing the car into the trailer. By the time I'd strapped down both ends and stowed everything away, I'd been outside in minus 25°C for about 15 minutes.

Shaune was standing nearby dressed in so many layers of clothes she had a hint of the Michelin man about her — I hasten to add it was all the clothes that made her look like that, for on a summer's day she'd rival anything on the Riviera.

On the other hand, I was not dressed for the occasion. I had just come from inside the heated exhibition hall so was only wearing jeans and a T-shirt that by this stage was drenched in sweat. It wasn't long before the T-shirt was becoming solid as the sweat froze and, according to some of the other workers, my face was turning blue.

One of the Swedes we were working with noticed with some alarm I was about to reach hypothermia and hustled me back inside to warm up and change into some dry clothes. The problem was I didn't have any. I had to wait until the ice melted before I could get the T-shirt off and then I had to wait until it dried before I could put it back on.

Two seasons in the snow and ice were enough for us. We were used to working in the warmth of summer so that was the end of our ski hospitality jaunt.

John Barnard and Ron Dennis had decided in the early 1980s that a turbo engine was imperative if the team was to win another F1 championship. John sketched out very strict design parameters for the new engine so it would fit his chassis, rather than designing a chassis to fit round an existing turbo engine.

This became known as the 'no compromise' car. I'd call this classic Ron thinking in that approaching an engine manufacturer and asking them to build a completely new engine was akin to giving someone a blank cheque. Like the carbon-fibre chassis three years earlier, Ron wasn't about to let cost get in the way of a good idea.

John and Ron chose Porsche to develop the engine because the German company had a huge amount of knowledge in building turbo engines, and Ron persuaded Mansour Ojjeh's TAG Group to finance its development. They began looking into the project in 1981 and tried to convince Porsche to invest 50 per cent in the project but they wouldn't. Not letting something as trivial as having no money get in the way, Ron told John to get to work on the engine parameters while he went about finding the money. TAG came onboard and the engine was announced in 1982, with the first rig tests in December that year. It was shown in 1983 running for the first time at the Dutch Grand Prix in August. The TAG Porsche engine was used up to the end of the 1987 season when the programme was ended and McLaren went to Honda.

Unfortunately the 'no compromise' car was compromised. In an endeavour to curb the increasingly powerful effect of the new 'winged' cars and their corner speeds, the FIA (Fédération Internationale de l'Automobile) deemed in 1984 all F1 cars were to have flat bottoms. As a result, the full effect of John's engine design parameters was never fully exploited.

I was fortunate to have seen some of the development of this incredibly powerful engine that at full turbo-boost could deliver way in excess of 1000 horsepower. Between the British Grand Prix in mid-July and the Austrian Grand Prix in mid-August, there was only the German Grand Prix at Hockenheim, which lies about 150 kilometres from the Porsche plant at Weissach.

As McLaren's then drivers Watson and Lauda, along with engine financier Ojjeh, would be visiting the factory, Shaune and I took the now christened TAG motorhome to the town of Weissach. It was not easy to get into the plant as the project was super-secret, but as TAG McLaren's people on the spot, Shaune and I had regular access. We were even given a Porsche 911 to drive. After three days we had to hand it back but to our surprise a beautiful cherry-red 944 turbo-engined model replaced it.

I could hardly believe it. The turbo 944 had just been announced to the motoring press and was not yet available in retail showrooms, but here we were driving one of the first of them out of the factory.

Prior to our taking control of the keys, the chief engineer of the TAG Porsche engine project, Hans Mezger, introduced us to the car. 'Please be careful because it is only new,' he said. 'It is one of the first road-going models and we need it back.' We covered about 2000 kilometres in two days, including a trip to Hockenheim that took half the time we usually allowed.

The month we spent in Weissach was interesting personally and commercially. Personally, because Shaune and I stayed in a hotel on the outskirts of Stuttgart near the Porsche Research Centre at Weissach, which meant we enjoyed the company of Porsche personnel nearly every evening. By the end of the project we felt like we were part of Porsche. Weissach is in a region of Germany where the people are known as Schwabisch. They are famously very Scottish when it comes to paying for things, although not when it comes to booze and fun.

Commercially it was enlightening to see just how much work the company was carrying out for other car manufacturers. I was staggered. Even if it was just a dashboard layout, Porsche seemed to be designing a component for every large-volume vehicle manufacturer in the world. Rolling roads ran 24 hours a day testing gearboxes and transmission systems. Even some of the world's best-known small-volume manufacturers had Porsche doing some sort of development work.

I well remember one 'experimental' vehicle that was undoubtedly not an officially commissioned project. Factory staff used an ordinary-looking, boxy-shaped Volkswagen minibus/van for carting people and parts around on a daily basis. The engine, however, to anyone with a discerning ear, was not as it seemed. I asked about this one day and was told the mechanics from the company's Le Mans race team had done an engine swap, inserting a full race 912 flat-12 4.5-litre engine that just happened to be lying about.

The story got better when I was informed on the way to a race meeting, the innocuous-looking van would pull up alongside some hyper sports car (preferably a Porsche) at the lights and throw down a challenge. Most of the time the Porsche mechanics received a cursory, dismissive look of disinterest, but occasionally some bloke with penis envy would blip his throttle in readiness to launch hard when the lights turned green.

The van full of giggling mechanics would match the sports car off the line and keep its nose just in front until both cars reached around 150 kph. At this point the van driver would ease off the throttle, despite having plenty in reserve, as his fellow engineers had determined that the van's windscreen was liable to disintegrate around then.

The TAG Group thought its turbo engine could be licensed for other applications once it had passed its useful life in the racing world. I know for certain the Messerschmitt aircraft company considered it for use as a helicopter engine but nothing came of the idea. After Honda became the engine supplier and it was clear that there would be no other application for the TTE, they were stored in the North Road warehouse of McLaren and the bulk of them ended up being sold as souvenirs to companies and collectors.

The engine might not have been used for anything else, but Ron persuaded Dr Udo Zucker, who developed the TAG Porsche's electronic fuel-injection system for Bosch, to come and work in England. He headed a McLaren International associate company, TAG Electronic Systems, that not only supplied the electronic control package for the McLaren Grand Prix cars, but has more than 50 customers throughout the world's automotive industry. Companies such as Toyota, Mercedes-Benz, BMW and Porsche buy its products.

He left there and started a new company within McLaren dealing in very high-end audio equipment called TAG McLaren Audio and by buying an existing company called Audiolab. That company ceased trading around 2003 and the electronics company is now called McLaren Electronic Systems. Udo left the TAG McLaren Group at the same time and the audio venture is no longer part of the McLaren Group's activities.

Chapter 4

Driving McLaren's motorhome

I still have the telegram asking Shaune and me to go back to England in 1977 to run a motorhome for Marlboro McLaren. It reads, 'JOB ON MARLBORO HOSPITALITY UNIT STILL OPEN AS PER OUR DISCUSSIONS LAST YEAR STOP WOULD WELCOME YOU AND YOUR WIFE TO WORK ON IT IMMEDIATELY.'

The telegram was not entirely unexpected, as I'd been fielding phone calls from Tony Thomas on a number of occasions and was still undecided over whether I wanted to return to England.

When I came back to New Zealand at the end of 1976, Shaune made it quite clear that being away for nine months each year wasn't really going to cut the mustard — and fair enough. In many ways I agreed with her, so my motor-racing days had come to an end, or so I thought.

In an effort to settle down in New Zealand we bought a house in an Auckland suburb, I got a nine-to-five office job and we began to try to find a domestic routine. Despite my hardest efforts at returning to a normal lifestyle, I was struggling with the whole 'get up in the morning, go to work, come home in the evening, have dinner, watch TV and go to bed' thing.

Something must have been stirring in the back of my mind when Tony first rang to see if I wanted to go back to take charge of the motorhome for Marlboro, because rather than turn him down flat, I said I'd think about it. So in a weird sort of way, I wasn't saying no to the idea of the job and nor was I reneging on my commitment to Shaune to stay with her in New Zealand.

The decision not to go back became even more difficult when during one of Tony's further phone calls, he said he wanted both Shaune and me to come and run the motorhome for them. By this stage it was getting increasingly difficult to come up with excuses not to go. Shaune's mum, affectionately known as Mrs J, didn't help matters much by saying, 'Get paid to travel around Europe? You'd be mad to miss an opportunity like that. And anyway, I'll move into your new house and look after it while you're away.'

We had just bought and moved into a house in Glenfield, so Mrs J had somewhere to stay and we had someone to look after our new place. After a couple of months we were going around in circles talking about it and getting nowhere. By the time Tony called for the fourth time, there was no more humming and ahhing, we just said what the hell, let's go for it.

Tony is a very persuasive man whom I first met in 1974/75 while I was helping to manage Ron Dennis's Formula Two team. He and I got on very well. Back then, Tony worked for Charles Stewart, a Marlboro-owned UK-based company that administered its interests in sports promotions, most notably motor racing.

At that time Marlboro was one of Ron's F2 team's biggest sponsors and large global corporations were beginning to realize the worldwide appeal of motor racing and the value of having corporate hospitality. Just look at the huge industry hospitality has become today. More deals are done in a corporate tent or box, watching one form of sport or another, than ever were done on a golf course.

So with nothing to lose, Shaune and I signed up for our next big adventure in the upper echelons of motor racing, having little idea what we were letting ourselves in for. Shaune suggested we sign just for a year to see how it would pan out.

We landed back in England not long after the final Tony phone call and immediately he suggested we take a look at the new style of hospitality he had in mind. Up until this point, at a race meeting you'd be lucky if the tent didn't leak over a wheezing barbecue, and warm boxed wine was all you got trackside. Sponsors were wined and dined at fancy restaurants, but that was always after the racing, or days if not weeks before. The unit we were about to inspect was being totally refurbished for the new season. It had been functioning as a kind of a press truck at various events, not as the motorhome Tony envisaged.

The Charles Stewart lot wanted to use the unit more as a mum-and-dad hosted hospitality unit. Eventually even folk older than us referred to Shaune and me as 'Mum and Dad'.

We may have had the first purpose-built and run hospitality set-up in the paddock but there were a few other teams heading in this direction. Texaco were doing something similar (it went on to become the Marlboro unit), Lotus had something and there was also a smattering of old vans.

What Tony and Marlboro had in mind was a whole new approach. Their idea was to get one of the biggest trucks in the paddock and convert it into a first-class catering and entertainment facility on wheels. The ultimate purpose was pure PR — to encourage businesses and wealthy individuals to dig deep and write out big fat cheques to sponsor our race-car teams. The Grand Prix circus was about to be revolutionized.

We all turned up at the United Services Garage body shop in Portsmouth and there was a shiny new TM Bedford tractor unit towing a 40-foot trailer beautifully fitted out with kitchen, lounge and a drivers' private room. Shaune and I looked at each other and thought, nice, this is going to be a great job. Almost as an aside I turned to Tony and asked, 'Very nice. But who's going to drive this bloody great thing?'

With a slightly puzzled look on his face, Tony turned to me and said, 'You are of course, you fool. Why did you think we paid your airfares to come over here?'

Bugger, I thought. I'm going to have to tell him I don't have a licence to pilot one of those monstrous things. As the colour drained from his face at that breaking news, he spluttered that I had driven Ron's F2 transporters all over Europe and beyond.

'Yes, Tony,' I replied patiently. 'That was a rigid-axle vehicle and this thing's an articulated lorry, a completely different kettle of fish. It needs a special licence.'

By this time Tony was looking decidedly uncomfortable. 'Christ, we'd better get you one right now.'

Within a few days I was booked into a training school in southwest London, where a 10-day course was being compressed into less than half that time, just for me. Meanwhile, Marlboro's behemoth of a rig was being delivered to the next Grand Prix in Monaco by another New Zealander, Max Amor, a Western Springs (Auckland) speedway rider who was on his OE. He subsequently moved to the US and went on to own a large earthmoving business before dying in 2009. Because I had a few days to fill in before my articulated truck course began, Shaune and I decided to join the trip to Monaco to learn something about our new roles as hospitality managers.

We travelled from London via the Philip Morris International office in Lausanne, Switzerland, driving a huge American Econoline van with an eight-litre V8 engine.

Eventually we made it to Monaco where everything had been set up for us. Shaune's initiation into the world of Marlboro entertainment was a little out of the ordinary, especially from a hospitality point of view. In her own words, 'I was introduced to a Marlboro consultant named Graham Bogle, who spent 20 minutes showing me how to make sandwiches, then another 20 minutes showing me where to hide them.' By this stage Shaune was slightly puzzled as to why you'd go to all the effort of making vast quantities of fresh sandwiches, only to hide them.

In a flash, Bogle enlightened us as to the reason. 'We don't want people eating them and enjoying themselves in this unit, because they'll hang around, and you don't want that to happen,' he explained.

We soon discovered what he was on about. Although the food was primarily for the Marlboro McLaren mechanics, the rest of the gannets in the paddock easily sniffed out where the good tucker was coming from, and descended on the motorhome like a pack of starving dogs looking for their last meal.

After my brief, eye-opening introduction to the world of hospitality at a Grand Prix meeting, it was time to get back to England and get organized for my attempt at getting a Heavy Goods Vehicle licence. Unlike sitting a car driver's test, which tends to be a series of multi-guess questions like how fast you're allowed to drive in a built-up area, and being able to get a few wrong, there is no room for error or guesswork when trying to get your HGV ticket.

Unlike that UK TV programme where a lady learner driver spends years failing her driving tests, there was no chance to go back to the testing station for another attempt when trying to get your HGV licence.

In the run-up to my test, I had many a nightmare about cones, because if you so much as looked sideways at one, it would topple over. And if that happened it was an automatic fail, no matter how well you did in other parts of the test. If I failed, it was goodnight, nurse, and I'd be on the first plane back to New Zealand.

The day of reckoning arrived all too fast and I found myself at the testing station trying to work out how I could stop my hands from sweating so much, knowing that if they didn't I'd struggle to hold on to the steering wheel.

Driving forward in, around and through the cones was difficult and nerve-wracking but nothing compared with having to reverse the truck and trailer unit. In this exercise I had to manoeuvre the truck and trailer backwards between the cones and come to a halt within 18 inches of a brick wall. Easy, you might think, but by this time my nerves were shattered and the cones seemed to have morphed into road spikes ready to puncture any hope I had getting back into Formula One.

It didn't bear thinking what Tony Thomas's reaction would be if I had to tell him I flunked the driving test. Anyway, I reassured myself that nobody's going to die if I hit a cone so what the hell, as I crunched the truck into reverse. The one concession with this part of the test was you were allowed to reverse with the door open, peering down the side of the truck with the occasional glance in the wing mirror on the other side to make sure you weren't about to run over someone.

Much to my surprise, it all went rather well and before I knew it I was at the wall with all the cones still standing. With a smug smile on my face and breathing a sign of relief, I pulled the door closed, but instead of hearing a satisfying clunk, I heard a dull thud as a cone prevented the truck door from closing fully.

'Fuckin' hell,' I mumbled, and a few other words to that effect. 'That's blown it, I've stuffed up royally.'

According to the rules of the test, the examiner still had to take me out on a road test in normal traffic. So it was with a heavy heart and half my mind on the process that we headed out onto the narrow lanes of Tooting and Wandsworth in the southwest of London. What the hell, I thought, I've failed so I may as well enjoy myself. I drove around thinking about what Shaune and I were going to do now that I couldn't drive the motorhome. I made it safely back to the testing station in one piece and I was going through the process of turning everything off when the instructor turned to me and said, 'I enjoyed that, a nice piece of driving and competently done. Pretty good for someone with as little experience as you've had.'

Nice of him to comment, I thought, but it's no damn use to me. I mumbled a thank you and left it at that. I hadn't really noticed he was filling out papers and signing them, rather than just giving all the paperwork to me with a simple 'FAIL' on it. He must have noticed my glum look so commented, 'I've looked at the rule book during the drive back and it says you must not hit or knock over a cone with a wheel or the trailer. It doesn't say anything about closing the door on a cone, so congratulations, you've passed!'

I must have looked like a fish out of water gasping for air as my jaw moved up and down trying to find the right words to say something. I felt like kissing him or giving him a bear-hug. Instead I settled on a stammering 'thank you, thank you very, very much'.

Unfortunately, or maybe fortunately, there was no time for celebration and before I could catch my breath, it was back on a plane and off to France again. While I'd been having kittens trying to get my HGV licence, Max had driven the rig from Monaco to Paul Ricard just east of Marseilles, where McLaren were conducting a test session. I arrived proudly waving my new licence in the air like a dog with two dicks, and took charge of the motorhome. Now I had to get it ready for the next stop, Zolder, for the Belgian Grand Prix.

What a great feeling that was, to know the big adventure was back on track. However, the euphoria soon settled down to excitement

George Harrison and Bob at the Canadian Formula One Grand Prix 2001.

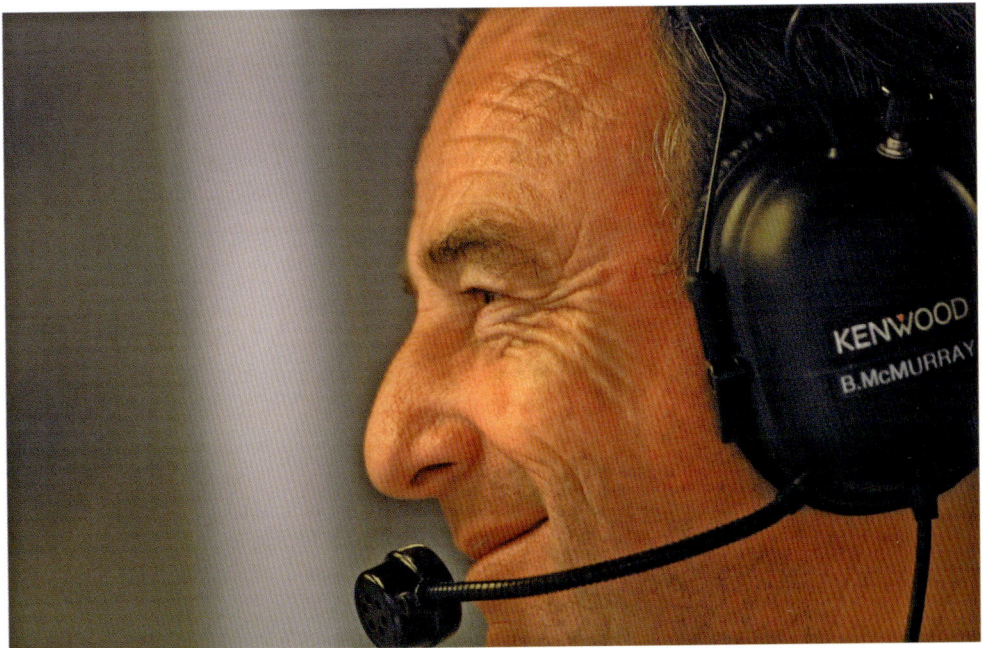

Contentment in the McLaren pits.

From left, Ayrton Senna, test driver
Emanuele Pirro and Alain Prost.

One of the craziest but most naturally
talented drivers ever to drive in Formula
One, Gilles Villeneuve was sadly killed
on 8 May 1982.

John Nicholson in the Lyncar 002 Formula Atlantic with trusty mechanic Bob McMurray
stopping it rolling away. England circa 1972.

Ayrton Senna presenting Shaune with the Blackbridge Road Tennis Tournament Trophy.

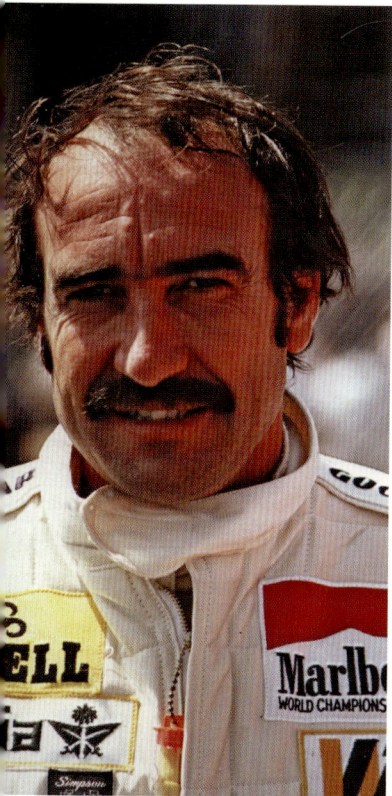
Gianclaudio Giuseppe 'Clay' Regazzoni, one of the old school of drivers.

Ayrton Senna's MP4/6 outside Number 10 Downing Street, minus the Courtaulds logo on the left sidepod.

Bruno Giacomelli with his 'cigarette' boat.

The jewel in the crown of Formula One, Monaco, with Jochen Mass's sailing boat in the middle of the harbour. It was later shipwrecked on rocks.

Ayrton Senna being 'arrested' in the McLaren factory by the local Woking constabulary.

Nothing else left to win. Mika Hakkinen and Bob with the spoils from the Barcelona Formula One Grand Prix 2000.

Jonny Reid in the A1 Team New Zealand car at the Taupo A1GP event in 2008.

Concentration in the garage: A1GP at Taupo.

World champion James Hunt followed by Jochen Mass and Carlos Reutemann driving Ferrari number 12.

Jonny Reid and Bob before the A1GP event at Taupo.

Ayrton Senna visiting Shaune and Bob at their home in Dairy Flat after the Australian Grand Prix 1993.

Bob with Stuart Hullah in the wheelchair. The chair had a Senna gear lever for Stuart to control the functions and was especially decorated by the McLaren paint shop.

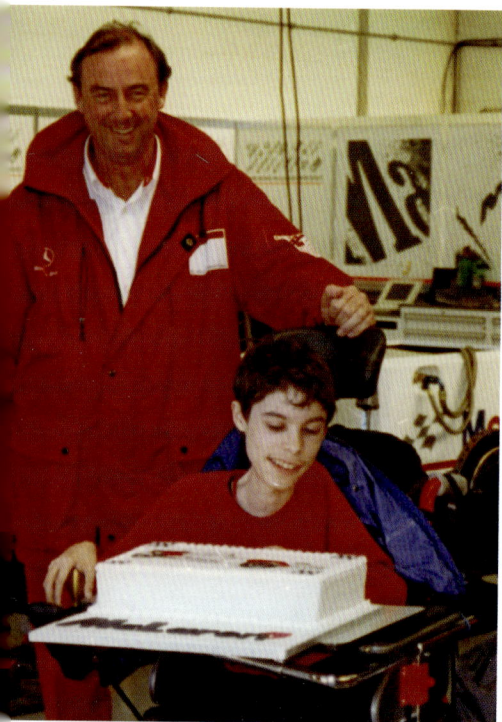

JAMES HUNT (GB)

James Hunt, world champion.

Sometimes the show cars had to get in some very tight places.

The Procar series cars racing past the famous 'Tip Top' bar out of Casino Square in Monaco.

Mika Hakkinen on his visit to Bob's house in New Zealand, with Shaune and her brother-in-law Ian Griffiths, known as 'Sinbad' in his early days at McLaren.

Doing a lap of the Malaysian Grand Prix track in the famous 1955 Mercedes-Benz 300SLR #722 as driven by Moss and Jenkinson to victory in the 1955 Mille Miglia. You can't quite see the big grin on Bob's face.

The McLaren team at the Rock Lobster fish and chip cafe in Adelaide. All dressed up for the end-of-season 'Not the Nigel Mansell' Courtaulds party, with eyebrows and moustaches in place.

Bob with Jo Ramirez.

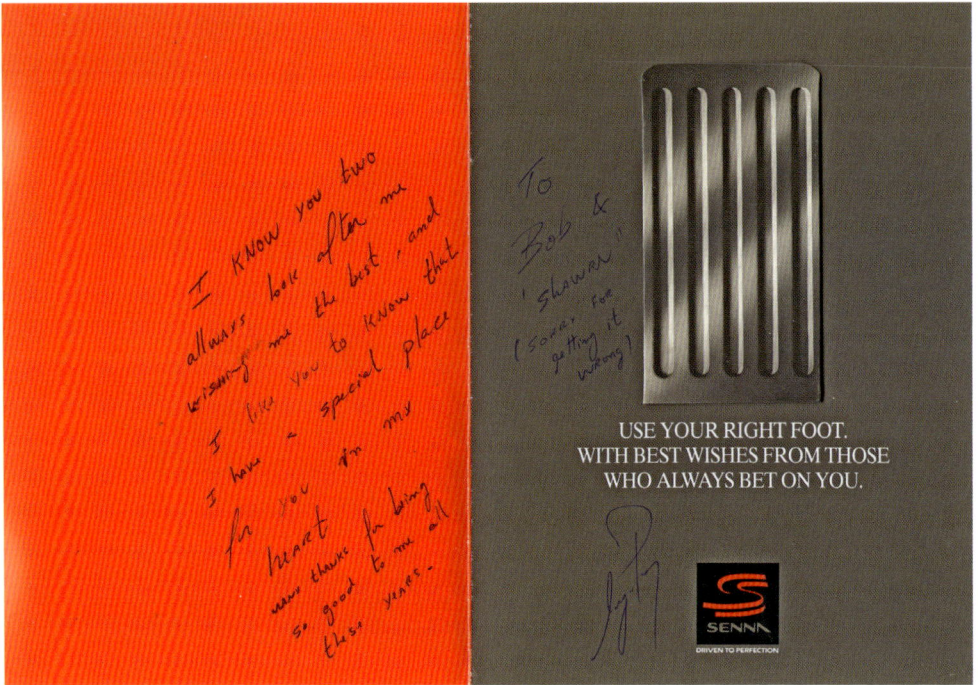

A touching Christmas card from Ayrton Senna.

A Christmas card marking the end of Peugeot engines in the McLaren camp and the beginning of Mercedes.

The Marlboro McLaren motorhome and Shaune's Ford Econoline waiting for a ferry from Bilbao to Portsmouth.

Ayrton Senna about to go and qualify. Always an exciting moment.

James Hunt in party mode at the Seneca Lodge Hotel in Watkins Glen, New York.

Mika Hakkinen in the office.

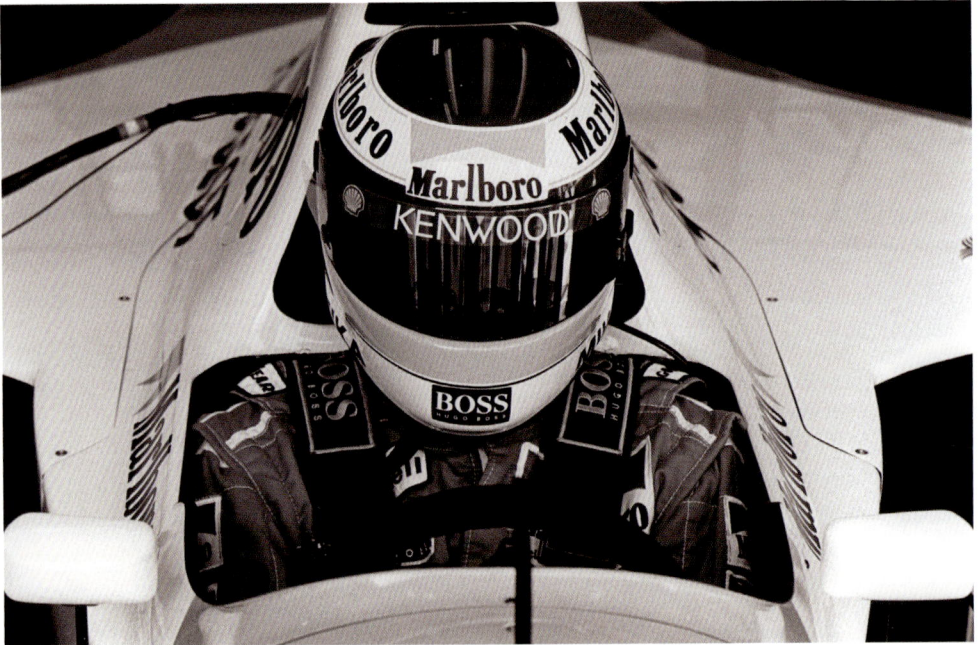

The Finnjet ferry from Travemünde to Helsinki. In the late '70s this was the largest, fastest and longest car ferry in the world and very difficult to back the length of in a truck.

Marlboro marketing and promotions boss John Hogan after a good race win.

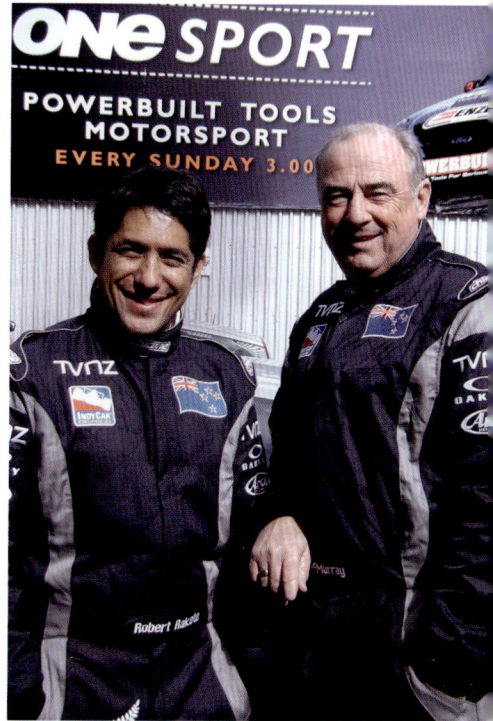

Robert Rakete and Bob in their party frocks ready to go to the Indianapolis 500 for TVNZ.

Catherine Zeta-Jones and Michael Douglas were regular visitors to the Grand Prix and it was always a pleasure for Bob to show them around.

Bob at his last Grand Prix for McLaren, the 2001 Japanese GP at Suzuka.

A1GP at Taupo. Happy as ever!

mixed with a little dread as Shaune and I sat in the motorhome on the day of departure and realized this trip wasn't going to be a Wednesday-afternoon jaunt around the back streets of Tooting. More like a fraught trek across a swathe of Europe, on the 'wrong' side of the road, in a huge million-dollar vehicle I'd never driven before. To add a little spice to our foray on foreign soil, neither of us knew whether to turn left or right out of Paul Ricard to point the rig in the direction of Belgium, let alone Zolder.

Many tense hours later, we finally arrived in Zolder and I collapsed on the motel bed in a mentally exhausted heap.

The next day we settled into the paddock at the track and got down to business. By the end of the Grand Prix, when we were packing up the motorhome, I was beginning to think this was the life for me. Travelling all over Europe in a mega-motorhome, meeting and greeting the rich and famous, living high on the hog while getting to see all the Grand Prix — how cool is that?

As we were getting ready to leave the track we were handed our next destination and it was a doozy — Sweden. We didn't have the luxury of time to drive the long way around, up through Finland, so we headed for the port of Travemünde near Hamburg.

Driving down to the port after an uneventful trip across Europe from Holland, I was looking forward to getting on the ferry and having a rest. The sight that greeted me as we pulled into the terminal complex made my heart sink. There must have been enough trucks of all shapes and sizes to fill 10 football fields and the ferry, or 'bloody great ship', made most apartment blocks look like Lego sets. We had decided to get there early so we'd have time to have a look around, but loading started at 10 a.m. for the 7 p.m. sailing. Some of the other drivers must have arrived the month before, because my turn to load didn't come around until 5 p.m.

As I pulled up to the cavernous opening at the front of the ship, all I saw was a narrow gap down the entire length of the ship right to its very end. It suddenly dawned on me, as my knees nearly gave out, that I was expected to reverse right down the length of the vessel with barely room on either side for a stick-thin catwalk model to squeeze past.

To make matters worse, I must have looked terrified because before long a crowd of drivers had arrived to watch me attempt this feat without damaging anyone else's rig, let alone put a ding in our brand-new artic. There was no use feeling sorry for myself, so up I hopped into the cab, swung the truck around and proceeded to reverse towards the loading ramp. This was the first time since I'd passed my HGV test that I'd needed to reverse the thing. At my first attempt I didn't manage to get all the truck onto the ship before I had to drive out again.

On my second attempt I got a bit further in and was thinking it was a bit like sex for the first time — pretend that you know what you're doing, and keep going. I was soon beginning to think I might just get away with it and convince the watching truckies that I did in fact know what I was doing. But ooh no — I was now within a whisker of scraping a shed-load of paint off a Swedish truck. So, back out I came again.

After yet another aborted attempt I could see the looks of utter contempt on the watching drivers' faces and as the sweat began to break out on my brow, I began to really worry I would hold up the sailing, or worse, the ship would leave without us.

Not one of the fat, unkempt, mustachioed, clog-wearing Germans watching so much as lifted an eyebrow to help me. Just as it began to sink in that there was more chance of the second coming than of my getting the damn truck and trailer down the chute, a face appeared at the window. In a thick Geordie accent that seemed to come from his boots he grumbled, 'Yiv neet done this befawa, have ya laddie? You'll na mare be giving these Kraut bastards owt more to laugh aboot. Yous'll be lookin' strite aheed at me and neet in ya mirrors, or anywhere else — understand?'

I nodded rapidly, swallowing dryly. With my eyes glued to his hands, I followed his signals to the smallest of twitches and after what seemed an eternity, he finally drew his fingers across his throat, signalling me to cut the engine. I had reached the bow of the ship. I was beginning to worry about myself by now, as this was the second Englishman in a couple of months I wanted to hug and kiss in thanks. However, by the time I'd managed to squeeze out of the cab, he'd disappeared. Mate, if you're reading this you'll know who you are and you'll know you have my eternal thanks.

Back on dry land again, I was coming to grips with driving the big rig and the more I came to understand how it all worked, the more I realized what a bitch of a thing it was. Under normal driving conditions on a good open motorway the motorhome was a dream to drive, but get it on a narrow road or in the middle of a town and it was quite a different story.

In a typical English trailer-design fault, all the wheels were at the rear of the trailer unit. That meant you needed all your lane, and most of the oncoming traffic's lane, to get around corners. While keeping part of your mind on where to position the rig on the road, you needed the other half to concentrate on keeping up the revs, because if they drop in a crash gearbox, it's all the way back to first to get going again.

The first time this gear drama raised its head was on an early trip through Belgium when I was heading down a hill, in the rain, towards an intersection controlled by traffic lights. I was attempting to change down when it all went wrong and I ended up grabbing a fistful of neutrals. I knew if I found too low a gear the wheels would lock up on the wet surface and the same would happen if I jumped on the brakes.

As I hurtled towards the intersection my life was racing before my eyes and I began to think what an inglorious end it was going to be to my all too short McLaren hospitality career. The good Lord must have been glancing in my general direction that day, for as we sailed across the intersection on a red light, the traffic to the left was all snarled up with its own problems and as I was too scared to look to the right. Somehow I had managed to miss everything and emerge unscathed.

At the time, our first F1 season in the motorhome seemed like a hell of a lot of fun, but in hindsight — a wonderful thing, as we all know — it was probably more nerve-wracking than anything. Piloting such a massive vehicle, decorated in Day-Glo red and bright white with MARLBORO WORLD CHAMPIONSHIP TEAM emblazoned on each side, on the wrong side of the road through a myriad of countries was an exercise in learning on the fast track. And I'm sure we must have caused some sort of aggravation, or had some sort of drama, at just about every track we visited that first season.

Because it was one of its kind in the paddock that year, the motorhome was a focal point at each round of the Formula One series. Shaune and I didn't just feed the McLaren F1 team, the Marlboro folk and their guests; our motorhome was also the place where the Formula One Constructors' Association and the Grand Prix Drivers' Association held their regular meetings. It really was the hub of all that happened behind the scenes at a Grand Prix. If anything was going to happen in the paddock, it happened in the Marlboro motorhome first.

Over time, Shaune and I got to meet and become friends with the couples running the much smaller hospitality units for other Formula

One teams. Of all the motorhome couples, none became better friends than Stuart and Diana Spires. This was a little puzzling as our first meeting was not auspicious. Stuart and I first met in the paddock at Zolder on the eve of the Belgian Grand Prix in 1977.

In preparation for all the Marlboro executives, and other notables, who'd be arriving the next day, I was proudly washing my beautiful new truck when the water from the hose suddenly cut off. Being slightly miffed, I went in search of the cause and it took only a few minutes to discover Stuart, who looked like a cross between Mick Fleetwood and Catweazle, had unscrewed my hose and replaced it with his own. He'd then proceeded to wash a strange box-like vehicle the money-strapped Surtees team had the audacity to call a motor-home.

'What the hell's your game?' I hissed through clenched teeth. 'I'm trying to wash the bloody McLaren motorhome, not some shit-box.' Within seconds we were yelling in each other's face and it nearly descended into fisticuffs. We managed to sort it out before it spiralled out of control and had a laugh about it later when we went on to become firm friends.

By 1980 Marlboro had developed a relationship with the Alfa Romeo team and was continuing its involvement in Formula Two. As you can imagine, Shaune and I really had our work cut out at the end of the 1970s looking after all these extra personnel. One thing I'll say, though, working the F2 races was more fun and far more relaxed than F1. They had a club feel about them, despite the cars being full-on wings-and-slicks racers with powerful two-litre BDA, BMW, Hart *et al* engines driven by Grand Prix stars of the time.

We were in the paddock for a stand-alone F2 race at Nogaro in the South of France in 1978 where there was an array of transporters in the paddock, one of which was head and shoulders above the rest. In fact, it would have put a lot of the F1 rigs to shame. It belonged to the Briggs-Briedenbach Racing Team, owned by two wealthy Americans whose money came from the Briggs' family business — the Flamingo casino in Las Vegas.

Their monstrous two-car Kenworth transporter surpassed nearly everything in European motor racing at the time and some bright spark came up with the idea that spectators might like to see the trucks that hauled F2 cars around Europe. After some discussion, the friendly French organizers readily agreed to a two-lap parade of the tractor units minus the trailers.

Eventually we lined up beside the local mayor, who was standing in a convertible, and when he waved the flag, off we went in a tidy, disciplined convoy. Not for long, though — when we came to the last corner of the second lap the plan changed dramatically. The first two tractor unit drivers planted their feet and amidst belching diesel fumes the trucks leapt forward, not quite F2-like, but fast enough. Without a moment's hesitation the rest of us followed suit and you could say truck racing was born at that very moment in 1978.

As we thundered past the mayor, who was frantically waving his arms trying to stop the drag race to the first corner, we soon lost sight of him as he disappeared into a cloud of exhaust smoke. However, it was a short-lived race as the now apoplectic mayor had summoned the local gendarmerie to the start/finish line, where we were all threatened with arrest.

Later on at Nogaro I met a fellow Kiwi, Murray Taylor, who was covering all the F2 races for the English publication *Motoring News.* It was great hearing another New Zealand voice and over time I came to know him quite well. Murray remembers the truck race and can confirm it took place. Truck racing is popular these days but some things don't change — the amount of black smoke pouring out of the exhaust stacks seems to be the same as it was back then.

Murray played his part in motor racing for many years, running his own Formula Three team for nine seasons. He helped launched the careers of several notable drivers including 1996 Formula One World Champion Damon Hill. He was also in charge when Paul Radisich made the racing world in Europe sit up and take notice by putting his car on pole in his first ever F3 outing. In 2003 Murray worked as media and communications manager for Team New Zealand in the America's Cup when it was held on Auckland's Hauraki Gulf. He is still working in New Zealand for, among others, the Toyota Racing Series, just as I am.

By now, some countries were beginning to have second thoughts about cigarette sponsorship in sport and Germany was becoming one of the loudest voices against tobacco involvement. The powers that be decided we wouldn't take the Marlboro motorhome to the German F1 Grand Prix; instead, we'd head up to Finland for the 1981 500cc World Motorcycle Grand Prix. Marlboro had a hefty involvement with Yamaha, Giacomo Agostini and Kenny Roberts and as there was no problem with tobacco advertising in Finland, off we went.

Way up there in Finland it was the first time, but by no means the last, that our hotel bookings had been messed up, so Shaune and I found ourselves in a backpackers. The Scandinavians have always been to the fore in unisex matters, as we were reminded. The Finns went in for unisex bathrooms, and after a long and tiring road trip, Shaune and I had no option but to join in.

Mixed nude showers are a trifle embarrassing when you're not used to them, especially after growing up in England — a place not known for its blasé approach to public nudity. 'What made it worse,' Shaune admitted, 'was that press people and all sorts of others we knew were there as well.'

Interestingly, 1981 was the last year a 500cc motorcycle Grand Prix race was held in Finland because the track, a public road, was close to the Russian border and was deemed unsuitable for further racing. You could see Russia from just outside of town. At one part of the circuit, the big bikes crossed a railway line at speeds that launched them into the air. Another shortcoming, as we soon discovered, was the complete lack of proper paddock space.

As an alternative I arranged to park on the forecourt of a petrol station that had a good view of one of the corners. Now that we had solved the dilemma of where to park, I turned my attention to another problem that had been on my mind for some time. The generator used to power the hospitality suite had decided to jump ship on the way to Finland. When it had come to rest after pinballing down the road it was battered and bent and after wrestling it back on board, I soon found it wasn't going to power a hair dryer, let alone a trailer unit.

Clearly the petrol station didn't have the required juice to cope with our power demands, so we asked politely at a nearby building that looked like a substation. Five cartons of Marlboro cigarettes and two cartons of smuggled German beer later, we were wired into the local grid with a hefty power cable that was probably 40 or 50 metres long and about 50mm in diameter.

Once everything was up and running, I made arrangements for the electricity guys to meet us back at the substation on Sunday night to unhook the motorhome so we could leave in time to get the ferry out of Helsinki. Come Sunday afternoon, I waited and waited but there was no sign of anyone. Remember that there were no mobile phones back then and leaving a live cable lying around wasn't a good idea.

By now there was no margin for error on the trip to the port so desperate measures were called for. I reversed the rig right up to the substation, got out, walked around to the back and wrapped the power cable around the bumper. I leapt back into the cab, told Shaune to hang on, crashed into first gear and floored it. The power cable snapped taut for a split second before it came flying out of the substation.

I hadn't really thought what might happen and even if I did, I couldn't have imagined the actual outcome. First there was a huge flash of light, quickly followed by a mini explosion and it was like a switch had been thrown. The whole village and gas station were instantly plunged into darkness. I hadn't just tripped the fuse, I had destroyed the entire bloody fuse box.

'Shit!' I yelled as I jumped down onto the road. I legged it around to the back of the truck, quickly unwrapped the cable and chucked the incriminating evidence into the locker. Hauling myself back into the driver's seat, I slammed the door shut as I floored the accelerator and raced out of Imatra faster than the truck and trailer had ever gone before. A risky way to disconnect a plug I know, but we only had two weeks to get to Zeltweg in Austria for the Grand Prix on 16 August 1981, and if we'd missed the ferry we were doomed. Not only was getting on the road to Zeltweg an adventure, the whole trip was one of the more memorable journeys of our careers.

Austrian road maps had never been known for their accuracy and while we could work out where Zeltweg was, it turned out to be more indicative than accurate. Although the legend may have said it was a main road, often it turned out to be more of a goat track. And that was the case as we got ever closer to our destination. After crawling along for miles on a switchback single-track road, it was becoming increasingly apparent there was no relationship between the map on Shaune's lap and what I was seeing out the window. Especially when up popped a stunning pink monastery perched high on top of the hill we were climbing at a snail's pace.

According to the map, the road went right through the middle of the Sekau monastery of Saint Christopher's, and the road we were on was the wrong one — a one-way track to the monastery, and the only place to turn around. As there was no alternative route, I had to shoehorn the artic through the entrance arch, slap-bang into the middle of the cloisters. Before long the monks were leaning over balconies, out windows and peering around doors with eyes on stalks, gawping at a huge Marlboro-liveried tractor and trailer unit blocking out the sun in the middle of their courtyard.

I was still learning how to drive the thing, so reversing it past the fountain was a non-starter. So forward it was, with me humming a few bars from 'Onward Christian Soldiers'. This was not in the hope of taking down half a building, but that the road would improve on the other side.

Wrong again. A rock and a hard place, the devil and the deep blue sea, Occam's razor and all the rest of those phrases whistled through my head. Just up ahead was a very narrow wooden bridge that seemed to get smaller as I walked up to it. The sign on one of the pillars stipulated a five-tonne limit. I glanced back at the rig, knowing it must weigh at least six times that and had another look at the sign just in case I had missed seeing an extra digit. No matter how many times I looked away and back again, it still said five tonnes.

Shaune and I returned to the rig, stopped and walked back to the bridge in the forlorn hope it was all a bad dream and the bridge had miraculously transformed itself into a two-lane, recently built concrete structure. Still no luck. We ran across the bridge repeatedly, jumping up and down in an effort to do our own stress test. 'Feels pretty solid to me,' I ventured hopefully to Shaune.

'If you say so dear,' Shaune replied. 'But you've lost an awful lot of your suntan, are you feeling OK?'

After more discussion we came to realize we had only two choices. Go for it and have a glorious end to our burgeoning hospitality career or head back the way we came, miss our connection and have an inglorious end. The saving grace was that the bridge was only about eight metres long, so if I got up a head of steam, our momentum might just carry us across if the bridge gave way. The truck and trailer unit was longer than the bridge, so if it started to collapse I hoped the tractor unit might be on the other side and could pull the trailer up and across. And if I went fast enough, I could get across before it all fell away.

Although Shaune was a little sceptical, it seemed like a reasonable plan to me, so with a determined mind I hauled myself back up into the cab. I told Shaune she would have to cross first in the 10-seater Econoline van to make sure the bridge could at least support some sort of weight. Also, I needed someone to chronicle my heroic attempt at getting to the next race on time, despite risk to myself, so if it all went pear-shaped, there'd be someone to tell the story.

I reversed the rig as far as I could without getting it tangled in knots, gave Shaune the thumbs up, crashed it into first, floored the accelerator and popped the clutch. The truck leapt forward, and with the exhaust bellowing, I hurtled towards the wooden structure that again appeared to get smaller the closer I got. Crunching through the gears, I hit the bridge at what seemed like a million miles an hour, shut my eyes, sent a few quick ones to the big man upstairs and rocketed across the flimsy structure. Apart from a brief sway in the middle, the bridge held and I shot off the other side.

By the time I had brought the rig to a halt my hands had stopped shaking and settled down to a mild twitch. Shaune sprinted over and we hugged in mutual relief. I was relieved I was still alive and Shaune was happy knowing she wouldn't have to explain the loss of a truck and trailer to McLaren, or that they'd have to find another driver.

With morbid fascination we walked back to see what, if any, damage had been inflicted on the bridge. Although still in one piece, it now had a bloody great sag in the middle where the weight of the vehicle had forced the two main piles deeper into the riverbed. Also, a couple of the top planks had broken and were sticking up out of the structure.

At last we set off again in search of a village that might be able to point us in the direction of the Zeltweg race track. Just six kilometres down the road we found one and asked a local where the circuit was. It transpired it was 200 metres up the road and the motorway we should have been on was across the fields running parallel to us. In the end what should have been a two-hour trip had taken us nearly seven hours and God knows how many years off our lives.

Despite that hiccup, the back-road journey showed us what great countryside there is to be seen throughout Europe and reinforced why we had decided to come back. Other than getting lost, our next biggest time-waster was the police. I have nothing against the police in any country pulling over bad, crazy or drunk drivers and giving them a hard time, but when you're trundling along minding your own business, they can be a right pain. I still don't know if they do it out of boredom or vindictiveness.

When we left Zeltweg, we left Austria and were travelling through Germany on our way to the Dutch Grand Prix at Zandvoort. Minding my own business driving along the autobahn, I was surprised to see flashing lights in the mirrors and to hear the wail of a police siren. On pulling over and stopping, I was approached by a German police officer who proceeded to tell me it was illegal to drive a truck on the autobahn in January on Sundays. I informed him I was aware of this, but the rig was in fact registered as a car and caravan.

What pleasantries there were at the start of our chat soon turned to custard as the pompous little git began strutting up and down waving his arms about like a windmill, banging on about how could something this big be a car and caravan? To shut the officious bugger up, I showed him the registration papers for the vehicle that stated, in black and white, that it was registered exactly as I had described to him.

By this stage the little man was close to popping a valve and demanded he measure the height of the trailer. I was feeling comfortable as the little sod got out his measuring stick, knowing we were a few inches under the four-metre height restriction. I glanced up as he marched over to the trailer and stopped breathing. Bugger, I thought — I'd forgotten about the guardrail that had been added to the roof of the trailer unit so it could be turned into a viewing platform at race meetings. Nobody had bothered to re-measure the height, so he might just get his wish and be able to write me a ticket.

The guardrail cleared the height at 3.9 metres at the first attempt, but not to be deterred, our officious officer tried all manner of ways to fail the rig on height. Just as he was about to give up in frustration, the rear door of the trailer flew open and out strode a by now very stroppy Judy Collins (not the singer).

Normally she was a very pleasant young American who we suspected was from a wealthy family, as every so often she would whip out the Platinum Amex and stay in some flash hotel. Judy was travelling around Europe following the Grand Prix and we had met in Monaco and agreed to give her a lift to the race meetings.

'Hey Bob,' she shouted, running out of patience. 'Tell the Krauts to fuck off so we can get a move on.'

One of the German policemen, who we had assumed didn't speak English, frowned and responded immediately, 'We do not like that language.' Even if he didn't understand the words, there was no mistaking Judy's tone of voice.

'Yeah, Judy, sure Judy, just go back inside the trailer, will you?' I snapped at her.

'No, no,' the head cop interrupted. 'It is not permitted to carry passengers in ze trailer.'

'Okay Judy, go and sit in the front with Shaune please,' I said between gritted teeth. The cops were really enjoying this now and I began to realize Judy's outburst was about to cost us dearly both in time and fines. Head honcho went on to tell me the vehicle was only permitted to carry two passengers in the cab. After much discussion, Judy was allowed up front as the rig had a single sleeper bunk she could occupy.

To this day, Shaune still recollects how tense it was in the cab for the rest of the trip. I had managed, along with a couple of Marlboro caps, to get the original fine down from 100 marks to 20. But because of my big-mouth friend in the trailer, it had rocketed to 500 marks. After that I didn't talk to Judy for the next three days. Having said that, she stayed with us for some time over that season and was pretty good fun.

I suppose it's like waving a red flag at a bull, driving a massive F1 truck across Europe liveried up with pictures of the race-cars. Some years it seemed as if every country's traffic police pulled us over in the hope of getting a piece of F1 merchandise. Almost all the drivers in the cars passing us would strain their necks looking up to see who was driving the rig. I was convinced they were expecting to see James Hunt, Niki Lauda or Mika Hakkinen in the driver's seat. More often than not they were surprised to see nobody driving, as the motorhome was a right-hand drive. The onlooking drivers could be a nuisance and a hazard on a busy motorway.

When we said we were not carrying any merchandise, their bottom lips would drop and they'd become officious and suspicious and want to see the mileage tachometer. That raised even more problems, as the truck and trailer unit was registered as a car and caravan and at that time there was no upper weight limit for vehicles with tachographs.

Many people might be under the impression Italian police are easily persuaded to ignore certain minor offences by the suggestion of a free hat or T-shirt. Not the case, in my experience. I'm reminded of an incident that occurred on the way out of Italy, near Ventemiglia, one day in 1982. I'd been pinged speeding in our executive motor-home so I pulled in between two trucks to see what would happen. The pursuing police Alfa raced ahead of us and pulled the three of us over. A lone policeman walked back to the first truck where a typical Italian screaming match took place, after which the driver was waved on his way. Same for the truck behind me.

I went through the whole 'American registered, doesn't require a tacho' thing, but to no avail. The cop now wanted to see inside the truck and unit. Not making the link between speeding and an interior, I politely, but firmly, declined to let him in. As the conversation started to escalate, the door of the police car opened and the most amazing sight began to unfold from the car. First a pair of knee-high black boots appeared, followed by a pair of legs that seemed to go on forever, encased in figure-hugging dark blue slacks with a gold strip down the side.

Topping the magnificent pair of pins was an impossibly tall and beautiful young Italian woman with hair down to the middle of her back. Not only was her chassis something to behold, the face matched — a very beautiful creature indeed. She adjusted her hat in the wing mirror, placed a pair of Ray-Ban Aviators on her perfectly formed nose and sashayed over to where I was standing. In near perfect, husky English she enquired if I had a tachometer. Gathering myself, I answered that I did not and explained why.

After a very pleasant and polite exchange, I was gently reminded that from 1983 onwards it would be a legal requirement to have a tacho, regardless of the vehicle's country of origin. When she had finishing gently admonishing me, she said I was to have a safe journey leaving Italy and waved us on.

Every year after that incident, I'd drive through Ventemiglia looking in police cars hoping to see the same woman. Sadly, though, I never did.

Poorly paid police are a fact of life in many countries. At the sight of a Formula One truck, Spanish and Portuguese police, for example, would do nothing to disguise their pleasure at the thought of a branded T-shirt or two. Some of the other European police, notably the French, German and even the British, are worse in my view, because they pretend to be honest. However, for straight out, in-your-face bribery and corruption, the Mexicans and Brazilians win hands down.

Another annoying hazard we had to deal with when driving across continents were underpasses. Having had the trailer and guardrail measured precisely by the German police, I knew it was a tad under the four-metre legal requirement so when I saw a sign on a Dutch underpass stating clearance was four metres, I couldn't see any problem.

We were on our way to Haarlem just to the north of the race-track at Zandvoort to fill up with LPG for the catering gear in the truck. Maybe the Dutch engineers should have used the German yardstick. A good way under the bridge there was a horrible grating and graunching noise and we ground to a halt. With head in hand I realized we were stuck, with traffic rapidly queueing up behind us, as it was five o'clock in the afternoon — peak hour on a Friday.

It wasn't until I got out to have a better look that I realized the road had been newly resealed and this had reduced the clearance to under four metres. By now the Dutch drivers were running out of patience and there was no way I could go forward and with all the traffic behind me, reversing wasn't an option either. Just when it seemed there was no way out of the predicament, a marshal from the Zandvoort race circuit wandered up and in one of the world's biggest understatements asked if I had a problem.

Indeed I did, I replied. We agreed the only way out was backwards and said he would sort out the traffic problem. With almost military precision, my Good Samaritan directed the banked-up traffic onto footpaths, up driveways and onto the median strip. After what seemed like an age and having deflated all the tyres on the truck and trailer, I managed to get the unit out from under the bridge and then had to park up and try to get them re-inflated. The incident made the local newspaper next day.

A lot of the racetracks and events are steeped in history and none more so than Monza, an old circuit in a beautiful royal park just outside Milan in Italy. I'll be honest, though, I've never liked Monza, probably because of what happened to us the first year there with the hospitality unit. The track may have a place in the motor-racing lore, but the fans are just a bunch of gorillas. We thought we were safe in our special compound, surrounded by wire patrolled by two armed guards.

Not so when Monza fans come equipped with wire-cutters. Just as we would take hats, sunscreen and a drink to race meetings, these fans evidently regarded wire-cutters as standard race-day equipment. Sure enough, after the race we spotted some people cutting their way into the compound. The guards seemed reluctant to act, so our sign language became more insistent and urgent. All of a sudden one of the guards marched over to the encroaching fans, pulled out his gun and jammed it in the stomach of the nearest trespasser.

For a moment I felt like an executioner having given the command to a firing squad. Before I could marshal my thoughts, the intruder had brushed the gun aside and joined his pals in the rush towards the motorhomes. There must have been at least 500 manic Italian fans inside our compound by this stage.

We fled inside the motorhome and locked ourselves in the safety of the hospitality unit. Paddy McNally, the Philip Morris executive, was sure he was in mortal danger. Strangely, though, the crowd stopped at the perimeter of the canopy. They didn't want to take the awnings as souvenirs or anything as ambitious as that. Bizarrely, all they wanted were some stickers, hats, or whatever we could find for them.

If some circuits were aggravating, others were delightful and none more so than Silverstone in the United Kingdom. In 1983 the Formula One Constructors' Association (FOCA) and the FIA decided motorhomes should be parked some distance from the racetracks. As always, ideas from eggheads who don't have to implement anything don't necessarily work. This initiative only worked at Magny-Cours in France and Silverstone, purely because in other places there simply wasn't the room to follow the edict.

At Silverstone we were banished to an area about 100 metres from the pit paddock, where we parked on the edge of the tarmac with our canopy out over the grass. One year my friend Stu Spires, from the Lotus motorhome, decided to mow the grass and that was the start of a tradition. The following year when he and his wife Di (who had moved on to run the Benetton outfit) turned up, they planted a flock of coloured, cardboard cutout sheep. Before long all the teams were trying to outdo one another.

As the years went by, white picket fences appeared, along with hanging baskets, potted plants, topiary and gnomes. Give or take two or three years, the Silverstone motorhome parking area was beginning to look like an English country fair, enough so that some compared it to the Chelsea Flower Show. One year we installed a water feature complete with fountain; that was fine until the inevitable happened — someone threw detergent in the water and it didn't stop foaming for two days.

In 1994 Ron Dennis launched the McLaren road car at Silverstone so he had his sister Marjorie, a plant expert, design and build a special garden feature as a presentation backdrop. With the same attention to detail that Ron possessed, she constructed a huge waterfall and rockery that eventually featured in a *Sunday Times* magazine article. Of course detergent was thrown in this water feature too, this time lasting for four days.

The organizers seemed to frown upon people having a good time, so in their inevitable way they decided to change how the paddock and motorhome parking was configured, thus destroying a little bit of countrified England inside a high-tech racing environment.

One final memory of Silverstone was when Marlboro marketing boss John Hogan suddenly decided to throw a barbecue for 300 people. Shaune scurried around the local shops buying enough meat, of any kind, to feed the impending multitude. Just as Shaune was pulling it all together, John changed his mind and called it off. The food was used that evening on a private motorhome event with all the rest of the teams. Later the mechanics' wives and partners took what was left over to a rest home. After any event, especially at Silverstone, it was a great social time and all the teams joined in to have a bit of a knees-up.

All our time wasn't spent in Europe, though. Right from the

start Marlboro often sent us to the United States at the end of the Continental season to take care of the team and its supporters. We would drive a hire car from New York City to Watkins Glen, a small town in upstate New York and home to one of the most famous road courses in the US. At that time of year, late September, this heavily forested area scattered with small lakes must surely be one of the most beautiful places I have visited. We used to stay at the Seneca Lodge, about six miles from the circuit, with members from other F1 teams. The name sounds grand, but Seneca Lodge was really just a rustic log cabin with smaller buildings for accommodation out the back. Perhaps because it was far from home, or maybe it was just the end-of-year feeling, but the trip to America seemed to encourage all kinds of strange behaviour.

The main transporter driver at the time, Roy Reader, who is still with McLaren on a part-time basis, would go without sleep for four days. One year there were about 14 of us in one big room on the first night because our bookings had been mucked up. Around 3.30 a.m. we all decided it was time for bed and it was all bit too much like the closing credits from a *Waltons* episode for my liking — all that 'goodnight, Bob', 'goodnight, Leo', 'goodnight, Shaune' stuff. Before long we realized nobody was going to get any sleep so we all went back to the bar.

Mentioning Watkins Glen brings another story to mind. The Glen was primarily famous for the US Grand Prix and a great place to go racing but it had a slightly sinister side that was equally well known by less savoury folk.

Most readers of this book will have heard of what used to happen on the mountain at Bathurst during the late 1970s and early 1980s after the sun went down and the police ran for shelter. Keep that picture in your mind and add a healthy dose of steroids and some seriously bad drugs because the Bog at the Glen left Bathurst for dead.

It was based on a similar premise to Bathurst where people would burn cars and the like. Many of the vehicles were bought and taken to the Glen for the express purpose of being destroyed and although I wasn't there in 1974 (I was there in 1977–80 but things had calmed down a bit by then), I got the story first-hand from some of the boys who had witnessed what happened.

Here's an abridged version of what they saw. Not forgetting for a moment the unfortunate death of Austrian rookie Helmut Koinigg, but it was a Greyhound bus that will be remembered the most.

A bunch of Brazilian fans had chartered a bus to go and support Emerson Fittipaldi over the race weekend. Fittipaldi was driving for McLaren at the time and was joint leader in the championship with Clay Regazzoni. It's conjecture but it appears the bus driver dropped his passengers off at the grandstand and parked the bus, leaving it unlocked. It was promptly stolen, driven to the Bog site (a patch of mud and dirt near the tunnel leading to the start/finish line), trashed and subsequently burned to the ground along with 12 other cars, some of which had been also stolen from a fan campsite nearby.

The odd thing is that up to this point, the police and track management turned a blind eye to this activity as long as it stayed in the Bog. Somehow I think burning a Greyhound bus and numerous other cars was the straw that broke the camel's back and the Bog was bulldozed into oblivion after the race.

Incidentally, Fittipaldi finished fourth to clinch the title with Regazzoni back in eleventh. It must be something in the air in America as it brings out the strangest things in people. Who would have thought it was possible to shift an automatic transmission from forward to reverse at full revs without the car moving? Tyler Alexander and Alastair Caldwell, both very senior engineering people at McLaren International, demonstrated their technique to me, proving it could be done. It meant driving our hire car to the track in first gear for the next few days, but as we were staying nearby it seemed a small price to pay for learning such a nifty little trick.

On more than one occasion, however, we were all reminded just how anally retentive American law enforcement officers could be when it came to high jinks. One year we decided to play a trick on a team mechanic, Ritchie Butler, who looked exactly like Barry Gibb from the Bee Gees. Ritchie was always a bit out there, so one night while he was out wandering the streets, we decided to strip his bedroom and rebuild it on the front lawn at Seneca Lodge.

Bed, lamp, bedside table, chair, even the pictures — everything was in exactly the same position as it had been in the room. The Lodge's proprietor, Jim, wasn't worried as he knew we weren't going to trash anything. Ritchie came back and we still don't why, thought it was perfectly acceptable to get into the outside bed and go to sleep. The mischief-makers, including me, were back in the bar when the local sheriff turned up and wanted to know what the hell a hotel bedroom was doing in the middle of the lawn.

To begin with we all shrugged our shoulders and said we hadn't a clue what was going on. It didn't take long for the sheriff, who by this time was rapidly coming to the end of his tether, to work out we were in fact the culprits. In no uncertain terms he ordered us to put everything, including Ritchie, back in the room.

It was probably the beer talking, but we all went, 'Yeah, yeah, yeah. Whatever. We'll do it in the morning.' Within seconds, like something out of *Gunfight at the O.K. Corral*, the sheriff had his shotgun up and pointing in our general direction. We may have been drunk, but I can tell you Ben Johnson wouldn't have been able to beat us out onto the lawn, even when he was juiced up.

There's something about American cops and their guns. A year later Shaune, two race mechanics — Leo Wybott and Hughie Absolom — and I discovered there were no rooms booked for us at the Lodge so we headed off to the circuit to find somewhere to sleep. On the way we passed a Holiday Inn where the welcome sign had had its signboard rearranged to say 'Fuck the Pigs' or something very similar. We pulled over, got out of Bill Smith's McLaren motorhome and ambled over for a closer look.

While we were peering up at the sign, a disembodied voice boomed out of the darkness and the place lit up like a Christmas tree on steroids. Slightly distorted by the bullhorn, it sounded like Arnie's Terminator was bellowing at us to assume the position. Looking like a startled rabbit in the headlights, I enquired, 'What position?' Luckily, Leo and Hughie knew what the command meant and grabbed me, pulling me down onto the ground as we assumed the spread-eagled position.

The headlights snapped off and when our eyes had adjusted, all we could see were the muzzles of various shotguns and handguns pointing at us. Again it took a good 30 minutes to clear up the misunderstanding but it was a bit worrying that every time we turned up in the States, we would find ourselves confronted by the muzzle of a gun or two. Mind you, there were times when we didn't really help our own cause.

A former director of McLaren USA, Bill Smith, once lent us his large GMC motorhome, which I drove from Montreal to Watkins Glen. Most of the mechanics thought this would be a far better way to travel than being cooped up in hire cars, so Shaune and I had about 14 passengers for company on the road trip. It wasn't long before a party started in the back, which of course I couldn't join, or so everyone thought. With cruise control set at 70 mph on the dead flat, straight freeway, I found I could take my hands off the steering wheel for stretches at a time and the vehicle wouldn't deviate from its course. After a bit of practice I knew I could get away with what I was about to do.

I swung round in the captain's chair, which allowed the driver to face backward when the vehicle wasn't moving, stood up and yelled I'd had enough of driving and proceeded to make my way towards the party revellers.

It was like time was instantly frozen — nobody moved for about a second — then pandemonium broke loose. Mechanics were crawling over one another in desperate lunges for the steering wheel. My little trick failed to end the raucous party, but it sure as hell quietened it down.

At the beginning of the 1980s Ron Dennis, at my suggestion, decided one of these GMC types of motorhome would be a great idea to have in Europe. So in typical McLaren fashion, we ordered the very best we could find and settled on a Revcon. The manufacturers refused to modify it for us at the factory so we shipped it back to the UK to have the work done.

When the Revcon arrived, I took it to coachbuilders USG, the company that had built all the Marlboro trucks. In a manner that put the Americans to shame, manager John Turner, who now works for McLaren, listened intently to the list of changes I wanted then quietly went about making all modifications requested.

It was a shame we left the Revcon badging all over it, though. We couldn't work out why every time we went to France, people would stop, point and snigger. Later, some friends in the South of France told us what the joke was all about. 'Rev' is part of the French verb to dream. 'Con' is a vulgar French term for a certain part of the female anatomy. Just as well we hadn't added any Marlboro identification.

It was rebranded soon after with Unipart Hospitality sponsorship.

However, all that did was to raise another language problem, again especially in France. Between the Monaco Grand Prix in May and the French Grand Prix in June we had four days to fill so it seemed like a wonderful opportunity to explore St-Tropez. We managed to find a space for the motorhome in a lovely camping ground in Port Grimaud, not far from St-Tropez itself.

About 9 a.m. the first day we were there, we heard a knock on the door. Shaune opened it to find a little girl about 10 years old holding up her finger in the universal sign of needing a plaster. Shaune duly found a Band-Aid and sent the child on her way. Not long after, there was another knock and this time it was a bloke asking, in faltering English, if we had any cures for dysentery. Not likely, Shaune told him. This pattern carried on for a few hours until we discovered that the locals took one look at our newly painted, red-and-white vehicle with the word HOSPITALITY on the side and decided it was a mobile hospital.

Things weren't always that amusing, nor did everything always go to plan. At Zolder, Belgium, we hosted the glitterati of the British and New Zealand motor-racing press at what is generally regarded as a slap-up lunch. When Patrick Fitzgibbon, the well-spoken Englishman who worked as press liaison officer for Unipart, said 'Gentlemen, lunch will now be served', the door of the motorhome flew open and I came down the steps carrying an enormous bowl of goulash that Shaune had spent hours preparing.

Unfortunately the wheels fell off my grand entrance when my shirtsleeve caught on the door handle. I remember watching in abject horror as this huge bowl sailed into the air, did a half-pike with a twisting somersault, and landed right side up on the ground. Pretty cool you might think, but not so.

Upside down would have been much, much better. As the bowl slammed into the ground its entire contents exploded out of the vessel like a modern-day Krakatoa, coating all and sundry within two tables with the mud-like goulash. Staggering upright, I nervously glanced around to see Shaune looking aghast. Patrick didn't miss a beat and immediately said, 'Gentlemen, we'll go straight on to the dessert now.'

Another time, Ron Dennis had the motorhome re-sprayed green and branded TAG in a shrewd tactic to persuade TAG owner Mansour Ojjeh to sponsor McLaren instead of Williams. The motorhome would give Mansour his own place in the paddock. Ron thought the Williams team didn't look after Mansour and his family in the manner a heavyweight sponsor might expect. They were often excluded from their paddock motorhome because it was used strictly as a race-support vehicle, not a hospitality unit.

Aware that sponsors needed to be encouraged and made to feel at home, Ron negotiated an agreement that ours would be Williams' second motorhome, where Mansour could entertain his own guests at Grand Prix. Shaune and I effectively joined the Williams team for that season. We even wore white shirts and green trousers so we looked like Williams' team personnel.

As dyed-in-the-wool McLaren people, we felt this was odd, to say the least. What's more, it led to a lesson in diplomacy for me. One day Ron talked to me about Charlie Crichton-Stuart, a socially well-connected Englishman who was an important member of Williams' management team. He was especially close to the TAG group and the Arab world in general. We talked about Charlie getting in the way of Ron's plan to attract the TAG Group to McLaren. Ron, as an aside, mentioned that there was an Exocet missile flying around the paddock and it was heading straight for Charlie's backside. I told Charlie, who laughed it off and told everyone in the paddock.

At the next race meeting Ron put a flea in my ear and had a few choice words to say to me about treating everything in Formula One, and McLaren especially, that he discussed with me either as a boss or a friend, as confidential. I swore to myself after that little incident that I'd never again repeat anything said to me in private.

Towards the end of 1987 at the Austrian Grand Prix, McLaren needed a new engine supplier so Ron and Renault's team manager, Jean Sage, were in the motorhome hammering out a deal. After what seemed an aeon, I was summoned inside to put my signature on the document as a witness to the signed contract between the two of them. I was sworn to the utmost secrecy.

When I left the motorhome, I returned to a shady spot where several other motorhome crews were relaxing. I'd been there only a few minutes when Jean sauntered into view. 'Hey Bob,' cried my good friend Stuart Spires, 'here's your Renault mate come to deliver the new engines for you!' At that moment I thought my heart would stop beating, especially as the smile on Jean's face vanished instantly. The rest of Jean's face didn't change much and he took it all in with a deadpan look on his face, made a bit of small talk and disappeared quietly and quickly. I was about to leap up and race after him to explain I hadn't said a damn word to a soul but thought better of it. If the others saw me running after the departing Jean, they might put two and two together and realize there might be a grain of truth in Stuart's chance remark.

When it seemed appropriate, I excused myself and went looking for Jean, hoping it wouldn't be too late to explain that not a word had passed my lips about the deal he and Ron had struck. By the time I found him, I was frantic with worry and had one eye on the lookout for Ron in case Jean had told him I'd let the cat out of the bag. To my enormous relief, by that time Jean had realized Stuart was just pulling our legs and that I hadn't tipped him off. In 1999 I reminded Stuart of the incident and he remembered it clearly. 'Now I know why you looked as though you'd seen a ghost,' he laughed.

Motorhomes criss-cross mountain ranges in Europe going to and from various race meetings, and as they are simply light-truck chassis with a huge superstructure bolted on top, breakdowns were a common occurrence. Packed to the rafters inside with all manner of equipment, coupled with steep switchback roads, the standard Cadillac car brakes had their work well and truly cut out. The first time this issue raised its ugly head was on a typically steep Austrian mountain road not far from Salzburg.

Every time I checked the mirrors the following cars were flashing their lights. After a short time I noticed a thin wisp of smoke trailing out from behind the motorhome. Before long this turned into a smokescreen blocking out most of the road behind. Just when I was getting rather concerned, the rear brakes promptly caught fire and we had to pull over. To cut a long story short, we had to wait for eight days for Cadillac to send new parts over and as no one would come and help I had to replace the damaged items myself. Fortunately our breakdowns were few and far between because we spent more on maintenance than most teams did.

One unpleasant side of travelling in a motorhome is that at some stage you have to empty the onboard sewage tank. One day we came out of the Paul Ricard circuit heading for Monaco, planning to empty the tank in a big tile drain we knew was on a nearby hill. At the drain I pulled the slide to empty the sewage but nothing happened. This was a common occurrence as all sorts of foreign objects were shoved down motorhome toilets. The usual way to fix this problem was to drive down the road and do a few violent swerves to dislodge the blockage.

The road down from Ricard to the motorway is winding and twisty, which would normally have taken care of the blockage. We reached the motorway and cruised along until we took a sharp swerve onto the other carriageway to avoid some roadworks. All through this manoeuvre a white convertible was behind me, following every weave I made.

Unfortunately on this particular day I forgot I'd left the disposal slide open. A short time later I was horrified when I realized the white car that had tailed us for a few kilometres was now being sprayed with 25 gallons of blue sanitized sewage. About five km further on I spotted the convertible parked at a tollbooth. I cringed, knowing there was nothing to do but stop and apologize. By doing so I hoped I might limit the amount of penalty for dumping sewage on a public road, not to mention on a following car.

As I drew up alongside, I saw the driver having an animated conversation with the local police. Reluctantly I got out of the motorhome and shuffled over to the group. Incredibly, I heard the man in the convertible simply asking for directions — no mention of flying sewage, yet I could see traces of blue sanitizer on the bonnet, screen and even the back seat. I could hardly believe it. The blissfully unaware driver folded his map, returned to his car and drove away. The cop looked at me as if to say 'next' so I lamely asked him if I was on the right road to Monaco, then got out of there as quickly as I could.

I wasn't the only one to fall foul of a blocked sewage outlet. Stu Spires had a similar problem a few days later. Without him seeing me, I shoved a French bread-stick up the outlet of his motorhome. When he came around the side to have a look I asked him what it was as he grabbed the stick and heaved on it. Unbeknown to me, by thrusting the loaf up the pipe I had dislodged the blockage and as Stu pulled the bread-stick out it was followed by the contents of the sewage tank — some 35 gallons, in this case. Poor Stu had his gloves on but that didn't stop human waste from spraying his shorts, his shoes and virtually the entire lower half of his body. Naturally I had a good laugh at his expense.

But along with the odd disaster there were plenty of good times, especially the paddock parties. For example, each year in Portugal the Minardi team would put on a wonderful Italian dinner — probably the best party of the year.

At the end of 1990 Shaune and I decided we needed something larger than the Revcon. As good as it was, the Revcon looked better than it actually functioned as a corporate hospitality unit. So once again we set off for Van Nuys in California where we knew we could order an Executive that had the advantage of a full-height interior. The Executive had decent brakes and hydraulic jacks at each corner so you could easily adjust the vehicle level wherever you parked.

Unlike the Revcon people, the Executive manufacturer was happy to incorporate the changes we wanted so we waited for six weeks while it was completed. We took delivery in the middle of nowhere on the California/Nevada state line to enable us to avoid California sales tax. Then we headed for the dock at Baltimore once more to get it shipped back to the UK. Unfortunately when it turned up at Southampton, every electrical item had been stripped out and stolen. No good in the US so I presume it happened on the boat, or on the notorious English docks. Everything had gone including the two European TVs that had been installed.

We kept that model for years before Shaune and I decided we needed a really big motorhome that could incorporate an office for Ron. Once again we did some research and discovered that the ultimate American motorhome was built on a bus chassis by a Miami company called Newell Motor Coach. This sounded glamorous but we soon discovered this Miami was in Oklahoma, not Florida. It was in the middle of the USA with the nearest decent hotel being in Joplin, Missouri, about 30 miles away. The new motorhome resembled a Wells Fargo armoured money carrier because its exterior was constructed by riveting aluminium panels to the framing.

Ron decided he liked the idea of a Newell coach, but not with rivets all over it, so in his inimitable way, he persuaded the Newell people to virtually re-engineer their entire production line using aluminium welding techniques and glue instead of rivets. The result was a new era for Newell. In fact, the product was so revolutionary for the company, a document was signed with McLaren in which Newell agreed not to duplicate the vehicle within one year. A year and two days later, Roger Penske's team in America had a Newell motorhome exactly the same as McLaren's. Newell vehicles have since become so popular that some Formula One drivers have bought their own and live in them at the circuits rather than fighting their way in and out during a race weekend.

When the Newell finally arrived in the UK, it was registered as a super-yacht under Mansour Ojjeh's banner and was generally regarded as the best motorhome in the entire paddock. A testament to Ron's philosophy that if you're going to do something, do it properly. The reason it was effectively a yacht was to accommodate a satellite phone with a dish so that calls could be made from any track in the world. This was before mobile phones had made an appearance and satellite phones were mostly used on boats at sea.

We were fortunate with the three motorhomes we had, the Revcon, the Executive and the Newell, as each was easily the best of its era. They were fitted out in the way Shaune and I wanted, as long as Ron agreed, which was vitally important as we worked and lived together in them seven days a week at times.

One ungrateful journalist who challenged my sense of pride in the motorhome wrote in the French sporting magazine *L'Equipe* that the Newell motorhome driver (me) had threatened to kill him with a bread knife. It so happened that during an interview with Alain Prost, he kept putting his feet up on the couch. Eventually I said to him in English that if he didn't take his shoes off the seat I would eject him from the motorhome. At the time I was drying the dishes and had a large bread knife in my hand that I was waving around while I remonstrated with him. I suppose he figured he got his revenge on me in print.

Shaune and I ran the Newell for four years until 1988 and in the end it became McLaren's on-the-road office rather than a hospitality centre. It also became an inner sanctum for drivers, or for Ron Dennis's special guests like Mansour Ojjeh. I was quite sorry when the Newell was sold to the Jaguar Formula One team. It was a heavy, solid and reliable machine that had been purpose-built for the job. Surprisingly, it was also a rocket. It was so fast it out-ran, on acceleration and top speed, the Ligier Range Rover crew vehicle over a 10 km blast from Seville en route to Jerez in Spain.

As time moved on, the hospitality unit grew into the big business it is today, with four chefs and five or six other kitchen-hands in the McLaren hospitality unit at each Grand Prix. Now they have 10 or 12 trucks and more than 30 people involved in the set-up and running of the McLaren Brand Centre, as it's now called. Shaune and I worked together for 21 years, managing the motorhome and its budget right up until the time I left McLaren in 2002.

Chapter 5

Ron Dennis: a man of vision

I couldn't possibly write a book about my time at McLaren without having a chat about the man who almost single-handedly brought the Kiwi-built team back from the brink. Ron Dennis is a man who always had a vision and he realized Bruce's old team would be the perfect vehicle to take him, and many others, to fame, fortune and Formula One glory. Ron always said to look at McLaren as a big book and he was merely a chapter in that book. Now that is literally true. Despite all that has happened over the past few years since I parted ways with the team, I still think of him as a friend, although in earlier days he had more time to be friendly.

It was with a heavy heart that I watched the once great team become mired in both perceived, and real, scandal. I'm not going to rehash the Stepneygate spy saga that tainted the 2007 F1 title chase and left a sour taste in the mouth — that has been done by far more knowledgeable people — but it was the Renault spy story that really made you sit up and think the motoring gods had abandoned Ron and McLaren.

I thought there was definitely a stench of back-room deals and old-boy networking in Formula One when Renault got away with its technical information shenanigans. How Renault avoided any punishment in their own spy scandal when they admitted data from a former McLaren engineer had been entered into their computer system, is anybody's guess.

In welcoming the news — well, he would, wouldn't he? — Renault boss at the time Flavio Briatore stated he'd like to thank Renault, title sponsors ING and all their partners for their wholehearted support during that period. This support, though, soon evaporated after Singaporegate, Piquetgate and crashgate.

Formula One is now on a par with professional cycling, and if F1 teams are not careful, major sponsors will pull the pin, like T-Mobile's parent company Deutsche Telekom did following the continuing drugs scandal with the cycling team they sponsored.

I am still none the wiser as to why McLaren was stripped of all their constructor championship points in 2008, and fined US$100 million, for the alleged use of Ferrari's data, when that was never proven to have been seen by any McLaren employee. The World Motor Sport Council agreed not to punish Renault, concluding that there was 'insufficient evidence to establish the information was used in such a way as to interfere with or to have an impact on the championship'.

Handing down its judgment at the time, the WMSC decided that three of the four drawings, showing McLaren's fuel system, gearbox and damper designs, were shown by former McLaren engineer Philip Mackereth to several other Renault employees, but that all three were 'either of no use to Renault or were in fact not used'.

Rubbish. I think that's like saying, 'I shot at him four times and missed, so you can't say I tried to kill him because I didn't manage to hit him.' In McLaren's case, there was no evidence that the team had access to anything, and yet they were still punished.

The end of that sorry saga, which did nothing for the public image of the FIA, Ferrari and Renault, left Ron a few million dollars lighter in the pockets, but firmly atop the moral high ground. I believe the fans and general public were on his side and when he and his team produced a new British F1 champion, Lewis Hamilton, for the first time in 12 years, McLaren could do no wrong — until less than a year later.

At the start of the 2009 season, McLaren shot itself fairly and squarely in both feet when it announced the sacking of their recently appointed sporting director, New Zealander Dave Ryan, for allegedly telling porkies to the stewards after the Australian Grand Prix about Hamilton overtaking another driver on the track under a caution.

It all started so well for Ron's team that year with the number-one plate, and the number-one driver in their new car. With the revelation of the Hamilton overtaking incident, McLaren's image and standing in the F1 community may have been irrevocably tarnished. Hamilton came out of it all right despite initially agreeing with the lie but it's Dave who will forever be regarded as bringing the team, and sport, into disrepute. Dave, however, strenuously denied these allegations to me, and I believe him.

While not condoning what Dave and Lewis allegedly did, I can't help but feel sorry for them both, and for Dave in particular, as the smallest slips of the tongue, even if uttered in the best interests of teams and drivers, can sometimes have spectacular repercussions.

Formula One is a sport fraught with underhand dealings, and more Machiavellian intrigue than Niccolo di Bernardo dei Machiavelli himself could have sown. Previously the team a notch above the rest ethically, McLaren now found itself embroiled in intrigue.

One wonders if Ron's move away from the racing side of things to concentrate on the McLaren Group has seen the steady hand of a man born to run race-car teams sorely missed. It's almost as if McLaren have mislaid their moral compass. Dave had given 30-plus years of his life to Ron and McLaren and although I knew Dave was part of the McLaren set-up in the 1970s, I didn't really get to know him until he became chief mechanic. When Dave was appointed team manager, the McLaren team really started to fly and the results soon followed. Although not liked by all the mechanics because he wanted things done his way, he was nevertheless well respected for his work ethic.

During his time as team manager, Dave was one down from Ron and to all intents and purposes ran the racing side of things. He was the manager of the race team and in charge of all racing activity, including getting the cars where they had to be and making sure the team worked properly. The only things not part of his remit were driver signings, car design, marketing and promotions — these were Ron's babies.

Martin Whitmarsh, team principal since Ron took the reins of the McLaren Group chairmanship, knew, as Ron did, that he could leave the running of the team to Dave.

Through all the fall-out, Martin was between a rock and a hard place — damned if he didn't do something about Dave and damned if he did. Sacking a bloke you've worked with for 20 years and whom you regard as a friend must be tough, but that's why he gets paid the big bucks.

As for Lewis's father Anthony getting in touch with FIA boss Max Mosley — a man himself not untouched by the brush of scandal — and moaning about his son's image being tarnished by all the headlines, he should have looked to his boy for some honest answers.

With the threat of McLaren being thrown out of the championship for bringing the sport into disrepute, Ron fell on his sword to save face with the governing body and severed all ties with the racing arm of McLaren International. As McLaren Group chairman, Ron reports to the shareholders (of which he is one) and the other companies including McLaren International report to the board.

It astonishes me how in a single lifetime one man can grab an F1 team on the brink of demise and through hard work, vision and passion take it all the way to the top, only to see it all crash and burn under the steerage of someone else. But Ron still had the sport, and his team, at heart and it takes a big man to walk away from something that's been part of his life for so long. During the 28 years of Ron's leadership, McLaren rose to win five world championships and become a shining example of a successful and innovative British business.

My friendship with Ron has dimmed a little over the years and time apart has made regular contact more difficult, but when you have a history that goes back so long, the embers of that relationship still glow in your heart. I make no bones about admiring Ron and his business and personal philosophies. In my mind he is one of only a very small number of people who have made Formula One what it is today. I worked most of my life for his company, they were wonderfully exciting times and I'll never regret it.

I have huge admiration for what Ron has achieved because he started life with no special advantages. In England that means you're practically disadvantaged. Ron was and is a Woking lad, and his workshops and factories have all been based in and around the area.

He had a normal education but decided to hit the streets looking for work rather than go to university. He once told me that as a teenager he simply didn't feel like studying any more so he took an apprenticeship as a racing mechanic.

He claims he was never that keen on motor racing itself, but was more attracted to the technical side of things. In fact, he always said he didn't even want to be a mechanic but thought it would help him get ahead in the motor-racing world, but as what, I don't think even he knew back then.

Ron was one of those people I'd always see around motor racing, probably at Brands Hatch or Silverstone in the early years. I'd also see him in a local Woking pub called the Four Horseshoes, on Chobham Common, having a drink and I'd sometimes go and say hi. By this stage I'd got to know a couple of people who worked for him, which made it easier to have the occasional social chat with him in the pub. I thought he was a really good guy and over time we became quite friendly.

However, when I finally got an invite to go around to his place, it didn't start out on the best note. Soon after I arrived and settled down into a chair Ron gave me a beer. After a quick drink I leaned forward and went to place the glass on the low glass table in front of me. To my horror, as I let the glass go it slipped through my hand and dropped into six inches of water.

After I got over my surprise, I realized it wasn't a table but a goldfish bowl. I still think it was an odd choice for a piece of furniture, or maybe it was Ron's way of checking how observant someone was. Apart from liking tables without tops, Ron's other major quirk was he simply would not give way in an argument (a trait I've also been accused of possessing). He was one of those people who would argue black was white, and would not let the subject drop until he convinced you he was right and you didn't know what you were talking about. And if you didn't quite agree he'd take it almost personally.

Ron had a small ski boat he kept at a place on the south coast of England called *Selsey Bill* and occasionally I'd go down there with him to have a bit of a yahoo. Once we were accompanied by Sally, his girlfriend at the time, with whom Ron used to have enormous arguments over the most trivial of things. After one of these rows we ended up back at his place in Woking where there was a beautiful cake waiting, probably dropped off by Ron's mother Evelyn.

On entering the house, Sally went straight over to it, picked up the cake and without a moment's hesitation, launched it at him, smashing it straight in his face. I hurriedly made my excuses and left, because I knew Ron just could not admit he was wrong and it would only escalate. Being as dedicated to motorsport as he was, it didn't leave much room for personal relationships.

Like everyone trying to get things off the ground in a business venture, Ron's early years were a financial battle, but to my knowledge he never let anyone down over money and everyone got paid what he or she was owed. It may not have always been in cash dollars, pounds or whatever the currency was at the time, but the people got paid. One occasion comes to mind, where Ron needed to pay me a considerable sum for overdue wages, and instead of cash he contemplated handing me an Italian-registered Porsche 911, glorious in red with the big rear wing. I'd probably have been more chuffed with an actual Italian-manufactured car but beggars can't be choosers. Eventually I got the money instead of the car, with Ron proving as always that he was true to his word.

Ron's attention to detail, not only in things mechanical, but in the way an entire team should be presented, became apparent very early on. When Jochen Rindt moved to Brabham from Cooper-Climax in 1968, Ron went with him and stayed for three years. By 1971 Ron and Brabham's chief mechanic, Neil Trundle (still with McLaren International), had joined forces and surprised the Formula Two world by launching a very professional — for the time — three-car team. Rondel Racing was loaned two Brabham cars by the company's business partner Ron Tauranac and the third car was financed by shipping magnate Tony Vlassopulos and his property developer mate Ken Grob.

The driver line-up wasn't too shabby either with Graham Hill,

Tim Schenken and Bob Wollek, with Carlos Reutemann joining the family when Graham left to run his own F2 team.

In 1972, with sponsorship from the French oil company Motul, Rondel expanded and acquired four new Brabham BT38s and Henri Pescarolo joined the driving team. Ron's legendary attention to detail could be seen in the immaculate presentation of the Rondel cars.

By 1973, Ron and Neil had parted ways, leaving Ron to build two new F2 cars. At the same time, Ray Jessup was playing around with designs for a Formula One car for Ron, to be driven by Tom Pryce in 1974. Money at this time was becoming tight and reluctant to be a mere bit-player at the back of the grid, Ron sold the F1 project to Ken, who campaigned it in the 1974 season with little success.

Deciding to stick with a category in which he was already enjoying some success, Ron ran two Surtees F2 cars that year for a pair of Ecuadorian hopefuls. With finance from tobacco giant Philip Morris, the team based itself in Germany with Ron staying in England dealing with the logistics.

The drivers and their cars were Fausto Morello, Ortega Ecuador Marlboro Team Surtees TS15A-BMW M12 and Guillermo Ortega, Ortega Ecuador Marlboro Team Surtees TS15A-BMW M12. Tim Schenken also drove for the team. The Ecuadorians soon found themselves out of their depth and it proved to be a turning point for Ron, as he realized the only way to get ahead was to do it on his own.

It has now become something of an urban legend, but I can attest that Ron did in fact come up with his new venture's name, Project Three, while lying in the bath. One of March Engineering's directors, Robin Herd, suggested Ron should enter the Italian Vittorio Brambilla in an F2 car as part of his own stand-alone team.

While thinking about things in the bath, Ron reckoned Rondel had been Project One, the Motul cars Project Two, so 'Project' should be part of the new team's name. Sometimes the simplest solutions are the best, so he decided to call his new venture Project Three. Project Three subsequently ran March F2 cars for Vittorio and Sandro Cinotti with middling results, despite Ron's passion for faultless preparation.

Ron's meticulous attention to detail first surfaced one night when we were getting ready to depart for Pau in southwestern France. This was for the 1976 race with Eddie Cheever and Gilles Villeneuve driving for Ron's by-then Project Four team. At about 8 p.m. I was helping load the cars onto a transporter at the Woking factory when Ron came out to check everything was going according to plan. As one of the cars was being run up the ramp into the truck, Ron, being Ron, noticed one of the rollbar drop-links had not been plated because we'd run out of time. Immediately he insisted the car was not to leave the workshop unless it was plated.

Where we were supposed to find a cadmium-plating outfit open in the middle of the night was anyone's guess. I thought his attitude towards race-car presentation was finicky, but you can't argue that it hasn't paid dividends over the years.

We eventually arrived late at Pau and consequently there was nowhere for us to park. Not having any of it, Ron went looking for the principal race organizer and commenced to berate him in pidgin French that no one could understand. To this day I still believe the French official just gave in to Ron to get him out of his face. It's not often you'll see someone win an argument in a foreign country when they don't even speak the language. All Ron managed was 'comme ci, comme ça' which roughly translated means 'so-so' or 'middling', while waving his arms about like a demented Italian.

My first professional introduction to Ron was at the Thruxton circuit in Hampshire in 1975. I was working for Bernie Ecclestone's

International Race Tyre Services when Ron wheeled in some tyres he wanted changed. During the season I frequently bumped into Ron professionally and at the end of 1975 he called me and asked if I would like to work for him the following year on the Formula Two team at Project Four.

This suited me fine as he was based in Woking near the Ralt factory and of course I felt I would have a real job in motor racing rather than a peripheral task. Tyres are an important part of racing of course, but as a tyre-fitter I felt as though I wasn't quite in the big-time yet. A job with a professional Formula Two team definitely seemed like a step up. When I began working for Ron I was still a tyre-fitter — of sorts, as the professionals did the job. I just took it to them and helped when they were short-handed, but my duties also included driving the transporter.

This entailed some very long drives through Europe and because the truck was not exactly a speed machine, it was a long time on the road. There was quite some time between races too, so on the longer trips it wasn't worth coming all the way back to England. On one trip we drove from Mugello near Florence with two weeks in between, so it was holiday in Sicily then from there to Estoril in Portugal to race at the Enna circuit around Lake Pergusa.

Ron knew a nice hotel on the beach at Taormina so that's where we stopped for a break. Life was leisurely, to say the least. We'd begin the day with coffee and croissants while watching our Japanese mechanic Kazu practise his karate kicks on beach umbrellas. During the day we'd take the cars out of the transporter and park them on the side of the road, do a bit of work on them and then load them up again. Considering how much dust and sand there was around, I'm surprised Ron agreed to this.

One night we all squeezed into Ron's hire car and went to a disco on top of a hill in Taormina. After a while all the mechanics wanted to visit another club but Ron and I decided to stay at the disco. He wouldn't let them take his hire car, suggesting they'd be safer in a taxi.

When we left the disco about an hour later, surprise, surprise — no hire car. We took a taxi back down the hill to the beach where our hotel was located. The road consists of two or three kilometres of hairpin bends. Strangely enough I remember feeling safer being driven by a Sicilian taxi driver rather than by Ron. We found the hire car at the bottom of the hill, leapt in and drove back to the hotel. Next day Ron gave his mechanics a verbal lashing but he was actually more frightened than annoyed. There was a steering lock in the hire car and why it hadn't functioned during the mechanics' downhill trip we never worked out. But it had clicked into place the moment Ron had twisted the wheel when we'd reclaimed the car.

Because he had his own water-ski boat in England, Ron was keen to hire a boat so we could do some skiing while we were in Sicily. Ron has a wicked sense of humour and I was about to find out just how warped it was. While I was happily skiing along, Ron put the boat into a whip and continued in a circle and I was like a ball on the end of a piece of string. I managed to hang on for about a lap and a half before falling off at what seemed like a hundred miles an hour. As I surfaced, spluttering, Ron cruised up to me gently, grinned slyly and offered a lame sort of apology like 'Sorry, Bobby.' That's all he said even after damn near drowning me.

In 1976, Ron's Project Four Racing team had just moved into its own premises in Woking and I can still picture the three-inch shag-pile carpet in the offices — very trendy at the time, although the office was just a mezzanine floor. To Ron it had everything he needed including a secretary, a very lovely woman named Rita Sale, who also looked after the accounts. Because Ron was loyal to his staff, they in turn stuck with him through thick and thin. Rita still works part-time for Ron in the accounts department at McLaren International.

Project Four's driver at that time was the young American Eddie Cheever, who had made a big name for himself in British Formula Three events. We started that season with a March chassis, later swapping to a Ralt built by Ron Tauranac's new company, which he'd founded when former Formula One world champion Jack Brabham decided to retire to Australia. Unlike today where the drivers are getting younger and younger, back then, having Eddie Cheever drive for us was quite unusual because he was still a teenager. Eddie had American parents but had grown up in Italy as his father, a former Mr Universe, owned a chain of health spas throughout the country.

One night, five of us squeezed into Eddie's Fiat 500 and headed out to an ice-cream parlour on one of the Seven Hills of Rome. I should have guessed what would happen on the way home because it meant coming back down that bloody great hill. Eddie, being a teenager and keen to show off his ability as a racing-driver, demonstrated how easy it was to negotiate hairpin bends by sliding the tiny Fiat about like a chook on an ice rink.

This was fine until we happened upon a wet patch of road. At this point there was not a hope in hell of the already sliding Fiat remaining in control and we smacked into the kerb. The little car catapulted into the air and after doing a barrel roll, landed on its roof, spinning like a top. Although none of us was hurt, I had a moment of panic as I could smell fuel and felt something dripping on me. Without a second thought I brought my knees up to my chest and kicked out the back window, clambering onto the road with everyone else following. While we were contemplating just what to do with the car upside down, a cop car came past and we just looked the other way. The cop carried on as if this sort of thing happened every day. As there were five of us, we simply lifted the car off the footpath, rolled it back onto its wheels, piled in again and limped back to Eddie's parents' house.

Before we headed back to our hotel, we helped Eddie park the somewhat battered Fiat in the garage. When Cheever senior saw the misshapen Fiat the next day he went ballistic and promptly grounded Eddie for two weeks. No driving, no social life, no racing, no nothing. This was rather inconvenient as Eddie was supposed to be our star driver the following weekend at Vallelunga, a circuit near Rome.

Common sense finally prevailed and Eddie's dad relaxed his ban so he could compete. Racing aside, Cheever senior banned his son from virtually everything for two weeks.

As the 1976 season progressed Scotsman Jimmy Tully and I were acting as team managers, although I don't think the title was widely used yet in Formula Two. We were responsible for setting up before races and even sometimes collecting prize money after the event.

This was typical of Ron, who liked to give people more responsibility as he came to realize he could place more trust in them. It allowed him to spend time back in England wheeling and dealing to make sure the team had the funds to keep going at a competitive level.

Not only was Ron big on being prepared to be able to fix anything, anywhere at anytime, we also had to have the necessary kit and smarts to fix things. This played out one time in 1975 when I was with two mechanics on the way to Mugello in the big ex-Wollek former Mercedes furniture van. Rattling down the road outside Rouen, the engine let out a howl of protest, followed by a death rattle and promptly expired.

After we had coasted to a stop we leapt out to have a look at the engine. After pulling it apart on the side of the road we discovered it had a broken pushrod. Our Japanese mechanic Kazu was promptly despatched on foot to find a Mercedes dealership that might have the necessary part.

In the meantime the other mechanic, a Kiwi called Ray (Kojak) Grant, and I started to unload the racing-cars to get at the welding gear and lathe Ron deemed were necessities in any decent racing transporter. Remarkably, Kojak welded the two bits of pushrod together, machined it down and we reassembled the engine. Five hours later we had the cars loaded back in the transporter, the engine running as sweet as a nut, and we recalled Kazu who hadn't ventured too far into the countryside.

I saw the same transporter about six years later and to my knowledge it still had the same repaired pushrod in it. Not only was the pushrod still going strong, Ray is still working for McLaren International more than 25 years later. There was no doubt that in the mid-1970s Ron's Formula Two team was the next best thing to the BMW factory-run March cars.

The March/BMW team had top drivers like JP Jarier and Patrick Tambay, so we tended to have the next best like Eddie Cheever and the Brazilians Ingo Hoffman and Chico Serra, themselves no slouches though. To keep up with, or sometimes stay ahead of, the BMW/ Marchs, Ron had no compunction about changing engine suppliers if he deemed it necessary. At one stage in 1976 we were using Lancia/ Ferrari engines supplied and tuned by the Brambilla brothers in Monza near Milan.

These engines had heaps of power but were too fragile, and more often than not they would fly apart during a race. After a while Ron got fed up with this and one night we all got down to it and reconfigured a Ralt to accept a Brian Hart-tuned Ford BDA engine. In commercial terms this might not have been the smartest thing to do, but in the end, all Ron cared about was winning races.

The Hart-prepared Ford may not have been quite as powerful as the Lancia/Ferrari engine but as it was still running at the end of its first race, Eddie said it was a great improvement. For a while after the Hart engine we used Schnitzer-tuned BMW engines, which led to Ron's involvement with the BMW M1 Procar series — not a smooth transaction, as it transpired.

I was helping to get the team set up for a meeting at Hockenheim when the police arrived and announced that the team's assets were being impounded. We soon found out that there was a dispute between Ron and Schnitzer. Under German law, everything could be seized by the authorities and impounded until the parties settled their disagreement. When Ron arrived at Hockenheim he found only a pile of parts and the chassis in the paddock. Everything else, including the transporter and me, was locked up.

Ron and I knew where the police had stashed the goods and we even contemplated — admittedly briefly — breaking it all out and legging it. Fortunately, Paul Schaefer, who owned the hotel we were staying in at nearby Speyer, was also a lawyer so his legal expertise was swiftly sought. Engines, transporter and yours truly were all released within a day and we were able to go racing, and Eddie won the event.

To this day, McLaren team members stay at Paul Schaefer's Goldener Engel hotel in Speyer. This is a typical example of Ron's loyalty to those who have helped him in the past. There are plenty of closer alternatives in or near Speyer and Hockenheim but Ron always works on the principle that one good deed deserves another.

The M1 ProCar races in 1979 were a spectacular promotional series that capitalized on the popularity of one-make races, which were in vogue at the time. Formula One drivers were let loose in a fleet of BMW Ml road cars for a 10-lap sprint race as a curtain-raiser to the Formula One Grand Prix event.

The Osella company in Italy was under contract to prepare some of the cars along with Ron's Project Four. When Osella lagged badly on the programme, Ron's company took over, so the bulk of the M1 grid was therefore prepared in England and he still owns a BMW M1 with chassis number three. And as all the earliest models were also destroyed in various crashes in the Procar series, Ron's is the earliest surviving model.

Despite Ron's having a large and interesting collection of cars and running a highly successful F2 team, the one thing we all dreaded was his getting behind the wheel of anything. Ron was always good fun on the expeditions to Europe, but no one who has been a passenger in a car driven by him can forget the experience.

At the Salzburgring one year, all the mechanics refused point-blank to get into anything if Ron had the steering wheel in his hands, so we hired another rental car for ourselves. That's how much his driving frightened us. Of all the scary moments, one memorable occasion at Pau in southwestern France stands out. We'd been out to dinner celebrating Shaune's birthday with Ron and the F2 team, plus American Fred Opert and the members of his team, who were mostly Kiwis and Aussies.

We decided to continue the celebrations in a bar near our hotel in the centre of Pau because it's famous for its vast array of Armagnac brandy. Being competitive team owners, it was odds-on the drive from the restaurant to said bar would be on for young and old alike. It was determined the last one to the bar would have to pay for the drinks all night. Not wanting to host a bunch of half-cut mechanics in high spirits, Ron's idea of race tactics was to use every bit of road, tarmac, footpath, roundabout or dirt he could find to get to the bar first. A convenient straight line shortcut across Pau's town square, scattering late-night strollers near and far and narrowly missing a fountain in the square, meant Fred arrived a distant second, protesting loudly about unsportsmanlike behaviour.

There were about 10 of us in the bar that night enjoying an Armagnac tasting session. Normally Armagnac was a tipple beyond the pockets of most racing team personnel, but that night — well, it was a big birthday for Shaune and Fred Opert was paying anyway. As the night wore on, we all became more adventurous as to what we wanted to drink. After the newer bottles of Armagnac were polished off, we began to move higher and higher up the shelves. Before long our glasses were being filled from bottles covered in dust, some of which were reputed to be over 200 years old.

The evening must have cost Fred a fortune because, strangely enough, he never went out with us for a drink again. As for the Armagnac, it was wasted on us all really. I couldn't tell the difference between one bottle and another, except it burned your throat on the way down or it didn't.

It has never helped that for 25 years Ron has hired and fired and kept company with some of the fastest drivers in the world, but that's never stopped him from thinking he too can go just as fast — and on public roads. Once he went through the windscreen of an E-Type Jaguar that left him with limited vision in his right eye. You'd think that would be enough to slow him down, but unfortunately it did not.

A few years ago I went down to Portsmouth with him in his S-class Mercedes. On the way back, from the outside lane, he suddenly veered across all three lanes to take the left-hand exit. Why he left it so late I have no idea, as I'd been telling him we had to get off at that exit.

The only reason I can fathom is he nearly missed it because he'd been distracted by our conversation. I figured he didn't want to kill himself, even though he nearly killed both of us, so I gave him the benefit of the doubt. I must have looked decidedly uncomfortable, because he asked me if anything was wrong. I swear to God he saw nothing strange about this rather radical manoeuvre in carving up three lanes of traffic.

Fortunately for his employees and the rest of England's motoring population, Ron now has a chauffeur to drive him on most occasions. I think Ron's willingness to take risks on the road — and I'd call them extreme at times — stems from his early years when he had to take great risks just to stay in business. I suppose everyone who tries to do something in the business world experiences the same heart-in-the-mouth journey at times, but it seems to me that in motor racing there's far less likelihood of a return than in most other kinds of business.

He took big risks with Projects Three and Four, but they paid off and he survived to go on to build one of the biggest organizations in motorsport. His public face may be a little stoic at times these days but he's been frightened, and frightened others, in the past.

It wasn't long after the Armagnac adventure that Ron got his competitive tail-feathers up again, and again it was in France. We returned from the Rouen-Les-Essarts track one day to find one of our rooms completely trashed in the lovely old hotel where we were staying on the banks of the Seine just outside of Rouen. Thinking it had been Ron having a bit of fun, we went straight to the room he and his girlfriend were staying in and emptied it completely. We hid the furniture and all their possessions in other rooms then we went downstairs for a quiet beer.

All hell broke loose when Ron arrived back and discovered what had happened. He actually kicked a couple of doors down looking in our rooms for his bed and mattress. When he finally restored some order to his and Sally's room, he came downstairs and announced we were all fired. A while later, he saw the funny side of it and we were all reinstated. Well, we had to be anyway — who else was going to help him race the next day?

I doubt if Ron puts up with pranks like that these days, but 30 years ago he was very much part of the team, staying in the same places and eating in the same restaurants. Because he knew the cars so well, it was easy to work for him and he had very good personnel and man-management skills even then. That's why so many people have stayed with him, even though he now runs a multi-million pound corporation, not just a racing team.

As Formula One changed and became more professional, so did Ron. He already ran one of the more professional outfits back in 1970s, so adapting to the times didn't take too much effort for Ron as he intuitively seemed to know the way it was all going to go. Instead of having dinner with his mechanics, he began to take potential sponsors and businessmen out, to convince them his team was the best to invest in.

Ron knew how to entertain people and is one of the best hosts I have ever met. One example was Shaune's 40th birthday. We were in Monaco for the Grand Prix and Shaune thought a quiet dinner in a small restaurant would be most appropriate. After all, how many people can say they've been to the Grand Prix at Monaco and celebrated a major birthday there?

I booked a little Italian restaurant I knew on the other side of Monte Carlo and we gathered half a dozen friends we knew who would not be attending the traditional black-tie affair at the Monaco Sporting Club that Friday evening. We walked around the harbour heading to the restaurant, past reputedly the largest ship ever to be allowed into the harbour at Monaco. Everyone who was anyone was staying on the *Sea Goddess* including the Philip Morris executives. Thinking it was worth a try, I marched up to the guard at the bottom of the gangway, told him we were McLaren people and asked if we could have a quick look. That was enough to get us on board, although Shaune was beginning to have some doubts about our welcome as we began to explore the ship.

The higher we went up the ship, the more Shaune protested, until finally we were confronted by a big staircase with double doors at the top. By now she was in a real panic, convinced we'd ruined our careers, never mind that we may have lost our original restaurant reservation. And then there was the matter of what was going to happen to all our friends who were meeting us at the restaurant.

By now I'd convinced Shaune it was all OK and just to stick close to me. At the top of the stairs I threw open the big doors, only to be confronted by Ron and his wife Lisa, Mansour Ojjeh and his wife Cathy, plus all the major sponsors of the team. All the men were in black-tie outfits and the women dressed to the nines in evening dress, about to leave for the function at the Sporting Club.

But first they sang Happy Birthday to Shaune. It was the most beautiful setting and to be honest, quite an emotional moment I'm never likely to forget. When everyone returned from the Sporting Club, a disco started with champagne, cakes and the works. I don't imagine Ron organized all the details but he was certainly part of the 'let's do it' committee.

'It was a wonderful surprise,' Shaune recalls, 'and I enjoyed the whole evening until Bob whispered to me "don't forget you've got to work tomorrow". Oh well, never mind!'

One of the tasks I did not enjoy at the end of each season was the discussion with Ron of our salaries for the following year. Until about 1984 or '85, Shaune and I would normally return to New Zealand for several months and Ron regarded this as somewhat traitorous behaviour. He said he thought we were a bit like Gypsies. It suited him, though, as he didn't have to pay us during the time we were away. We were quite entitled to do this, as we were self-employed to a large extent.

Once Shaune and I headed off to Europe during the racing season we were very much on our own. Hospitality was our responsibility — one less item for Ron to worry about. If something wasn't right we soon heard about it, but principally we made sure our department ticked along smoothly. The total cost of the hospitality exercise was probably no more than £20,000 in the 1984 season, but after a while Ron began to sit down with us at the end of the season and suggest the food and hospitality could be improved for the following year. As a result he increased our budget by about 10 per cent for each ensuing year.

As time went by, the team increased in size, the working hours grew longer and eventually we had to adopt a different method of payment. When Project Four became McLaren International, Ron, Shaune and I formed a company called Upper Crust Ltd that charged McLaren International a flat fee for its services. Whatever economies we could manage added to our end-of-season profit. We certainly didn't cut any corners, as any attempt at being miserly would have quickly spelled the end of our contract.

By 1989 the annual cost of the hospitality unit was around £35,000, but the task had expanded considerably. Knowing Shaune and I depended on making a profit from operating the hospitality unit, Ron decided it was hardly fair to us if he wanted a couple of bottles of £200 wine for entertaining after a particularly satisfying victory. In the early 1990s we changed to a new system that gave us a float for every event. Our negotiations with Ron were always perfectly amicable and they took very little time. As I'm not a great negotiator, it was a simple matter of telling Ron what the cost would be for the coming season. Knowing I wasn't about to shoot myself in the foot by overcharging him, he'd agree to the price and that would be the end of the matter. If things differed greatly for some reason, we'd adjust it later on. It was a great way to do business.

The way Ron did business with people he trusted, it made me wonder how he got on with then vice-president of Mercedes-Benz Motorsport, Norbert Haug. In my view Ron is everything Norbert is not, which made the German one of the least popular people around the Formula One paddock. He tended to talk only to people who might have some influence in his world and he struck me as a self-important, pompous individual. At McLaren that attitude was simply not welcome. I'll say this for Norbert, though — he certainly knew how to celebrate.

He had a very different attitude to corporate McLaren, where a Grand Prix victory simply meant the job was being done properly. To Norbert, a win was a reason to celebrate. The parties in the Mercedes motorhome became legendary, at times lasting all night and sometimes until Monday morning. I felt sorry for the other poor motorhome people when these parties got going because the chef might be bludgeoned into cooking spaghetti bolognese at 4 a.m., but that's why they were on the payroll I guess. Norbert's capacity for partying late, then getting up the next morning apparently unaffected by his vast consumption of alcohol, was astounding.

Ron's partying days were tailing off as he strove to forge his F1 team into the best in the paddock. Accordingly he was not a regular at Norbert's parties, preferring to get back to England and start planning for the next race. You could say Norbert had a lot of spare time on his hands and appeared to do little apart from entertaining.

I think most of the oomph in the McLaren-Mercedes union was provided by the hard-working Jurgen Hubbert. He was a Mercedes-Benz DaimlerChrysler board member and an absolute gentleman who, like Ron, always had time for everyone. Jurgen was a serious player in the paddock and one of the proponents of the manufacturers' Formula One championship.

The transformation of Project Four into McLaren International did not happen by accident. When Ron started McLaren International he believed standard, tried-and-true business practices and methods could, or perhaps should, be applied to motor racing. He would go to seminars and study business methods and he learned what a lot of businessmen never do — you can't possibly have all the attributes yourself to run a large and complex modern business on your own, so you need to surround yourself with talented people who have the requisite skill-sets. Without following some alleged business guru's prescription for success, Ron was putting the right people into the right slots. When you have good engineering, accounting and marketing people looking after your core business, you can concentrate on leadership and development of your enterprise and that's something Ron has always been brilliant at.

McLaren's managing director, Martin Whitmarsh, was a typical Ron Dennis managerial appointment. He came to McLaren in 1991 from British Aerospace with no motor-racing knowledge. Ron would have noticed his keenness but I've no doubt what he wanted was Martin's management ability. I first met Martin in the workshop one day when neither of us had time for more than a brief chat.

He impressed me immediately as an intelligent and serious person. Martin joined McLaren as Head of Operations. I next came across him in a small bar the evening after the Japanese Grand Prix. The Log Cabin is famous principally because it's the only bar around Suzuka that stays open after 10 at night. Because it was difficult to get a flight out of Japan the night of the race, most of the teams' personnel, including management and drivers, would turn up sooner or later for a beer.

In 1991 Gerhard Berger and Ayrton Senna had finished first and second. Ayrton had gained enough points to assure himself of his third championship in a McLaren, so we all felt we had plenty to celebrate that evening. As the night wore on, everyone was getting more and more merry — fairly drunk, in fact — and more beer was being poured over people than down our throats. When things were at their rowdiest, who should walk in but a very sober-looking Martin. He made a beeline straight for the bloke I was standing next to and started talking to him.

As I had a couple of bottles of beer in my hands I offered to pour two of them over his head. Looking me straight in the eye he said, 'You wouldn't dare.' Not being one to turn down a challenge, I promptly dumped the contents of both bottles over his head. And 10 out of 10 for Martin, because he never tried to get away; rather, he took it in good humour.

He must have got into the spirit of the occasion quickly, because it wasn't long before I noticed him pouring beer over other people. It's true the beer-pouring episode may have favourably influenced my attitude towards Martin, but I always found him friendly and helpful. As I never dealt with him directly I may have had a perspective that other McLaren people did not enjoy, but certainly Martin is a person for whom I have plenty of respect.

For all the appointments he's made from the outside, Ron has also promoted long-time employees who have been loyal to him, and can do the job, to senior positions. Director of McLaren marketing Ekrem Sami started as a gofer while he completed his business studies at university. Financial director Bob Illman came to McLaren in 1983 and stayed until 2003, having worked for various other small Formula One teams that had folded, hence his early nickname 'Folder'. Bob is a motor-racing enthusiast above all else and despite his senior management position at McLaren, he still dons his overalls as a race marshal at club events around British circuits.

Fiscally speaking, Bob is a smart operator with incredible attention to detail that, I'm sure, is vital when you're responsible for managing the money in a motor-racing team — not a business generally regarded as a secure investment. One day I was out fishing with him on the stretch of river he leases in a beautiful area of England near Alton, where I actually managed to catch a fish for once, when my mobile phone rang. How Ron knew that Thursday afternoon I would be standing in the middle of a river trying to land a fish I'll never know. It added to the urban legend that Ron had hidden cameras everywhere and knew exactly what every team member was doing every moment of the day and night.

Many people have also speculated Ron has hidden microphones and cameras around the factory but I'm sure there weren't any. Nevertheless, Bob and I spent some time on that river bank assuring ourselves that Ron's call to me was a coincidence and that he could not possibly have a camera installed in the trees nearby.

Even back in the days of Project Four, we used to reckon Ron was working on Project 24. We just knew that mentally he was already far ahead of the existing project. It was almost as if you could safely say if Ron's current idea was up and running he'd already have moved on to his next big adventure.

You always sensed something new was around the corner. I believe it's why so many people stay with him for so long. And of course he's very good at talking you out of something — like resigning — which, I suppose, is as important as being able to talk you into something.

Working for Ron was good fun, as it seemed more like working for a mate who ran the team than for a boss. Ron may not have seen things this way, but that's how I and several others regarded the relationship. He attracted some top mechanics to the team and because he was a good boss they stayed with him.

I'm still not sure how he inspired such loyalty; perhaps it's the fact he is extremely good at talking to people. If you went into his office steaming about something he'd listen to the problem briefly, then talk for 15 minutes. By the time you'd left the office you'd be happy, although a little puzzled the problem may not actually have been solved. We called this Ron's 'gift of the gab' but it could, if not kept in check, descend into another name we had for it: 'Ron-speak'.

You really had to be there to listen to it, but he'd use the latest business buzz-words and convoluted sentences. It didn't appear to confuse him but it sure as hell did most of us. It might have been a kind of defence mechanism or smokescreen for his perceived lack of formal education. Why that should have worried him I have no idea, but to me it's an example of how you can be disadvantaged in England if you don't have a university education and the accompanying social advantages. It seemed to me that the former head of FIA, Max Mosley, sometimes attempted to speak down to Ron, as if he was some kind of upstart.

Of the two, I think Max is the one whose pedigree is suspect, with his father being the late fascist leader Sir Oswald Mosley. In 2008 a British newspaper exposed Max enjoying a sado-masochistic orgy with five prostitutes — now that's what I call strange. Ron has an aversion to the way Max talks to people and so he should. You should treat people, as Ron does, as you want to be treated yourself.

The Dennises are a normal family, fairly close without living in one another's pockets. Ron's mother was a guest at the British Grand Prix each year for as long as I can remember, until she passed away. Ron was also very good to his father, Norman Stanley. Norman had his first heart attack in 1984 and I recall how this got me into deep trouble with Ron at Brands Hatch during the British Grand Prix that year. Ron had asked me to go to the back of the grandstand outside the circuit to hand some paddock entrance tickets to his dad and two heart surgeons Ron insisted accompany his father.

Because it was a bit of a trek, I rode out on a scooter — not the wisest choice of transport. Norman wanted to ride back with me, to which I naturally objected, as the heart specialists couldn't ride with us. However, they didn't mind so Norman leapt on the back and we sped off to the McLaren hospitality unit in the paddock. When Ron saw his father astride the scooter waving his arms and generally enjoying the ride, he went absolutely berserk at me. When the surgeons arrived they copped it as well because Ron felt, not unreasonably, that if they were being paid to look after his father then that's what they should be doing. The fact nothing happened to Norman seemed to escape his dutiful son's logic for the moment, but it revealed his deep concern for his family.

In 1991 Britain's *Management Week* magazine posed the question on its cover, 'Is Ron Dennis Britain's Best Manager?' Although I'm not qualified to answer that, I would describe him as certainly one of the best managers of his own brain I've ever met. His workload was huge, yet his time management was so good it allowed him to keep most weekends free for family pursuits.

Ron wasn't a total working machine and he and his then wife Lisa had a place in the South of France that started out as an old villa.

They'd lavished love and attention on this property, and a fair chunk of money presumably, but the place was absolutely magnificent. It's where Ron could get away from all the pressures of racing and his growing business.

Shaune and I had the privilege of staying at the farmhouse many times and we agree our sojourns there have provided some of the most enjoyable days of our lives. Lisa is a fantastic woman and a good friend, one who came to a lot of races and who's equally at home talking to the president of a large corporation as she is to the person cleaning the toilets. She knew all the mechanics by name, so everyone who worked on the team appreciated her down-to-earth manner.

Ron and Lisa have supported Tommy's, a campaign for the protection of unborn children and as part of her involvement, Lisa gave a massive amount of time to the organization of a race as a supporting event at the British Grand Prix in 1992. She is also a published author with a series of childrens' books about Mac and Lauren, who live in a fantasy world of Grand Prix racing.

McLaren's favourite charity is The White Lodge, which provides activities and opportunities for disabled people of all ages, for their families and carers. This organization relies substantially on McLaren for its income. Ron's philosophy is he'd rather give a large amount of money to one organization and make a difference, than smaller amounts to many, where the effect would be minimal.

Few would be aware of the compassionate side of Ron Dennis's nature. After all, most people don't go around bragging about the good works they do and strangely enough, a lot of people in the Formula One world wouldn't understand it. Ron feels the need to spend his money where it will do some good and a substantial amount goes into kart racing to promote British drivers (Lewis Hamilton springs to mind). McLaren International fosters engineering training, even supporting some promising candidates through university courses.

I'm unsure whether you'd call the following story loyalty or charity, but it illustrates Ron's unwavering devotion to those he cares about and who contributed to his early companies. A former McLaren employee, who worked for Ron at Project Three and Project Four, appeared to lose his way when McLaren International came into being. Although this man wasn't the brightest spark, Ron gave him an opportunity to work in different departments to help him find a task that suited him. However he was a bit of a free spirit and he suddenly resigned. Ron continued to pay his wages out of his own pocket for about two years, so the man would feel he still had a job. Stories like this filtered down through all levels of the company, even though there are hundreds of people working for the organization now.

To me, Ron has always been a man who leads by example and not by telling people what to do. Having said that, there is a limit to his charity. When Ron acquired his first aircraft, a Falcon jet, its purchase was mentioned at a factory get-together. He was at pains to point out the plane was not a personal toy but a business tool belonging to the company. It would enable him to attend more meetings, visit more potential sponsors and generally be a more efficient manager.

George Langhorn, a long-time employee who'd run the paint shop at McLaren for many years, asked Ron to confirm if he understood correctly the aircraft belonged to McLaren International, 'so you could say it's ours', he quipped.

'Absolutely,' Ron confirmed.

'Then it will be okay if I take Thelma and the kids to Spain next weekend, will it?' George queried.

Everyone except Ron, who looked the other way, roared with

laughter. I'm not sure he ever saw the funny side of this, but I know he has made good use of his 'business tool'. He even used it once to check on progress of the Newell motorcoach and make sure Shaune and I were OK when we were stranded during the winter in Joplin, Missouri, overseeing the vehicle's construction.

On that occasion Ron had taken delivery of the ex-Julio Iglesias Falcon 20 executive jet in St Louis. His chief pilot, an ex-Royal Air Force Vulcan captain named Bob Frith (whose initials were RAF), phoned to say they'd be in Joplin at 9 p.m. After we waited and waited at the airport and were about to give up, an emergency was announced over the Tannoy. Fire engines turned up with flashing lights and wailing sirens and bang in the middle of all the commotion we saw a small jet land and presumed it was Ron. It wasn't until later we learned it was his jet that had caused the emergency response.

The extreme cold had caused a malfunction in the system that lowered the undercarriage. That meant they were preparing for a belly landing in the dark. Ron had been up to the cockpit to give his pilots the benefit of his advice but according to co-pilot Geoff Hardwicke, on his first trip, Ron had been told in very plain language that there were two captains on board and he should go back to his seat and put his belt on.

Fortunately they managed to lower the undercarriage on final descent and disaster was averted. 'Closest I've ever been to death,' muttered a somewhat white-faced Bob Frith in the bar later that evening. It took two or three whiskies before this former RAF career man admitted he was quite shaken by the incident.

Ron has not forgotten the people in the factory who have played such a huge part in the team's success. For years he would make a point of sitting down in the staff cafeteria on Monday morning after a Grand Prix and telling the inside story of what happened at the track. He'd give the real story warts and all, so the factory staff, who normally never see a race live at a circuit, would know exactly what was going on. I understand that he doesn't always have time for this now, but managing director Martin Whitmarsh carries out this duty in his absence.

One of the ways Ron showed his appreciation each year to his staff was to throw a really good Christmas party. Shaune and I organized a couple of these functions for about 60 people at Project Four. Now the McLaren Christmas party can only be described as an extravaganza attended by about 2000 guests.

One year we had the whole of London's Alexandra Palace filled with a fun fair and snow. Another time we went to a film studio that had been built to resemble a 1930s Chicago speakeasy where every guest was given play-money to gamble with at roulette tables. Another year we had a lady who did amazing things with a very large pet snake. Manhattan Transfer was the band and on the return trip to London the lady lost her snake. Just how anyone could lose such a large animal in such a small bus I'm not sure, but we heard there was a half-hour delay while the snake lady, the bus driver and members of Manhattan Transfer searched for the missing reptile.

Another year we had a Cirque du Soleil troupe perform for us because Ron had become a friend of owner Guy Laliberté. McLaren Christmas parties have become legendary because that's just the way Ron does such things.

When it was finally time to leave McLaren, I went to see Ron to let him know I was on my way to other adventures. We had a good chat about all sorts of things spanning the last 30 or so years — an overview, I suppose, of what I've tried to convey in this book.

He was sorry I was leaving, said he wished I wasn't but as much as he wanted, couldn't get involved in my decision-making. He kindly went on to say if I needed anything in the future, not to hesitate in contacting him. Then he wished me luck and I realized my years at McLaren had come to an end.

To be honest, most of the conversation was a bit of a blur, as it's pretty damn hard to part company after nearly a lifetime of working for a good bloke like Ron Dennis. One thing he said to me, as I was about to walk out the door, stuck in my mind.

'Never look back. Move on, my friend.'

Chapter 6

Mansour Ojjeh: a watch on Formula One

I have made numerous references already to Mansour Ojjeh and his effect, influence, support and friendliness at McLaren and consider it appropriate to devote a chapter to the family.

Mansour's father Akram, who was born in Syria but became a wealthy Saudi entrepreneur, founded the TAG (Techniques d'Avant Garde) group in 1977 and cultivated connections within Middle Eastern governments by acting as an intermediary in arms dealing. He avoided publicity as much as he could but hit the headlines when he purchased the liner *Le France*. Mansour's mother was French and he spent much of his childhood in France although he also attended schools in America, graduating in 1974.

Mansour's passion for motor racing developed after he attended the Monaco Grand Prix in 1978 as a guest of the Saudi royal family, which owned Saudi Airlines, Williams' sponsor at the time. His enthusiasm for the sport led to TAG becoming Williams' principal sponsor in 1979. The influx of capital enabled Patrick Head to build competitive machinery and Williams scored its first F1 victory at Silverstone in 1979. Alan Jones then won the World Championship in 1980 and Keijo (Keke) Rosberg repeated the feat in 1982.

When Ron Dennis approached Mansour his idea was to get him aboard McLaren as a partner rather than a sponsor. Mansour agreed to invest US$5m in a Porsche-built turbo engine in 1982. Mansour and Dennis then established TAG Turbo Engines in September 1982 and the company's new engine was unveiled at the Geneva Motor Show in 1983. It raced for the first time at the Dutch Grand Prix in August. The following year McLaren-TAG drivers Niki Lauda and Alain Prost dominated the world championship series with 12 wins from 16 races. By year's end Mansour was the majority shareholder in McLaren, although the deal was not made public until March 1985. (Source grandprix.com)

Although that's the outline of the deal, in a previous chapter I explained exactly how Ron came up with a cunning plan to entice the Ojjehs away from Frank Williams' team by offering the McLaren hospitality motorhome as a base for Mansour to use while entertaining his own guests at a Grand Prix. Ron realized early on that a man who poured a vast amount of money into a very expensive sport should be cared for like a rare flower, lest his interest wither and droop.

I got to know Mansour before he married his American wife, Cathy, and later Shaune and I became acquainted with his stepmother and brothers too. We were more or less running the motorhome as the family's regular get-together haunt at Grand Prix. Mansour's younger brother Aziz was an enormous, well-built, square-jawed character like Dolph Lundgren. At first glance you'd be inclined to take a wide berth around him, but he turned out to be a gentle giant.

We found the Ojjeh family to be a fantastic bunch of people despite having enough money to acquire a Third World country or two. In our line of work we often came across the very well heeled and many of them were not the most pleasant people to deal with.

There's an old adage that often sprang to mind: money can't buy you happiness, all it does is make a shitty life acceptable. I could never quite work out why the very rich often seemed quite miserable in their demeanour. But not the Ojjehs. They were about as normal as you could possibly get, despite the fact they could have bankrolled any F1 team in the paddock.

I think the Ojjehs were just as happy having a beer with the race mechanics as they would have been sipping a 1958 Latour Pauillac wine with the President of the United States. I don't know whether they ever socialized with the President of the United States, but if they did, I can't imagine any of them being overawed by the experience. As you can imagine, they moved in seriously wealthy circles and we once heard a Texas oil man, Tommy Thompson, say he'd burn his little pile by comparison if he had Mansour's stack.

This made Shaune and I decide to do a little bit of research so we could understand the sort of people we were dealing with. We quickly learned the TAG Group is privately owned, self-financing and extremely wealthy. It has interests in everything from hi-tech activities like Grand Prix racing, America's Cup yachts and executive jet leasing to farming in the USA. But as it's a private company, there's no way of learning exactly how much they are worth.

We knew for several years Mansour had been building a massive motor launch, and finally it was about to get its great public unveiling at the 1983 Monaco Grand Prix. It was truly magnificent by all accounts. So much so that an Arab prince, who had been a guest on board, couldn't stop saying how impressed he was by the workmanship, the fit-out and the styling.

Following a time-honoured tradition in the Arab world, Mansour gave the boat to the prince there and then and the prince sailed it away the day after the race. This odd behaviour on Mansour's behalf niggled away at me for months until I couldn't take it any more. When the time was right I delicately raised the subject and asked what motivated a man who had spent months and months building something very bespoke would, in the blink of an eye, simply give it away.

'Ahh Bob,' he said with an American-French accent rather than Arab, 'it is true I gave it to the prince. But if the yacht cost me $10 million to build, it is but a drop in the ocean when the new owner will give me $100 million in new business.'

I realized something important that day — it doesn't matter if it's a $100 lunch or a $10 million boat; it's only the numbers that are different, not the long game.

Thinking about it, part of the attraction of working for McLaren over the years was meeting such a huge array of people including the Ojjehs and their friends. And Shaune and I got along with all of them.

While on the subject of the rich and famous, there was a night at the iconic Jimmy'z bar in Monaco in the early 1990s when it wasn't so much of a flocking of the rich, but definitely the famous. For all intents and purposes it was a gathering of the motor-racing gods of two eras: Jackie Stewart, Alain Prost, Juan Manuel Fangio, Jack Brabham, Niki Lauda and others. And there we were, along with Mansour and his younger brother Aziz. It was a *Twilight Zone* moment (not the prissy vampire movie but Rod Serling's original), where you had to pinch yourself to make sure it was real.

'You are part of this family now,' said Aziz. This simple but sincere statement made a big impression on me. Here was this man whose family could easily buy half the world's airlines, and a few ships to boot, proclaiming Shaune and I were part of his family.

Those who maintain that the extraordinarily rich are all flash and no substance have never met the Ojjehs. There was many a time I witnessed first-hand that their sentiments were genuine. On one occasion at the Canadian Grand Prix in 1984 Mansour and Aziz appeared deep in conversation with people who I assumed were wealthy customers looking to buy aircraft or something equally expensive. On spotting both of us, the two brothers immediately made their way over to us and engaged us in conversation.

While being very down to earth, the Ojjeh family also moved in circles we mere mortals rarely visited. Their friends and guests included people who were stars in their own right. Michael Douglas was a regular visitor to McLaren with his wife Catherine Zeta-Jones. I still regard it as one of my top-20 days when I had the privilege of showing them around the team base. She may be a big Hollywood star but she's no airhead and has a marvellous sense of humour bordering on the coarse, especially when telling jokes. But with that voice coming out of that astonishingly beautiful face, how could anyone take offence?

As naturally befits a man of wealth, Mansour, as head of various successful companies, had access to a company-owned jet piloted by his long-time employee André Amar. Before he was given the cockpit of the private jet, André flew Mansour's personal helicopter, and when the boss wasn't about or using the thing, he'd indulge himself with a bit of — how can I describe it? — pushing-the-envelope flying.

Around 1987 we arrived at the Paul Ricard circuit, which lies not far from the Mediterranean coast in the South of France. The circuit is a 40-minute drive east of Marseilles. To the south lies the popular beach resort of Bandol, a charming French holiday town with a lovely enclosed harbour and some fine restaurants.

There wasn't much happening on the track that afternoon. The Formula One cars sat in their garages and the mechanics lounged about with bugger-all to do while the drivers were nowhere to be seen. Just as everyone was winding down even further in the mid-afternoon sun, the tranquillity was shattered by the *whoop-whoop* of an approaching helicopter. The noise got louder until the chopper landed in the carpark behind the garages. Some of us sauntered over to see who had dropped in and I wasn't surprised to see André jump down from the cockpit. He'd been on his way to return the rented aircraft to the airport in Nice and decided to make a short detour to see his boss.

After a quick chat with Mansour, André looked around the garage and after a moment fixed his eyes on me and drawled in a thick accent, 'Boob, 'ow would yoo like too curm for eh quick ride in zee 'elicopterr to zee airport? We will collect our own machine which 'as been serviced zair.'

While André had an adventurous streak, I had no qualms about going for a flight with him at the controls. It was reputed he'd flown all through Asia and had spent time in Vietnam just before the Americans arrived. I can only imagine it must have been when the French were having their own tête-à-tête with the North Vietnamese. If André did have some combat experience it would make sense that Mansour had him on the payroll, as the guy would really have known how to fly. Over the years I've learned rich men value their lives highly and avoid taking unnecessary risks like hiring cut-price pilots or flying in single-engined helicopters. In any case, I'd flown with André before and had every confidence in his ability.

Every time I set foot in a helicopter and it claws its way into the air, drops its nose and begins to move forward I'm filled with a sense of wonder. I can't for the life of me work out how it goes up in the air let alone straight ahead. The 20-minute flight to the airport was pleasant enough and after landing and returning the rental helicopter we walked over to Mansour's private machine.

This thing was no small Robinson R44 or such like but a rather large French-made six-seater Squirrel powered by twin turbo-charged engines developing goodness knows how much horsepower. You could get to places very fast in that beast. As André spooled up the rotor while we were buckling in, he casually mentioned the afternoon was ours and we should go for a sightseeing trip. When all the dial needles reached their correct positions and André had finished his pre-flight check, we suddenly shot up into the air like a scalded cat and buggered off out over the Cannes bay. That day I learned a helicopter can, in the right hands, do a power dive.

André had spotted what he decided was an Italian battleship anchored in the port. With a smile verging on the manic, the formerly sane Frenchman, whom until then I'd had implicit faith in, suddenly mutated into a deranged World War II fighter pilot. As the horizon tilted to a seemingly impossible angle and the deck of the battleship rapidly filled the windscreen, I realized I was on the verge of panic.

Just when I was beginning to think things might turn out to be OK, André started to yell 'RATA-TAT-TAT-TAT' at the top of his voice, mimicking a machine gun. At this stage we were still hurtling, almost vertically, towards the metal behemoth and I thought I was doomed to die in this maniac's pseudo naval battle.

Within mere seconds I was able to see the whites of the eyes of some seriously worried sailors on deck. Just as thoughts of the divine wind entered my head, the colour outside the cockpit turned from a dull grey to an azure blue as we shot skywards again.

I don't think we grazed the ship's radar mast but I wasn't paying too much attention as I was preoccupied with feeling mightily relieved we were still in the air. André quipped 'we should go now', to which I nodded vigorously in agreement, as I still hadn't recovered my voice. I looked around at the view and contemplated how sweet life seemed after all.

Not content with just having avoided crashing into a warship, he then put the thing in a vertical climb, sort of stalled it and went back to have another go at the ship. I think he was going to continue doing this over and over again until he was informed by the Nice Airport controllers that there was a plane coming into the airport on finals and he should clear off.

My moment of euphoria didn't last long. When my breathing had settled down and I had decided not to have a right go at the guy holding the controls in case it sparked yet another crazy stunt, I turned to André with a wan smile. That was soon wiped off my face when about 20 minutes after the ship episode and in the middle of nowhere over the Alpes Maritimes I noticed he'd slumped forward in his seat with his eyes closed.

By this stage I'd stopped trying to work out how many gods I must have offended in an earlier life. I'd just missed being turned into a pancake on the deck of a warship, only to find myself contemplating the thought of spiralling into the Mediterranean, and all because some dumb-arse helicopter pilot had decided to relive the old days and have a heart attack. Great.

In shear frustration and fear I kicked out at André, catching him in the calf with a good shot as I anticipated what things would be like in the afterlife. André snapped awake and glared at me, asking what the heck my problem was. He'd set the autopilot and was having a catnap and didn't appreciate the rude awakening. I wasn't convinced helicopters have autopilots and went about making sure André was *compos mentis* for the rest of the trip.

He became bored with my antics and announced he may as well test the newly serviced aircraft to see it was airworthy. Why you'd check something's airworthy while it's 3000 feet in the air is beyond me. If it all goes wrong there's no recourse. Away we went up to about 4000 or 5000 feet and it was a hell of view until the bastard turned off both engines.

If you think a stone plummets earthwards fast, you should see a helicopter — preferably not from the inside, as it was the most terrifying thing I have ever experienced. Not only did my life flash in front of my eyes, but I couldn't avoid the thought 'what if the engine doesn't start again or André has a heart attack?' After mere seconds of heading straight down with only the sound of the wind howling through the auto-rotating blades, I cracked and screamed at André, 'Why the fuck don't you do your bloody testing on your own?'

Without heeding a word, the mad bastard continued to fiddle with knobs and switches and in his own sweet time, he powered up the engine again. Almost immediately our rate of descent slowed and some semblance of control returned, giving me faith I wasn't about to become pavement pizza.

That was the first time I really lost the plot with André. In the past he'd erred a little on the crazy side, but in general he was great fun to fly with because there was rarely a dull moment, though that day's flying was the most extreme. However, others who had the 'pleasure' of flying with him did not always share my sentiments.

On the odd occasion, when the big boss wasn't too close at hand, it was possible to get André to take someone up for a joy ride. During the 1995 Portuguese Grand Prix, English couple Jamie Watt and Jo Davies were working with Shaune in the motorhome. As a reward for their hard work I arranged for them to go for a quick spin in the helicopter with André.

They were a little apprehensive to start with but André turned on the French charm and in a sort of lounge-lizard accent promised them the ride of their lives. After a brief discussion, they all clambered aboard and what happened next is still indelibly imprinted on my mind.

André cranked up the big engines to full revs and just as it appeared it was going to shake itself apart, he released whatever you release in a helicopter cockpit and the thing shot skyward with such speed it would have put the Apollo space rocket launches to shame.

As the chopper disappeared into the heavens, I started to have misgivings about suggesting the two of them should go for a ride. My anxiety wasn't improved when I spotted the helicopter in a power dive moments later, heading straight down towards the paddock.

Having been in that similar situation before with the mad bugger, I wasn't overly concerned about them hitting the ground but what he did next almost overturned the laws of physics. He pulled up abruptly and flipped the aircraft on its side, and more, which suspiciously looked like a wingover manoeuvre — except helicopters don't have wings, now that I come to think about it.

He soon righted the helicopter and at a slightly more sedate speed and trim, disappeared with the pair on a sightseeing trip. On the their return, Jamie and Jo climbed out of the helicopter on slightly wobbly legs but otherwise unscathed after André's initial moments of madness.

McLaren International — with the Ojjeh connection and not Marlboro this time — also had a connection with skiing. When he wasn't at the Grand Prix, Aziz Ojjeh was a speed skier who was determined to break the world record. It wasn't long before he started looking longingly at the wind tunnel used to assess the aerodynamics of the F1 car.

Aziz soon convinced everyone that if the tunnel wasn't being used for car testing, he could make use of it to get his stance right and reduce his drag through the air. After getting his crouch as aerodynamic as possible in the tunnel, Aziz then moved on to his helmet. At the speeds some of the skiers were travelling, getting your head and helmet in the wrong position could result in your head nearly being ripped from your shoulders.

After a few attempts with the new helmet and body position out on the slopes, Aziz wisely decided while he still had all his arms and legs in good condition and while he was still in full command of all his faculties, he'd give the record attempt a miss. It was a dangerous pastime, especially if you came unstuck at the speeds some of the skiers including Aziz could reach. They can attain speeds in excess of 250 kph. That's faster than most junior formula classes can get up to and even F1 cars don't often go that fast.

Deciding he still wanted to be involved in skiing, Aziz arranged personal sponsorship through TAG Heuer for World Cup skiing competitors Harti Weirather, Helmut Höflehner and Marc Girardelli. During the mid-1980s Girardelli was easily the most successful of this trio, winning the World Cup five times before retiring from racing in 1997. Aziz remains involved with the TAG Group and is now the vice-chairman. TAG remains a 15 per cent shareholder in the McLaren Group.

Chapter 7

Personalities and politics: colourful characters of the pit lane

The following pages concern some of the more colourful characters I came across during the years of my involvement in motor racing. There is no particular chronological order to the various observations and stories; it's more about who did what to whom rather than when.

My first story is about being in the right place at the right time. For about seven years we had an Italian driver called Arturo Merzario. He was a skinny, weedy character but he could drive a car with some skill. In fact, he was contracted to Ferrari for three years and had some success driving sports cars in endurance races.

Art is perhaps most renowned for being one of the drivers, along with Guy Edwards, Brett Lunger and Harald Ertl, who saved Niki Lauda from his burning car during the 1976 German Grand Prix. His Formula One career wasn't so hot, but having a big fat Marlboro sponsorship in your back pocket has its advantages. He drove for a number of teams during his career — Williams, Fittipaldi, March, Wolf and finally his own Merzario team.

I remember Art very well because he was way ahead of the curve when it came to the look and feel most us know Marlboro for. He was prone to wandering around the circuit wearing a cowboy hat, even before the cigarette company rolled out its long-running cowboy imagery. Art was probably wearing the wide-brimmed headgear to keep the sun and rain off him, so it could well have been more a practical response to the weather than a style decision. Nonetheless, he had the look of the future Marlboro Man about him.

As well as his big cowboy hat, Art always wore dazzling white racing overalls on which the bright red Marlboro logo stuck out like a sore thumb. One particular day the stars must have been aligned, the moon rising in Venus's quadrant, and Jupiter was in Mars' ascending whatever, because Art could hardly have planned what was about to unfold. He was about to secure his racing future in a way no other driver could have done.

I was in the motorhome watching the 1979 Grand Prix at Monza (a bad year actually, as it was in this race that Ronnie Peterson was killed), enjoying myself in air-conditioned comfort, a particularly pleasant way to watch racing in a hot and humid climate. I wasn't on my own, or I'd have had a cold one nearby, but there were a couple of Marlboro executives with me so I was on my best behaviour. One of the big shots was none other than event marketing boss John Hogan, an Australian who had done rather well for himself, having climbed all the way up the corporate ladder.

As the cars returned from their out lap to form up on the grid for the 10-minute wait before the actual race start, the cameras focused on Arturo, who was driving for his own team Merzario Ford, sponsored by Marlboro that year. Not even David Ogilvy of the Ogilvy and Mather dynasty, who remains one of the most famous names in advertising and one of the handful of thinkers who shaped that industry, could have written the script for what happened next.

When his car eventually coasted to a stop, Art unbuckled his belts, stood up on the seat of the car, leaned back against the rollbar and took off his helmet. All this was done with such an air of nonchalance that all of us watching half-expected him to pull out his bloody cowboy hat from behind the seat and plonk it on his head.

Then our jaws dropped. In fact Art did have the damn hat almost straight away and he proceeded to unfold it and place it carefully and deliberately on his head. I'd never come across a folding hat before but what came next was pure theatre. Seemingly without a care in the world, Art pulled a flip-top packet of cigarettes out of his top pocket, which just happened to be emblazoned with the Marlboro logo, and proceeded to light up. As he brought the similarly emblazoned flip-top lighter to the cigarette, the packet was still in his hands, rotated so it was directly facing the camera, which was filming the car parked on the grid.

When the cigarette was alight, he dropped his hands and the world got to see a Formula One driver wearing a cowboy hat, standing in the cockpit of his Formula One car, on a Formula One grid, smoking a Marlboro cigarette as if it was the most natural thing to do before the start of a Formula One World Championship Grand Prix. That little photo-op was of course pure gold for the brand.

The whole display was so way beyond cool it was verging on the unbelievable. Here was a man who was about to dice with death in one of the premier events of the motorsport calendar, and apparently he couldn't give a toss. Or from a marketing point of view, he was having a Marlboro while calmly contemplating what might be about to unfold.

It was almost enough to entice me to take up smoking the sponsor's product. I turned around to ask the Marlboro executives what they thought of Art's antics, only to see them looking at the television screen, transfixed by the sight of their product being used so blatantly on a global broadcast — and it hadn't cost the company a red cent, beyond the sponsorship of Art's team.

Shortly afterwards the producer switched to another camera shot and general pictures of the other stars on the grid filled the screen once again. The spell was instantly broken and all I heard was a deep intake of breath and I'll never forget the words that marketing boss John Hogan uttered next.

'Well, as far as I'm concerned, Merzario has just renewed his contract for life.'

Multinationals aren't necessarily known for keeping their word, but in this case Marlboro stood proud and followed through on Hogan's comment, continuing their sponsorship of Art for many years. He ran his own Formula One car in 1978 and 1979, and even today his driving school has support from Marlboro.

In the early 1970s Formula One underwent enormous changes. Commercial sponsorship became a reality and eventually the purists realized it was the way forward for the health and growth of the sport. The Formula One Constructors' Association (FOCA), under the leadership of then Brabham team owner Bernie Ecclestone, started lobbying circuit owners to improve safety features and event promoters to pay Grand Prix teams more money. The growth of the sport was accompanied by political manoeuvring that continues to this day. The politics didn't affect me in the 1970s but I realized there were some pretty extraordinary things going on.

In South Africa in 1982 there was disagreement over the wording in the Super Licence contracts, which the governing body the Fédération Internationale du Sport Automobile (FISA) wanted all drivers to sign. The clause read, 'I am committed to the above team to drive exclusively for them in the FIA Formula One World Championship(s) until the [date].' It went on, 'I will do nothing which might harm the moral or material interests or image of International Motorsport or the FIA Formula One World Championship.'

The two parties were so far apart that the drivers, led by Niki Lauda, actually went on strike. He saw the Super Licence as a document that committed him to racing in Formula One and nothing else. In a hotel about 20 miles from the Kyalami circuit, the drivers locked themselves in a room with two heavies on the door to prevent anyone walking out, should one of them weaken. For light relief, when the discussions got a bit heavy, accomplished pianist and Lotus driver Elio de Angelis would hit the keyboards and bang out a few classical and contemporary tunes.

The following day, an agreement of sorts was reached, allowing the drivers to return to the circuit in time to fit in one timed practice session. On another occasion, this time in 1975, the drivers expressed considerable concern about the safety of the crash barriers on the Montjuic Park circuit in Barcelona and refused to race. The organizers' response was to threaten to impound the cars. With such a draconian measure slapped down on the table, the drivers had no alternative but to go racing.

The world champion at the time, Emerson Fittipaldi, cruised around in his Marlboro McLaren at the back of the field for a few laps, allowing the team to pick up its start money, and then promptly pulled into the pits and parked the car, citing a mechanical issue that would prevent the car from racing. At that time Emerson was almost a racing deity, and probably still is in his native Brazil, so in the eyes of the public he could do and say no wrong.

His concerns about the safety of the track were tragically proven well-founded when Rolf Stommelen inherited the lead after Niki Lauda and Mario Andretti had a coming together. Twenty-five laps into the race Rolf lost his rear wing — not dissimilar to what happened to Graham Hill in 1969 when he had an accident on the same circuit in the same place — and his car leapt the barrier into the crowd, killing four people and injuring many more. Rolf was badly injured and the race was stopped shortly after.

As an aside, one of the very few women to start an F1 race was also competing that day. Lella Lombardi was circulating in sixth place (last actually, as seven other cars had crashed out earlier) when the race was red-flagged. Consequently she became the only female to gain a point in F1. In fact it was recorded as half a point: since the race had been stopped on lap 29, the drivers filling the first six positions were each given half the points normally allocated to place-getters in the event.

In retrospect it's clear that the accident proved conclusively the drivers were correct in claiming the track was a deathtrap. In doing so, they gained the upper hand and had to be listened to. As well as becoming a force in how the world championship would be run in years to come, they were just beginning to command the large sums of money that superstars would one day see as their right.

Because many of the fledging Grand Prix Drivers' Association meetings were held in the Marlboro motorhome, I was privy to some of what went on. Much of the time the discussions were rather childish. For example, the first 20 minutes would be taken up with an argument about the air-conditioning. Niki Lauda would say 'It's not for me' and Emerson Fittipaldi would snap back 'We must have it.' This sort of thing could go on and on, prompting up-and-coming drivers like James Hunt and Alan Jones to walk out and leave the rest of them to their bickering.

James and Alan always struck me as drivers who just wanted to get on with the job and go racing rather than become embroiled in the Machiavellian machinations of Grand Prix politics. Having said that, though, Alan wasn't entirely disinterested in the outcome of those verbal fracas, and was apt to discuss his personal agenda with others on the quiet.

Moving forward a few years, another who couldn't be bothered with all the argument was Jacques Villeneuve who, much like his dad Gilles, was 'not interested in the politics, just in racing cars'.

For example, Jacques really didn't want to know about the Head and Neck Support (HANS) device that was introduced but not mandatory in 2002. HANS became more or less compulsory in 2003; in much the same de facto sort of way seat-belts became compulsory 30 years earlier. Even Formula One's resident medical expert Professor Sid Watkins campaigned for the adoption of the HANS device for a long time, so you'd have thought all the drivers would buy into the idea.

Driver politics have played a part in Grand Prix teams since the day manufacturers started having two-car teams. In fact, if my memory serves me, at the 1956 end-of-season Italian Grand Prix, Peter Collins, who could have won the world championship, was forced to hand over his car over to Ferrari team-mate Juan Manuel Fangio. The Argentinean went on to finish second and both drivers shared the points, giving Fangio enough to win the title. Can't see Lewis Hamilton handing his car over to Jenson Button towards the end of a race in order for Button to win another title — the circuit would run with rivers of angst.

While other teams were rife with infighting, I can comfortably say, with hand on heart, when I worked at McLaren it wasn't all that bad. Of course there was always a bit of niggle, but nothing compared with the situation in some other camps. We usually managed to have driver pairings where one was unquestionably faster than the other, so there wasn't much friction.

James Hunt and Jochen Mass, for example, got along fine. I don't think they were great mates, but then they were very different personalities and from diverse cultures and backgrounds. Patrick Tambay was a gentle person, rather like Jochen, and neither was as vocal as that irrepressible ladies' man James. The difference in driver skill may have contributed to the lack of egotistical infighting among drivers at McLaren, as in motor racing the alpha dog will always be the driver who is consistently the fastest. Of course that doesn't always stop the young pup from trying to get one over the old dog.

In some cases we had a driver who was more passive than the other and didn't always want to pick a fight or be the centre of attention. This successful style of combination may have had its roots back in the days of Bruce McLaren and Denny Hulme. Bruce was the team owner and boss, while Denny was the quiet one who got on with the driving and proved to be the quicker of the two.

I doubt if Denny was even worried when he was paired with Emerson Fittipaldi. Denny won the first Grand Prix of 1974 in Argentina so he could hardly be regarded as a slow-poke. Although he was in the final year of his F1 racing career, Denny undoubtedly felt considerable loyalty to the McLaren team, as he stayed with them from 1968 until 1974, finishing third in the world championships twice after winning his world title with Brabham in 1967.

Emerson, on the other hand, was a completely different character. He was at the peak of his European career when he arrived at the team in 1974 and promptly won his first world title, finishing second the following year. Emerson was one of the drivers, and no disrespect to him, who probably wanted the best and didn't care who supplied it. After he left McLaren, though, things didn't work out so well — with his own team he never quite reached the heights of his McLaren days in F1, his best result being 10th in 1978.

It may sound like it was all a bed of roses at McLaren, but a few thorns found their way to the top and sparks flew on occasions. None more so than when Alain Prost and Ayrton Senna ended up together at McLaren. How Ron Dennis handled those two without losing a limb, I'll never know.

Alain and Ayrton were two of the most political animals I have ever come across. Millions of F1 viewers witnessed the culmination of the simmering rivalry when it all exploded at the 1989 Japanese Grand Prix. Up until 2009, when it was discovered Nelson Piquet was ordered to deliberately crash his Renault to allow his team-mate Fernando Alonso to win the 2008 Singapore Grand Prix, this was one of the most notorious incidents in the history of Formula One.

After a season of bitching and infighting as team-mates at McLaren, their penultimate race of the 1989 season was to determine who would be world champion. Ayrton needed to finish in front of Alain to keep his title hopes alive. Alain led for most of the race and in what looked like an audacious passing move, Ayrton fired into the side of Alain's car, forcing both off the track.

Ayrton restarted and made it back to the pits for repairs, rejoined the race, and went on to take the win. Alain, on the other hand, parked his car and walked back to the control tower and placed an official complaint. During the podium ceremony it was announced Ayrton had been stripped of his win and disqualified from the race for using the escape road to rejoin the race, handing the world title to Alain. The race was eventually awarded to Alessandro Nannini in a Benetton Ford.

All hell promptly ensued, to such a degree that Ron Dennis hauled both of his warring drivers into the team offices and slammed the door on anyone else trying to get in. After half an hour both drivers emerged and nothing more was said about the incident. To this day, as far as I know, only the three of them know exactly what was said behind those closed doors.

But if that relationship had its issues, those two didn't hold a candle to the Ferrari pairing of Canadian Gilles Villeneuve and Didier Pironi during 1982. Talk about a collision of personalities. Gilles was cut from old-school cloth, where you did an apprenticeship when new to a team and supported the top driver, as he did with Jody Scheckter in 1979.

When Didier arrived to partner him, Gilles expected the same sort of respect from the Frenchman as he had shown Jody. He was about to be sorely disappointed. During the 1982 San Marino Grand Prix the Ferraris were running one and two with Gilles in front. Towards the end of the race, the Ferraris were so far in front of the rest of the pack one of the pit lane crew held out the 'slow' sign.

Gilles lifted off, expecting Didier to do the same and follow him home. Not so. Didier had other plans and shot past him on the last lap, leaving no time for Gilles to retake the top spot. Spitting tacks, Gilles swore he'd never speak to Didier again. The saga had a tragic outcome when Gilles pushed his car too hard in an effort to out-qualify his arch-rival for the Belgium Grand Prix at Zolder. He crashed and was killed.

Unfortunately it didn't end there. It's almost as if Didier was cursed from then on. At the start of the Canadian Grand Prix that same year, Didier stalled on the grid and Riccardo Paletti ploughed into the back of his stationary car, dying instantly. Later in the season while leading the championship Didier launched over a slower car, crashing heavily and breaking his legs so badly he had to retire from racing.

Still his bad luck continued. He took up offshore powerboat racing, only to be killed, along with his two crew, when his boat flipped over in a race near the Isle of Wight off the coast of England in August 1987.

After his death his partner gave birth to twins and guess what she called them? Didier and Gilles. Go figure.

On a personal level, Gilles was a truly lovely man and Shaune and I got to know him and his wife Joann quite well as they also lived in a motorhome at the circuits. When Jacques (who went on to race F1 and win a world title in 1997 after a successful career in CART/ IndyCar) was still a little boy we used to bounce him and his sister Melanie on our knees. Didier, on the other hand, took a very political view of everything in Formula One and tended to bend whichever way the wind was blowing.

Although there's been a fair amount of politics happening within Formula One over the last few years, I'd still have to say, on balance, the 1980s were by far the worst. As early as 1980 FISA and the Formula One Constructors' Association (FOCA) were at each other's throats like rabid dogs. Too much ink has already been spent on that tussle, but I'll add my spin anyway.

Suffice to say that in 1980 Australia's pending second F1 world champion, Alan Jones, got caught up in the two governing bodies' shit-fight. After the running of that year's Spanish Grand Prix, which Alan won for Frank Williams' team, FISA (which at the time ran F1) declared the race illegal, so no world championship points were allocated. The decision to devalue the race as counting towards the world championship was over an issue of unpaid drivers' fines. It was a petty reason in the bigger picture perspective of things. However, despite all the political infighting within the various governing bodies, Alan went on to win his world title.

The battle between the two bodies flowed over to the 1981 season when that year's South African Grand Prix was cancelled due to further disagreements. Eventually everyone concerned at a governing level decided to put most, but not all, their personal agendas behind them and the Concorde Agreement was signed so the sport could move on. Although it was an improvement, the Agreement didn't solve all problems, and every now and again the odd issue still raises its ugly head.

I was at Imola for the San Marino Grand Prix in 1982 when FISA announced that Nelson Piquet's Brabham and Keke Rosberg's Williams had both been disqualified from the results of the Brazilian Grand Prix a few weeks earlier. As you would imagine, this decision went down like a lead balloon with Frank Williams and Brabham's Bernie Ecclestone. Both were powerful FOCA personalities, so they lobbied the rest of the organization's members and decided to boycott the San Marino event.

The only FOCA member whose cars raced in anger was Ken Tyrrell. His main sponsor, the appliance manufacturer Candy, indicated their sponsorship agreement would be terminated if the Tyrrell cars withdrew from San Marino. Ken was quite politically motivated and a leading figure in FOCA. Nevertheless, he was realistic enough to realize he needed to race to keep the money coming in. I'm still convinced he felt slightly grubby about being forced to race by his sponsors, whereas from a moral stance, he'd have preferred to have sided with FOCA and withdrawn his cars.

That weekend we were told to pack up and get across the Italian border into Switzerland as fast as physically possible. Personally, I felt rather sad about the decision. As much as I never liked Monza, I always enjoyed Imola. I thought the people in Imola were kind and gentle. Anyway, our instructions were to pack up, but look as if we were *not* packing up. Just how we were supposed to pull down an awning without looking as if we were in fact pulling down an awning, I've never been sure.

However, we did it, and with the transporters and motorhomes loaded we hightailed it to Switzerland that night. We left the others, including Ferrari and Renault, to do battle with a grid of just 14 cars.

Most of the problems that occurred in Formula One between 1979 and 1982 can be attributed to the complete lack of agreement on where the sport should be heading. Jean-Marie Balestre, head of FISA, and Bernie Ecclestone, head of FOCA, were constantly at loggerheads over whose plan was superior. With two of the biggest players in the sport at odds with each other, it was no wonder things were in a state of upheaval.

Balestre was one of the old blazer-wearing, armband guard who wanted to run the sport as it had always been. More of a daredevil gentleman's club, for gentlemen racers who regarded it as more of a hobby than a business. Balestre was also prone to tell anyone who'd listen that he, and FISA alone, ran the sport and no one else. It didn't take too much working out that this attitude got right up Ecclestone's nose. With the growing power and influence of the fledgling FOCA group, it was inevitable Balestre's old-school management style would eventually succumb to the new powerbrokers.

Eventually it all came to a head when Max Mosley finally managed to depose Balestre in 1991. Balestre was ousted and replaced by poacher-turned-gamekeeper Max, who had left his March engineering company in 1977 and sold his shares but remained a director for a number of years. Ecclestone, in contrast to Balestre, had much grander ideas for the sport. He had visions of its growing up and becoming a truly professional entity and he wanted to run it as the multi-million dollar, multinational promotional juggernaut it is today.

While Formula One's highly regarded big wheel has not been officially involved in the governance of the sport for many years, nothing happens without an acquiescent nod from Bernie. The ageing patriarch of F1 has been involved with the Formula One Management company from day one, and as a result has the biggest say in what happens to the sport — despite what some say to the contrary. Never one to shy away from speaking his mind, Bernie has in the past shot from the hip and, at times, almost shot himself in the foot.

Who can forget his comment a few years ago when he said, 'You know I've got one of those wonderful ideas . . . women should be dressed in white like all the other domestic appliances.'

Or, when talking about how he preferred totalitarian states because things get done under such regimes, he said in an interview with *The Times*, 'In a lot of ways, terrible to say this I suppose, but apart from the fact that Hitler got taken away and persuaded to do other things that I have no idea whether he wanted to do or not, he was in the way he could command a lot of people able to get things done.'

The controversy over the last two years that has dogged F1 must have Ecclestone shaking his head in disbelief at the lack of direction of his life-long passion, as well as its moral bankruptcy. There were the various controversies already touched on in this book, and the biggest upheaval of them all — when Renault allegedly ordered Nelson Piquet Jnr to deliberately crash so his team-mate Fernando Alonso could win at the Singapore Grand Prix in September 2008.

However, Ecclestone has his own spin on such things. 'Things that perhaps went on years and years ago are known now because we are so super-professional. We keep our eye on every single thing. Homosexuality has been going on for years and years, and years ago nobody knew anything about it. Then all of a sudden things come to light, and when it's all brought to light people start looking at things and making sure people are following the rules or not.'

Ecclestone has been involved in motor racing for over 50 years, building Formula One into the behemoth it is today, and he still retains the drive of a much younger man in his quest to improve the sport. 'My contribution is I helped the sport to where it is today. I just want to keep growing F1 and I shall continue doing what I am doing as long as I think I can deliver.'

Everyone who has a passing interest in F1 has heard of Bernie Ecclestone, but not many know how he got to be where he is today. So here's a rough overview of how Bernie came to be known as Formula One's 'puppet master'.

He began his involvement in racing in the late 1950s when he bought the F1 Connaught team and even tried to race at Monaco in 1958. He was Jochen Rindt's manager in 1970 when Rindt was posthumously awarded the world championship. Two years later he bought the Brabham F1 team and went on to have success with Nelson Piquet winning two world championships.

In 1974 Ecclestone, along with Max Mosley, Colin Chapman, Ken Tyrrell, Teddy Mayer and Frank Williams, decided the sport needed organizing and they set up the FOCA. By 1975 FOCA had won the battle with the FIA for a revised entry system and money to be paid to all the teams. Those teams suggested getting F1 set up on a more professional basis, as there was a general lack of direction and leadership. As everybody was doing their own thing, Bernie thought he'd try and put it together properly. Max Mosley also had his own team at the time. He was a lawyer and was helping Bernie as well.

Of the founding FOCA fathers, it was Bernie who was always foremost in looking for every angle to make the sport more popular and exciting. Shortly after the battle erupted for TV rights, it was Ecclestone who emerged with his hands on the prize.

After so long in the sport, Bernie has seen his fair share of drivers and trying to single out one driver would be nigh on impossible because you can't compare eras. In an article published in the *New Zealand Herald* he was reported as saying, 'When I had my team, Jochen Rindt was a great driver back then and today it's that Sebastian Vettel or even Lewis Hamilton or [Fernando] Alonso. There's lots of good drivers and it's hard to pick one; they're all pretty good.'

The *New Zealand Herald* article went on to say that Bernie may be short in stature at around 1.6m, but his influence casts a long shadow over the world of motor racing. The billionaire is one of the best-paid executives on the planet and as far back as 1996 was reputedly being paid $118 million a year. Although his vast fortune may have taken a hit with his recent divorce from his 1.9m-tall Croatian-born wife, there's still more than enough left in his coffers for Bernie to continue wielding the enormous power he has in Formula One.

Ex-president of the governing body of motorsport, the FIA, Max Mosley could not have been more different and how he and Bernie remained friends for so long is anyone's guess. Max studied physics at Christ Church, Oxford, graduating in 1961 and went on to study law at Gray's Inn, London, qualifying as a barrister in 1964. During the same period he joined the Territorial Army and trained as a parachutist.

Many people tend to think the FIA and Mosley are intrinsically linked, but his introduction to the sport of motor racing was anything but planned. He and his wife were given tickets to Silverstone, and from that day onwards Max was hooked after watching the likes of Stirling Moss, Bruce McLaren, Jack Brabham and all the other big names of that era. Max was soon flinging himself around various British race circuits in a Formula Junior, but following a couple of big shunts while racing he soon realized he was no world champion in the making. Max retired from the racetrack and joined forces with Robin Herd, Alan Rees and Graham Coaker to form March Engineering (the M stands for Mosley).

When some of the other team owners realized Max was a trained lawyer, they started to take him along to the negotiations between themselves and the promoters to discuss prize money and other issues. He found the complete disorganization of F1 offensive to his sensibilities and when Bernie Ecclestone turned up a year later, both of them were appointed to represent all the teams.

By the time the early 1980s rolled around, Max had had his fill and took some time out from the sport. However, after a short time, he couldn't resist the temptation to get back into the governance of motor racing and accepted the chairmanship of the manufacturers' arm of the FIA, then known as the Fédération Internationale du Sport Automobile (FISA).

That didn't last long as he could never get to talk to the then president Jean-Marie Balestre. He decided to stand against him and promptly won the day with backing from New Zealand's own Morrie Chandler. Max steered the boat until 2005 when he retired, but was soon convinced there was no one who could do the job so he stepped back up to the plate. In 2009 he stepped aside again, handing the mantle to Jean Todt.

During his last years as president of the FIA, Max battled to reduce the cost for teams to participate in F1 racing. His rationale of wanting to limit the annual budget teams are allowed to spend was at odds with some of the bigger players in the sport. But he knew what repercussions were just around the corner and was proved correct when a few years later Toyota, Honda and BMW pulled the pin on their F1 racing arms.

Due to the economic climate at the time, the main boards and CEOs of these companies simply did not have the time to focus on Formula One. Racing was a peripheral activity to them; they had much more important priorities — like saving the parent company. Max always struggled to get people to think outside the Formula One paddock and see the bigger picture.

And don't forget, whoever is president of the FIA, their job is not just overseeing Formula One, but global motorsport in general.

This includes liaising with motoring organizations around the world. However, as F1 is the Blue Riband of motor racing, one would hazard a guess that it takes up much of the incumbent's time.

After 16 years in charge of the FIA, Mosley has managed to change a vast number of things in the sport, some contentious and some revolutionary. However, being a mere mortal, he admits he hasn't managed to get everything done that he wanted to. 'It's absolutely clear to me that if we could get our national sporting authorities in different countries all over the world to foster karting energetically, we would then get a new generation of drivers emerging. It would take five-plus years but any country that gets the grass roots of competition racing and rallying going is going to produce a world-level driver.'

Through all the contentious ups and downs during his tenure at the helm of the FIA, including intrusions into his private life and the unfortunate death of his son, Max still retains his enthusiasm for motorsport. On stepping down from the presidency, he's not walking away from the FIA, as he'll be taking up a position on its senate.

During the 1980s and 90s, Max and Bernie dragged Formula One kicking and screaming into the modern era and kept the sport at the forefront of media coverage. Along the way they turned it into a billion-dollar industry, paying drivers what some would say are obscene amounts of money.

One of Bernie's more colourful and famous comments was when he was asked how many millionaires he had made in the paddock. After he had slowly and carefully looked around he commented, 'All of them.'

The two of them also realized the sport was spinning out of control financially in the early 2000s and they put plans in place to reduce costs and introduced a spending cap. Love them or hate them, you have to admit F1 would not be as big as it is today without their vision, energy and leadership. The two friends have built Formula One into a spectacle watched by more TV viewers than any other sport except the Soccer World Cup, an event that is held only once every four years.

Soon after Balestre was ousted, the new regime instituted pit passes and eventually the task of who got what fell under the purview of a Sardinian named Pasquale Lattuneddu, who relished the role of Paddock Policeman. It's common knowledge that Formula One Management, incidentally part-owned by Ecclestone, employs him and that he's one of Bernie's closest lieutenants.

Before Pasquale's ascendancy to the pit pass issuing throne, the job of managing transporters, trucks, cars and people entering the pit area was handled by Allan Woollard, who eventually started handing out passes allowing various people access to the pit garage and the paddock. He was also responsible for organizing where the ever-increasing number of motorhomes and transporters were to be parked.

Not only was Allan a really nice guy, he also had a practical streak. He was very approachable and would listen to anyone who had a particular problem or a case to present. If ever I had a problem parking, or as far as I know, anyone had a problem parking, then Allan would work out a solution to keep everyone happy.

He had this job for many years, and as much as organizing hundreds of people and scores of vehicles was always going to be a nightmare, no one to my knowledge ever complained.

Allan had such a knack for logistics it wasn't long before he was put in charge of Formula One airfreight and Pasquale became his understudy for several years. Compared to Allan, Pasquale was and still is, in my view, unnecessarily rigid.

Those of us who had been driving motorhomes into Grand Prix paddocks for years took some time to accept the legitimacy of

Pasquale's role, especially as Allan was still on the job and generally regarded as being in command.

Don't get me wrong, as F1 grew into the massive logistical nightmare it is today, we could all see the sense and need for some sort of regulation or system to restrict access to the pits to only those who actually needed to be there. However, when Pasquale took up the reins in 1989 he soon turned into an uncompromising enforcer and nobody could understand why his rules were so harsh. One could hazard a guess he had a Napoleon complex and wanted to make his mark on the rest of the world.

Pasquale wouldn't let anyone into a paddock until Wednesday night, which thoroughly pissed off all and sundry who had the job of setting up everything before a frantic Thursday when the rest of the team and drivers would arrive. What infuriated everyone was Allan's system had worked like clockwork. Almost overnight the Sardinian slapped a hundred-and-one new rules and systems in place, and just like the Italian parliament, everything ground to a bureaucratic halt.

It got so bad at times that there were a few light-hearted discussions around the paddock about organizing a collection to employ a bloke from a dubious Sicilian family to undertake an illegal commission.

By 1991 things were coming to a head with Pasquale's heavy-handed approach. At the Silverstone Grand Prix he turned up in the paddock area on Friday morning wearing sunglasses. None of us had ever seen him wearing glasses, let alone sunglasses, but he wouldn't let on why or what had happened. It wasn't long before we found out he'd been given a right hook by an irate Italian truck driver who'd spent all day and night driving from Italy to get his team's gear to the circuit. We were told that when he arrived at the paddock gate, Pasquale refused to let him in for another four hours. The trucker, most unimpressed, jumped down from his cab and lumped the officious Pasquale, leaving him flat on his arse. Poetic justice, maybe.

Team owners weren't immune to Pasquale's overbearing manner either. Even McLaren's Ron Dennis had to jump through numerous hoops if he wanted an extra pass. He had to write to Bernie Ecclestone requesting any extra passes and then Bernie would authorize Pasquale to issue the requisite.

By 2003 everyone, including guests, had to have their picture on any issued passes. Although it was another layer of bureaucracy, the F1 paddock area is probably the safest place on earth these days, thanks to Pasquale the Paddock Policeman.

NASCAR, which is America's favourite form of motor racing, prides itself on its drivers being accessible to the public because paddock entry is unrestricted. However, I noted that as far back as 2001, some of the leading NASCAR drivers were complaining they couldn't concentrate on their jobs because they were being overwhelmed by autograph-hunters.

Perhaps the need for a legitimate paddock pass and restricted entry is not always such a bad thing. But in my view, Pasquale took his job of managing who comes and goes into the paddock to a level of self-importance that would rival any number of Roman emperors, who saw themselves as demigods. If Pasquale had just taken Allan's model of how to operate a paddock area and modified it to suit the times, all would have panned out well. Instead he must have decided to run the pits and surrounding area as his own personal fiefdom.

Pasquale can be seen to this day hanging on to Mr E's every word as Bernie surveys and inspects his paddock and grid. Pasquale would always be seen at the elbow of any celebrity visiting the starting grid or on the pit wall, sometimes known as Prat's Perch, of whichever team was leading the race. He'd be poised there with a radio in hand, and the roving eye of a trained Doberman, probably just salivating

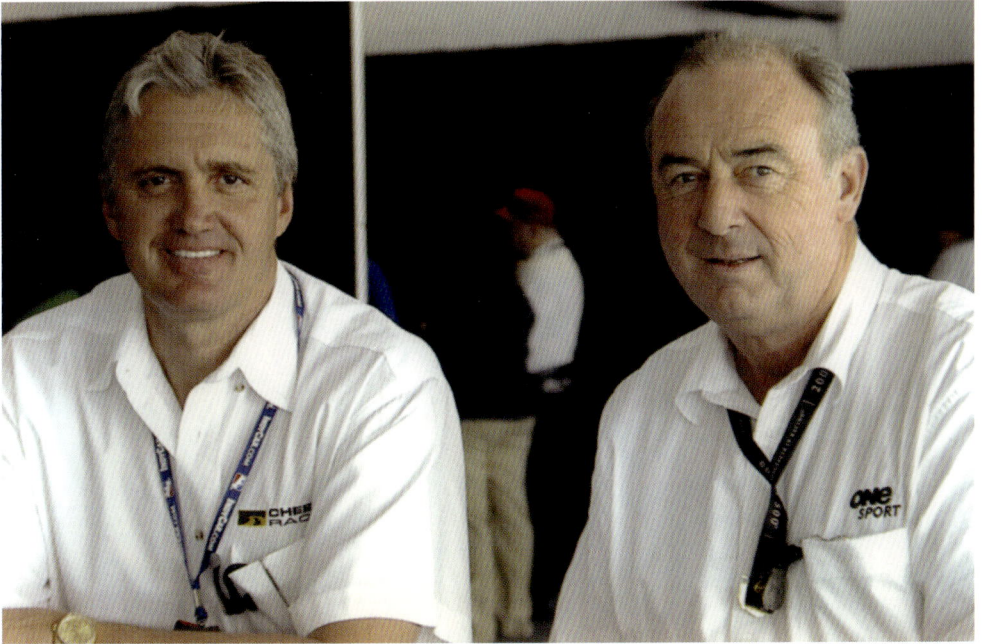

Eddie Cheever and Bob at the Indy 500 in 2008.

Eddie Cheever in the Project Four Racing March 752 Hart at a very wet Salzburgring track in Austria. From left, Peter Hodgman, Ron Dennis leaning into car, Eddie driving, Jimmy Tully, Japanese mechanic Kazu, and Bob on the front left wheel.

Williams designer Patrick Head (left) and Aussie Formula One driver and 1980 world champion Alan Jones.

Bob with Mika Hakkinen (at left) and Martin Brundle (at right) — 'Good guys, both of them.'

OPPOSITE PAGE TOP: A memorable day. The 2008 Indy 500 winner Scott Dixon with tactician Mike Hull at left and wife Emma.

OPPOSITE PAGE FOOT: From left, Ron Dennis, Mika Hakkinen and Bob.

Who looks best in drag — Bob or Dame Edna?

Ayrton Senna explaining the quick way to get around the Hungaroring circuit to the McLaren guests in the Paddock Club.

From left, Mansour Ojjeh, Alain Prost and Aziz Ojjeh with Creighton Brown looking on.

Bodyguard duties to the Paddock Club driver appearance with Mika Hakkinen and his manager Didier Coton on left.

After Ayrton Senna had an 'issue' with Eddie Irvine at the Japanese Grand Prix in 1993, the mechanics attached a little present to his steering wheel at the next race in Australia.

The winning moment: Scott Dixon at the Indy 500 in 2008.

The amazing Porsche-built TAG Turbo engine at the Porsche test track Weissach, 1982.

The Target Chip Ganassi IndyCars of Scott Dixon (9) and Dario Franchitti (10) on the grid at the Indianapolis Motor Speedway.

Sten Pentus in the Toyota Racing Series FT40 in the wet at Manfeild Park race track, Feilding, New Zealand.

Series champion Mitchell Evans in his Toyota Racing Series FT40 negotiating turn 6 at Hampton Downs race circuit in Te Kauwhata, New Zealand.

at the thought someone might break one of his many rules. He also had the uncanny knack of knowing just which driver to be deep in conversation with as the cameras panned in for a colour pre-race shot. The consummate professional, perhaps.

Of all the stars, celebrities, royalty, wealthy and the faux-important who strut around the Formula One paddocks of the world, few can approach the dedication to make it to every race like an Austrian tramp called Henry. (At least we think he was Austrian or German or Swiss, as he spoke with a Teutonic twang.)

Henry was of an indeterminate age; he could have been 30 or he could have been 60. I had him pegged at closer to 60. He had long, unkempt hair that wouldn't quite make it all the way into dreadlocks and a moustache, which drooped over his top lip and mouth like some long-neglected grey plant growing over the entrance to a disused tunnel. While not exactly antisocial, Henry could do cantankerous rather well if things weren't going according to his plan, or he'd given the booze a nudge. It didn't help matters he was diabetic and wasn't too particular about keeping his blood-sugar levels at somewhere near the right numbers.

For a bloke with a slight build, Henry had a strong heart and a capacity for hard work.

I first met him in our debut season with the Marlboro motorhome when he boldly came up to us during a race weekend and announced he was working with Marlboro. Along with his self-appointment to Marlboro, he also had his own job description worked out. Henry explained he was there to help with washing down the truck and any general maintenance with the rig over the weekend.

A little taken aback by his forwardness, I nevertheless gladly accepted his help with washing the rig and erecting the enormous canvas and aluminium-poled canopy that extended from the truck some six by twelve metres along the length of the motorhome. A big job for Shaune and me on our own, but with Henry around it was much easier.

It didn't take me long, about one hour to be honest, to discover that Henry, although he had a 'special' relationship with us and Marlboro, was helping just about anyone else in the paddock that needed a hand, be they McLaren, Ferrari, Minardi or Lotus. At the shout of 'Henry' he would be there in a flash to render any kind of assistance. He never received any payment in the conventional sense, surviving instead on handouts and gifts from the motorhome community. Come to think of it, he was never all that bothered about food and drink either, although it was also freely given if he wanted anything.

Henry was definitely an oddball but he was worth having around the place. In the days when the motorhomes were just trucks, buses and American campervans with canopies and extensions, they were damn hard work when you got to the paddock. This was before the days when 20 or more people were specially employed to set up and operate the enormous structures that are crammed into the paddocks today. Not so much a tent city, more a scaled-down version of downtown Manhattan.

He drifted from Grand Prix to Grand Prix by thumbing lifts on the open road or cadging a ride with a French or Italian truckie delivering produce in the nearest town to the next race. Sometimes Henry would even stow away in a trailer and in almost two decades I can't recall him missing a single European Grand Prix.

Like any self-respecting hobo, Henry had few belongings and most of those were emblazoned with a team name, or was a sponsor's giveaway. When he got too much stuff to carry he gave it away to someone more deserving whom he'd met on his travels. He even made it to the occasional race away from the Continent like the Brazilian

Grand Prix, or some other country whose border was not as closed as others. Nobody in the paddock ever knew Henry's history or where he came from. He really was a man of mystery and I never saw his passport. The nearest we got to anything like the truth, we think, was when he mentioned he could never risk being stopped by the police in Austria as he would then spend very much more time in that country than he intended. We think he may have deserted at some time from the Austrian army but the story could never be confirmed.

It wasn't just Formula One Henry seemed to be able to get on the inside of. Often he'd turn up at a race meeting festooned with triple-A (Access All Areas) passes from top-notch concerts. I saw him with passes from The Who, Queen, Status Quo, AC/DC and Elton John gigs. When we quizzed him about how he had not only got into the concerts but also how he got his hands on triple-A passes, he always replied that he was part of the stage crew.

One time in 1987 we managed, by pleading with Marlboro Holland management, to get hold of some highly coveted tickets to the World Speedway finals in Amsterdam. All the management came through with were some general admission tickets that we duly, and happily I might add, took. As we were settling down in our seats way up the back in the stands, whom did we spot but bloody Henry. He wasn't with us mere mortals somewhere in the stand, he was marching across the track infield wearing an official vest with all manner of official passes hanging from his neck.

I think the Formula One paddock was his spiritual home, as so many different nationalities were represented and few questions were asked. If answers weren't forthcoming, no big deal was made of it. After a good wash with a couple of bars of soap, he didn't scrub up half bad either.

He even managed to convince some of the more relaxed European-based teams that he should guard their motorhomes at night . . . from the inside where there was a comfortable bed. Henry was seldom actually given a pass, and Formula One Management tolerated his presence to a certain extent. He even had conversations, albeit brief, with Bernie Ecclestone himself at one stage.

Henry's F1 world started to come apart when Pasquale assumed control and introduced the dreaded paddock pass. From that time, anyone at all who wanted to set foot there had to have in their possession a pass authorised by Pasquale himself. It's got to the stage now that all the passes are electronic and have to be swiped over a pad that registers if you're leaving or entering the inner sanctum. No more blagging at the gate for Henry, who had some of the best stories going for unsuspecting marshals as to why he should let be inside.

Once he even marched an unbelieving gateman to the very door of Bernie's private motor coach and banged on it, telling the stunned official that Mr E will be very pissed off that his private assistant was denied entry. The gateman backed down and Henry took up his rightful place inside the paddock area. Time and progress caught up with Henry and he slowly drifted away from the F1 scene.

I believe he died a few years ago. Nobody who was part of paddock life from the late 1970s to the early 1990s will forget Henry and it's a shame he's gone. It's almost as if the demise of Henry was indicative of the end of a more relaxed and personable era of Formula One. I have a feeling Henry wouldn't have liked the new 'business' of motor racing.

It wasn't just the drivers and crew who could be politically incorrect — very senior team members were prone on the odd occasion to say something controversial. Tyler Alexander was one of the original founder members of Bruce McLaren Racing, finally retiring from McLaren International in 2009 after 45 years with the team. At the 1993 British Grand Prix at Donington, Princess Diana visited the garage. We had been warned about the impending royal visit and were all lined up ready for her appearance. When she arrived I stepped back a little and found Tyler right behind me. When Diana moved through the garage her ladies-in-waiting blended into the background with us.

I never thought she was particularly attractive. She was too skinny but Tyler said she looked quite good. By this time Diana had her back to us and was leaning over the car having a look inside the cockpit. All of a sudden Tyler in his Californian drawl said in a stage whisper, 'God fuckin' damn I could give her one.'

The lady-in-waiting, whom Tyler hadn't seen standing just behind him, snapped back, 'But you'll never get the chance.' Game, set and match to the royal entourage.

The Dutch Grand Prix held at Zandvoort was a particular favourite of ours. Not only because of the fantastic fries and mayonnaise that is a delicacy there but for its proximity to Amsterdam. That city has long been known as a great place for after-dark — in fact all-day — entertainment of the more liberal kind. Together with a few friends, we would make the one-hour drive to the city during the evenings and sample what some of the less salubrious establishments could offer.

Once the word got around I was asked by some of our team to take them into the city on a free evening. 'With pleasure,' I replied; 'the more the merrier.' As time went on and the word spread about our planned expedition, my little adventure was turning into a guided tour of Amsterdam at night. They even gave our jaunts a name — Bobby's Tours to Amsterdam. I felt like some Japanese tour leader with eight or ten people, male and female, in tow from one dodgy club to the next.

We went to live shows where anyone had the opportunity of helping nubile young ladies undress, to bars where ladies did extraordinary things with £1 notes and ping-pong balls. When those novelties wore off we'd go window-shopping, as the ladies of the Amsterdam night were wont to sit in their window displaying their wares. We went to so many places with so many different people that two of the establishments gave Shaune and me free entry each visit in appreciation for bringing our tour groups. Shaune even got to know the naked girls gyrating on top of the bar so well that she had conversations with them along the lines of 'How do you keep this secret from your mum?' Quite bizarre.

Chapter 8

The drivers: stars of the F1 circus

Formula One has changed a lot over the past few years with a number of less than savoury skeletons falling out of various closets. I've touched on some of the more colourful episodes in other parts of the book and the ones I've missed can be found on various news or motor-racing websites.

I'm not about to jump on my high horse and make moral judgments about some of these incidents and issues, but to my mind, a lot of the alleged underhand dealings and dodgy decision-making by some senior F1 team members were all about the business of going racing and not really about the racing per se.

I'm not one for saying 'back in the good old days', because the good old days were neither good nor bad — they were just different. However, the drivers were larger than life. In fact, these celebrities were the main focus of interest and their personality clashes and lifestyles were what made the headlines, not what the team or governing body were up to.

The late 1970s and early 80s were the nascent days of the sport, as there was only a limited number of good mechanics and top drivers. You'd see drivers doing Formula One, Formula Two and Formula Three. They were more than happy to jump into almost anything and go racing. That's why New Zealanders and Australians were able to see the Tasman Series with stars like Jim Clark, Jackie Stewart, Bruce McLaren and Chris Amon going at it hammer and tongs.

All sorts of people involved in the sport moved around because they enjoyed racing. Ken Tyrrell and Graham Hill would often do a Formula Two race with Ron Dennis then follow up with a Formula One event. Drivers were racing for a job and weren't overly concerned about what class they raced in, or who the team owner was who provided the car. There was none of this 'I only race Formula One' attitude that is prevalent these days. IndyCar drivers are different. They tend to get involved in other forms of motorsport on occasion and sometimes will contest open-wheelers and tin-tops in the same season.

It wasn't only the drivers and mechanics who moved around; the sponsors were also happy to spread themselves across a wider field. Marlboro, for example, had their fingers in Formula One, Two and Three. They sponsored both McLaren and Alfa Romeo in Formula One, and supported motorcycle racing and an American hotdog skiing team.

It would appear the demands of going motor racing are so much more these days that the fun and camaraderie may have been squeezed right out of it. Never mind, I'm not involved in it any more, sad to say, and I have some great memories of many of the drivers who were around when I was part of F1.

Two-time world champion Mika Hakkinen always springs to mind when I think back on the drivers I came into contact with at McLaren. One of the more memorable times was when he was in New Zealand for an advertising shoot for then McLaren sponsor West. It was at this time I had my best boat trip, ever, on a huge super-yacht sailing across the Hauraki Gulf at lunchtime with Mika, Didier, Mika's then wife Erja and one or two West people. Relaxing on deck under huge sun umbrellas, getting wined and dined and waited on — pure luxury!

Shaune and I were having a barbecue and since Mika was staying at Gulf Harbour Lodge Hotel, we invited him and about 20 other people along. I had put a lamb on the spit and could see him eyeing this up with a quizzical look on his face. He kept glancing at it but wouldn't go anywhere near it. He seemed very concerned about this lamb going round and round on a spit.

When it was cooked, two of us took the lamb off the spit and placed it on the table. As most Kiwis know, when lamb is cooked properly the meat just falls off the bone in a beautiful greasy heap. We all dived in to grab a piece while Mika was standing back with an uncomfortable look on his face. I'm sure he'd never seen an entire animal cooked that way. I called him over and handed him a succulent morsel from the spit roast, which he gingerly placed in his mouth. Mika was soon at the front of the queue stuffing handfuls of meat into his mouth.

While he was visiting Auckland I thought it would be a good idea to take him to the annual Wings and Wheels event at Whenuapai Air Force Base. Mika wandered around looking at all the old race-cars, including a few F5000s, and signing the odd autograph. There were a couple of helicopters buzzing about and every 10 minutes he'd come over and ask me where the 'wings' part of the show was. 'Soon, soon,' I'd tell him, wondering when they'd start clearing the runway.

He spent some time in the McLaren Trust tent, signing more autographs and chatting, while all the time keeping one eye on the runway looking for the fixed-wing aircraft and asking all the time, 'Where's the wings, where's the wings?'

After another hour or so I asked an official when the planes would arrive. As it turned out, this was the first year Wings and Wheels had no wings, so it was back to the house. That's all Mika wanted to see — wings. I guess he got to see wheels every day in his professional career.

When we arrived home, Mika said he was always wary about going out to restaurants and other public places, as autograph-hunters and people wanting their photograph taken with him would mob him. I told him that apart from the Wings and Wheels event, he was unlikely to be recognized anywhere else outside of a racetrack in New Zealand. 'Yeah, yeah,' he said and we bet $100 on it.

His wife Erja, who was a TV presenter in Finland, manager Didier, trainer Mark Arnall (who became Raikkonen's fitness man) and a few others were at Gulf Harbour having dinner on his last day in Auckland. During one of the courses the waiter came over and told Mika he recognized him. Mika went on about how he'd been correct that someone would know him and I was thinking my $100 was as good as gone. However, something prompted me to ask the waiter if he could identify my guest. He said he'd seen him in the restaurant the other day and it was nice to have a customer come back again. He had no idea he was serving an F1 world champion, so my money was safe after all. Mika loved New Zealand. He often said it was as close to his beloved native Finland as he could get.

David Coulthard was a different sort of bloke. At times he was fun. But in the race-car when he was driving, there always seemed to be something wrong. He had a loose rear end — mechanically speaking, not in his private life. He was prone to complaining about the car rather than finding a way around the problems.

He was a good guy but a little too stiff for me so I gravitated towards Mika, who was more fun once he got to know you. I spent a lot of time with Mika being his unofficial bodyguard, shepherding him around the paddock and making sure he made it from one off-course event to another.

Off the racetrack Mika marched to his own pace, which was at times lackadaisical, but put him in a car and he was blindingly fast. The first time he got into the McLaren in 1993, after Michael Andretti had left, he kicked Ayrton Senna in the arse, out-qualifying him first time out at Estoril. On his day he was absolutely fantastic and Mika's overtaking move on Schumacher at Spa in 2000 is the stuff of legend.

It was through Mika and his friends that I first met Kimi Raikkonen. After a race in 2001 we were all in the motorhome when a world championship ice hockey match was playing on TV. The game didn't start until 9 p.m. and as both Finns were fans of the sport, they settled down to watch it. When evening turned into morning, I began to realize Kimi had a pretty good capacity for vodka. He even told me the only way to get through an entire game of ice hockey was indeed to have a supply of vodka handy. Back then Kimi was a Sauber driver. He would later be contracted to McLaren and after that to Ferrari.

Mika and David Coulthard were the two most recent drivers I spent a whole season with. I always said I'd leave when Mika did and when McLaren moved into their new facility. I met Lewis Hamilton occasionally, the first time at Spa when he was just 10 years old. That was of course when he was a karter; I never worked with him when he was a driver at McLaren. Ron Dennis and Martin Whitmarsh had plans for that boy way back. McLaren, Mercedes and Martin Hines of Zip Karts had a karting championship scholarship going for the best and brightest young drivers.

I don't have much recollection of Lewis, as he was just another eager kid who was into karting, albeit quite a quick driver, but he sure as heck went on to achieve great things. I met him for the first time as an adult in 2008 in his first year as a McLaren F1 driver and he struck me as a self-assured and confident young man. I read he's getting a bit cocky lately, but that's what happens sometimes with success. You would be hard-pressed to name a decent race-car driver who didn't have a healthy, or unhealthy, ego. And boy have we had some egos over the years at McLaren.

I've often been asked if McLaren ever wanted to get hold of Michael Schumacher, as he'd been contracted to Mercedes for ages and we were using their engines. Michael started with Eddie Jordan and soon moved over to Benetton. I remember there was some discussion about his coming over but I doubt he would have got on with Ron. It was as much of a personal thing as anything and I don't think he would have fitted into the team anyway.

Schumacher was one of the drivers I struggled to get along with and one incident springs to mind. We were all at the Log Cabin in Japan and he'd just won the Grand Prix. This bar in Suzuka was pretty crowded as it was a popular haunt for teams and fans alike on Sunday evening after a race.

In 1995 Schumacher had won the race and the title. The Log Cabin is a very small place and not equipped to take the hundreds of race crew and drivers who descend on it. Because it's a tight fit and getting to the bar can be a mission in itself, there's an orderly queue for beers and everyone from truckies to tyre-fitters to world champions all just waited their turn. But not Schumacher. He tried to push his way to the front of the queue and demanded he be served right away. I objected and told him to pull his head in and wait his turn.

Some heated words were exchanged and I ended up shoving him against the wall and suggested he pack it in. Just as it was about to go off, his chief mechanic at the time, Mickey Ainsley-Cowlishaw, intervened and calmed things down.

I don't know who had the biggest ego, but the biggest ego battle would possibly have been between Ayrton Senna and Alain Prost. It was ridiculous and that's the only word for it. I've mentioned elsewhere in the book the worst of the incidents between them in 1989, but that was only the culmination of their animosity. My good friend Jo Ramirez always tried to mediate between them as he was on Ayrton's wavelength and could also talk with Alain. Unfortunately even the likeable Jo couldn't always keep the peace.

Alain and Ayrton were equally quick on the track but in different ways. Ayrton was super-fast most of the time but had lapses, while Alain would be able to pace himself and was always able to look at the longer game. Ayrton took each race, or even each lap, as it came. However, the way their on-course battle degenerated into a personal battle within the team was just plain ugly.

For the first time I could remember, and I'd been involved with McLaren on and off since the late 1960s, the team split right down the middle, with some in Ayrton's camp and others in Alain's. It was a horrible time. It got to the stage where one of them would go to the bathroom in the motorhome before a race and deliberately stay there too long so the other one would be absolutely busting and couldn't go about his business when he needed to.

They wouldn't talk to each other either. If they both found themselves in the motorhome at the same time, one would leave immediately. I can't put my finger on any one incident that caused this rift the size of the Grand Canyon, but it was as if it just slowly ground its way into existence until it was too late to do anything about it. Then all hell broke loose.

It got so low that Alain became convinced Ayrton was getting better equipment than he was and that's when it started to get nasty. I don't think that was the problem. Ayrton had a strong relationship with Honda, which Alain lacked. It's a shame really, because if the two of them had worked together McLaren could have ruled the Formula One world for a long time.

Just before Ayrton's death in 1994 the two of them reconciled.

When Alain retired from F1, Ayrton said he missed him as the competition made them both stronger. Their relationship had got so bad, one of them had to leave and it was Alain who went to Ferrari, and of course the already damaged relationship deteriorated even further. It got to the stage they were knocking each other off the race circuit. It was a complete farce in the end but how do you tell two people they have to like each other? It's just not possible.

Ayrton was Brazilian, so I guess his temperamental nature came with the territory. Everyone remembers the time in Japan when he had an issue with Eddie Irvine, went to find him and gave him a whack. That all came about because Eddie had the temerity, after being lapped, to unlap himself and overtake Ayrton, who thought it was dangerous. Eddie being Eddie didn't care who or what he passed, he just wanted to go racing.

I have a photograph of Ayrton's car at the next race in Adelaide, where the mechanics had taped a pair of boxing gloves to the steering wheel. Ayrton would often descend into a dark mood but then he could be the nicest person you'd ever meet. When he came to our house, my mother-in-law couldn't stand him to begin with. And when Mrs J doesn't like you, you're in big trouble. Even when Ayrton was at his most charming he couldn't turn her around. She thought he was arrogant and boastful but she was polite to him all the same.

While he was in Auckland, at the end of his last season with McLaren in 1993, we'd go down to the helicopter base and fly over the city and the Gulf islands. I've never seen anyone take so many photographs and be so enthusiastic about a place. Out of a race-car and away from the track he was fantastic company, a completely different bloke.

There was this one time with Ayrton in Canada, which was one of the fun places to go, when after the race was over we'd all go to what was euphemistically called the ballet. The place was called the Orange Box Club by most of the people involved in F1 because the girls would stand on orange-coloured boxes in front of you and do their private dances. We had the whole team there after the race on Sunday night from truck driver to owner to Ayrton and his younger brother. Ron gave me a fistful of dollars and set me the task of trying to get a girl for every single member of the team. So off I went and after two hours I'd somehow managed to get a girl for everyone in the team and arranged them all in a circle, including one for Shaune.

I've still got two visions in my head. One was of Ayrton's brother Leonardo, who probably shouldn't have been there at all, sitting there with a naked girl dancing in front of him, with his jaw on the floor. I doubt he'd even seen a naked woman before. The other being I was the only person in the room who didn't have a girl as I'd spent the whole time rounding them up to dance for the others.

I finally got over to where Shaune was sitting and her girl was by now crouching down on the box, naked, and they were deep in conversation. This time it wasn't quite 'does your mother know what you're doing tonight?' More along the lines of what college she was at and how her studies were going. It was an oasis of sanity in this rather down-at-heel club. Ayrton liked to let his hair down on occasion but only when he knew his fun time would remain within the team.

Essentially, though, he was a religious kind of bloke and when he was in the motorhome with just us, he'd go up the front, sit with Shaune and read his Bible. This was his time for reflection and Shaune would be the only one near him as she quietly went about her chores. When he came out of his reverie to go and get ready to race, he'd go over to Shaune, give her a kiss and be on his way. He had a soft side the race fans never got to see. On the track it was like the red mist had descended and the Berserker rage had taken over.

He was absolutely convinced he was the fastest thing on the track and nobody else had the right to be there, let alone be quicker than him. If things didn't go according to plan he'd start to think there was a conspiracy to undermine him. If he got passed he took it as a personal insult. I liked him, though, and got on well with him, occasionally acting as his minder as he moved around the paddock.

In Japan, Ayrton had an almost god-like status, to the extent we could never get him through a crowd. It needed a small phalanx of helpers to protect him on his journey from the pit garage area to the Paddock Club. For some unknown reason the short trip also included fighting our way through public access zones.

After some trial and error we worked out the easiest way was to mimic a boxer entering the ring before a fight. Ayrton would put his hands on my shoulders, dip his head to his chest and follow in my footsteps as I barged through the adoring crowd like an icebreaker in the Ross Sea. We had other guys on either side of him acting as buffers to prevent unwanted incursions into our flying wedge. Despite all this, Ayrton loved the adoration and would sign stuff where and whenever possible, but there were times it got damn scary, I can tell you.

Ron and Alain began well but the relationship started to sour when Alain decided to change teams. Things got so bad that when Alain won at Monza in 1989 he threw the winner's cup over the side and didn't give it to Ron. In absolute disgust, Ron threw the Constructor's Trophy at the feet of Prost. Alain, who on that day extended his record haul to 39 victories, was complaining of unfair treatment and favouritism on engines towards Senna, whose engine had actually expired during the race. The Honda management were not about to favour Prost at all after that outburst.

McLaren and Ron have every trophy they've ever won and would have a replica made and give it to the driver to keep. If Ron had to give a trophy back he'd get another made — in fact, I think they've still got the very first, original Belgian Grand Prix trophy, which they never returned.

Alain could be as mad as a cut snake at times. One time he was inside the motorhome and there was a meeting going on at a table outside with Mansour Ojjeh, Ron and a couple of other people. Alain asked me what was going on and I shrugged my shoulders and told him I didn't have a clue.

He then went on to say that when he nodded I had to quickly open the door of the motorhome. I said OK and went over to the door. Once my hand was on the handle, he nodded his head and I flung the door open. Alain went past me in a blur, leapt high off the top step, somersaulted in the air and landed with an almighty crash flat on his back in the middle of the table where Ron and company were sitting.

Bodies, chairs, papers, pencils and sunglasses went flying everywhere. Those at the table were looking at Alain like stunned mullets while he picked himself up, dusted himself down and walked off saying, 'I'm sorry' with a Gallic shrug of the shoulders.

I'd have to say, though, while I thought it was bloody funny, Ron was livid about the incident.

Relationships depend on the sort of person you are. When Alain and Niki Lauda were fighting it out for the 1984 championship, it came down to the wire at Estoril and there was only half a point between them. Niki eventually won the title that year but there was no animosity between them. Sure it was competitive but it never remotely descended to the level of animosity between Alain and Ayrton.

Niki was one of those guys who had a star aura about him. He could walk into anywhere and the room would quieten a bit and people would gravitate towards him. He did, however, have an annoying habit of wandering about with his fly undone a lot of the time.

Although Niki had been retired for a couple of years, Ron was totally convinced he still had the goods to make an impression on the championship. He was right as Niki settled into the swing of things quickly and soon was going as fast as anyone else at the time and duly won the 1984 title for Ron that year.

That was the start of eight glorious years of McLaren being right at the top of their game. We won seven of the next eight world championships, a feat not even Ferrari can claim. Alain learned a lot from Niki and although he wasn't blindingly quick over a lap, he could string a race together just like Niki. The two of them became wily racers and Alain's famous quote was, 'The best way to win a race is at the slowest possible speed.'

Niki and James Hunt were great friends and they used to have a great time together. Niki was after anything in a skirt that moved. It was just amazing. In fact, Niki and James would alternate using the back of the motorhome for, we suspected, the occasional romp. When it was James' turn a strange smell would emanate from down the back. I always thought it was the air-conditioning; it couldn't have been weed as he was a highly tuned athlete.

You have to give a lot of credit to Niki when he arrived at McLaren. Not to beat about the bush, after almost being burnt to death in 1976 when plastic surgery wasn't as advanced as it is today, his badly scarred face wasn't exactly a painting, but that didn't hold him back from taking the piss out of himself.

Niki didn't take himself too seriously, even after such a horrendous crash, so the odd joke at his expense soon started to circulate. I think it was Paddy McNally, or he and John Hogan between them, who coined the nickname 'The Rat' for Niki, and to show how much it didn't matter to him he had Niki 'The Rat' Lauda painted across the front of his helmet. He loved all that banter and joking. He would crack jokes all the time about his ear and within the team we all found it all quite amusing — that's just how he was.

It's probably been replicated a hundred times elsewhere but in case you missed it, one of his favourite quips was based on a Winston Churchill quote. If someone was giving him a sideways look and thinking he was ugly, before they were able to open their mouth Niki would say, 'Yeah that might be right, but I had to go through a fire to look like this, what's your excuse? Were you born like that?'

The guy was one in a hundred million. You don't get to win Grand Prix, pilot jumbo jets and have your own international airline if you're not really switched on.

James would still have to hold the mantle as the most out-there driver Formula One has seen. We used to have to smuggle him away from the track at the end of some Grand Prix races and into a nearby campsite so he could relax away from all the busybody prying eyes in the paddock area. There were a bunch of us including mechanics, fans and friends (his 'friends' were called 'The Sutton and Cheam First Eleven' and his brother Norman was the leader of the pack — about eight of them at any one time and all serious lads) who wanted to have a few beers away from the garages and just chill.

More often than not, when James joined us in the tent a strange herbal smell would be wafting out from between the flaps. At Zandvoort one year there was an argument brewing between Gary Anderson and James about the fastest way around the Dutch track. Somehow, unbeknown to me at the time, Shaune got involved in the discussion and they all decided to go for a drive with Gary, who was a mechanic, showing James the fast way around.

During their trip around the circuit, I was looking for Shaune and couldn't find her.

Sometime later she arrived back at the tent, looking a little dishevelled, in the company of James, who had a reputation for being a ladies' man, and Gary. You can guess what the first thought that flew through my mind was, but I quickly realized from their conversation they had been howling around the track in the hire car, so it was no wonder Shaune looked a little second-hand. It didn't help matters that it was dark by then and they'd done a few laps.

In 1977 and '78 it was party time. We celebrated his birthday at Watkins Glen — it wasn't actually James' birthday as he was born on 29 August, but it often turned out to be his birthday party for some reason. It was also my celebration, with the 1977 race being on 2 October, three days after my birthday. After he'd won on the day, James spent the entire night and most of the next morning wandering around absolutely plastered, with a plastic helmet on his head topped by a flashing red light.

You could always have fun with James. In the Tip Top bar in Monaco one time the police were coming down the street clearing away all the party-goers and drunks. Shaune and I were standing with James and his girlfriend at the time, supermodel Jane Birbeck (or Hottie, as she was known to the team), and we took shelter in a doorway. The police arrived shortly after and proceeded to whack us all over the heads until they realized who they were laying into.

James was livid but couldn't do much about taking on a squad of hardened CRS coppers.

During that time James, Paddy McNally (the Philip Morris bloke who was a sort of mild-mannered minder), Niki Lauda and at times John Hogan and very occasionally Tony Thomas all got up to some interesting antics. James would pretty much be up for anything, anytime, anywhere. When he won the world championship in 1976 he organized a lady for every member of the team.

I suppose you could say James was the George Best of not only Formula One but motor racing in general. He broke the mould of the gentleman racers of the late 1950s and early '60s to become the darling of the motoring press and of course the ladies.

From a team perspective, McLaren got a lot of mileage out of James. He was on the front page of a lot of newspapers and magazines during his time at the top and they weren't all motorsport publications. For the first time, gossip and women's publications were paying attention to one of the 'hunks' of racing.

As well as enjoying the high life, James still knew where his roots were when it came to racing. 'Look after the mechanics, and they'll look after you' wasn't just his motto — a lot of drivers believed that — but James had his certain away about doing just that. Watkins Glen was a prime example. As we all know, if a driver finishes on the podium he'll get a bottle of champagne. Back then it was real champagne, not the fizzy water drivers get given today, and James would sign the bottle so the mechanics could auction it afterwards to get some beer money for themselves.

This went on for a while until some of us realized one of the team, a Kiwi named Tony van Dongen, could do James' signature quite well. Without too much persuasion some of us went off and found a case of champagne. Tony signed all the bottles, mimicking James' signature. At the next race, after James had left the garage, we started selling the individual bottles as 'James Hunt's Watkins Glen 1977 Race-winning Champagne Bottle'. We sold five or six of those and there could still be one or two out there on someone's mantelpiece, with the owner believing they have the original.

When Ron took over the team this auctioning of stuff took a different turn. He was a lot stricter on what could be auctioned from the pit garage. Ebel watches were a team sponsor whose representative

Pierre asked Ron for a driver's race suit. Pierre Alain Blum was the grandson of the Ebel watch company's founders. Ron said no and that was that, or so he thought. Later in the season Alain Prost would give us a suit or two of his own to auction over the pit wall down from the hospitality suites. Pierre Alain turned up at the auction of a couple of race suits and bought two of them and they weren't cheap either. They had to be a couple of thousand each. He then went straight around to Ron, held out his prize purchases and said, 'I've got my race suits now.'

Ron went berserk but in an almost friendly sort of way as the relationship between Ebel and McLaren was always a good one. From Ron's point of view, the selling of old or unwanted car bits, T-shirts, race suits, gloves, helmets, shoes or whatever over the pit wall or out of a barn was demeaning for his team and he was always trying to clamp down on it. I tended to agree with him, especially if a team didn't change its uniform from one year to the next. The McLaren uniform was always new each year but sometimes the colours stayed the same and to the casual observer it looked the same as the previous season's.

It was quite possible to turn up at the opening Grand Prix the next year to see four or five people hanging around the pit garage in team uniform who had nothing whatsoever to do with the team. So Ron pulled the pin and we all thought bugger, there goes our party money. Having said that, though, Ron would at times hand out cash, or put on a big party, in lieu of the money we used to get from selling team gear. Inevitably there was the odd person who managed to smuggle something out of the garage and sell it on the black market.

Most of the time Ron could work out who or where the rogue stuff came from, because even if the name on the pocket was unpicked, more often than not there'd be a laundry mark on the inside collar identifying the original wearer of the garment.

When Gerhard Berger joined the team he sure as hell brought a lot of colour and character with him. He was one of the best practical jokers I've ever come across and the stunts he and Ayrton pulled on each other are legendary in the paddocks. As well as being incredibly creative when coming up with ideas for stitching people up, Gerhard was also damn good behind the wheel of a Formula One car. He didn't have the mercurial talent of Ayrton but he did out-qualify him eight times and put his car on pole four times, winning three Grand Prix.

One of the classic pranks Gerhard pulled on Ayrton was when he replaced the Brazilian's passport picture with a snapshot of a large pair of testicles. Ayrton was unaware of this until he handed over his passport at customs in Argentina on the way home to Brazil. It took him nearly 36 hours to get out of Argentina so he could get a replacement passport.

It didn't stop there. Gerhard heaved Ayrton's briefcase out of a helicopter once — while it was in the air. Then there was the time in Australia when Gerhard filled Ayrton's bed with animals. Ayrton came into the room saying, 'I've just wasted an hour getting a dozen frogs out of my bed.'

To which Gerhard's deadpan reply was, 'So, you didn't find the snake then?'

From all reports he's been like that all his life. A really nice, fun fellow to be around and one of nature's all-round good guys. He handled all his own contracts, no agents or managers.

But Ayrton wasn't always the fall guy. He glued all Gerhard's credit cards to the inside of his passport with superglue so Gerhard couldn't buy anything anywhere. Ayrton's comebacks were more irritating than monstrous like Gerhard's, as he didn't quite have the Austrian's imagination.

The two of them were always challenging each other to contests away from the track as well. At an after-race function Gerhard slapped down the gauntlet and challenged Ayrton over who could drink a bottle of Dimple whisky. Neither of them was the world's biggest drinker, with Gerhard maybe just having the edge. Ayrton didn't trust Gerhard, so he asked the restaurant owner to get two new unopened bottles from out the back.

They sat down at the table, agreed to take alternate drinks, and off they went. Halfway through their respective bottles Ayrton was beginning to roll in his chair like a sailor in rough weather. Gerhard by comparison wasn't looking too bad. By the end of the bottles Ayrton wasn't so much off his face, more like lying on it flat on the floor while Gerhard was wandering around, apparently sober as a judge.

It transpired a little later that Gerhard had arranged earlier in the day to have two bottles delivered to the restaurant ready for the challenge. One of the bottles of whisky had been watered down to the strength of cold tea while the other was pure whisky. Money had changed hands to ensure the diluted bottle was plonked down in front of Gerhard while Ayrton had to drink the hard stuff.

Incidentally, that episode was part two of my hat trick of inducing a world champion to be sick by sticking my fingers down his throat. First was Prost, now Senna and later there was Hakkinen.

Jacques Villeneuve paid a fleeting visit for a test once but didn't appear to like what he saw and moved on. Phillippe Alliot drove the Peugeot-powered McLaren as he had been promised he could be a 'Peugeot' driver, and he probably underwent one of the most remarkable transformations of any driver I ever saw. I don't mean in driving ability but looks. Within days of quitting Formula One his hair turned from dark brown to white. He'd stopped dying it overnight. Martin Brundle was another who dyed his hair, we think, and every time he had a shower in the motorhome our nice white towels turned a sort of chestnut colour afterwards. According to Martin he never used hair dye so I'm not sure what he was drying.

Michael Andretti was another driver at McLaren for half a year until he got the sack and Mika took over for the rest of the year. Michael didn't help his cause much by buggering off back to the States after each race. He just couldn't get his head around living in Europe. I didn't meet too many blokes who would rather live in America than on the Continent.

He would blame his lack of pace or performance on McLaren for not giving him any testing, but he was never there to do any testing because he'd always gone back home. So Ron had this brilliant idea at the start of the year that Shaune and I should cruise around the South of France and look for a house for him and his family to live in. We went to villa after villa and Michael would visit them all. Some of these homes were absolutely beautiful but Michael always found fault with them.

Michael's then wife, Sandy, turned up at the first Grand Prix in full Indy racing gear — a black-and-white chequered flag made into a very expensive pant-suit.

She was wearing a full chequered suit, enough gold for Africa, the big hat and high heels — I thought she looked like a typical American trophy wife. During the first race she marched straight through the garage, across the pit lane to the wall and inserted herself right next to Ron. This was in the days when women weren't really encouraged at McLaren to be part of the racing side of the team.

No racing-drivers' wives or girlfriends, or mechanics' partners for that matter, were allowed inside the team. Ron nearly fell off the step and probably cricked his neck, his head spun around so fast in surprise. He sort of stuttered in disbelief before he found his full voice and then stated categorically that she wasn't allowed to be out at the pit wall and was to remove herself immediately. She really went off the deep end, stomping and shouting like a shrew, or a fishwife, that it was her husband out there and she had every right to be there. This went on for three or four Grand Prix until Ron snapped and told one of the McLaren girls to take her shopping in the run-up to the race and over the weekend.

I thought Michael wasn't as mentally tough as the other drivers and it didn't help matters he had Ayrton as a team-mate. He had a few good drives but Ayrton was leagues ahead of him and he just couldn't compete.

Another good character was Keke Rosberg who would smoke like a chimney before, during if he could, and after every race. The most memorable cigarette moment was at Brands Hatch during qualifying in the wet. Keke was sitting in the car, smoking a cigarette, hoping the rain would stop and the track dry a bit before he went out. No such luck.

With about 10 minutes to go he realized it was going to stay wet and as he grabbed his helmet from the cowling in front of him, he took one last drag and casually flicked the burning cigarette out the side of the car and pulled on his helmet. The car was fired up and he roared out of the pit lane and put in a blistering lap in the wet, which most drivers couldn't have done in the dry, and plonked the car on pole.

Alain Prost's team-mate when he moved to Ferrari, Nigel Mansell, was a McLaren driver for a while. He drove two or three races in 1995 before Mark Blundell came back into the team. He was a McLaren test driver in 1992. That was the time when we had the MP4/10 and Nigel couldn't fit in it. He was too big so there were all these stories floating about how he was sitting on his wallet and it was too big and fat after a season in the US. I'm pretty sure Mercedes brought him back against Ron's wishes because they wanted a star in the car. Nigel was an F1 world champion, had gone to the United States and won the CART IndyCar World Series and finished third at the Indianapolis 500.

On his return to Formula One and to McLaren in particular it was discovered the cockpit was too narrow for him. In the time he'd been away, car shape and construction had changed to confine the driver more. Nigel had always manhandled a car around a racetrack using his shoulders a lot, so he needed more room.

Within the space of just three weeks the engineers and chassis designers had drawn up, manufactured and fitted a brand-new tub to the car. This changed the whole look and aero so everything else had to be tweaked to get the whole package to work. Internally this new and then subsequently modified car was called the MP4/10B. Although the car was actually released as the MP4/10B, it quickly became known by the press *et al* as the MP4/10WB — Wide Bodied, this in homage to Nigel who had come back from the States where the food portions were rather large and the more 'relaxed and open' seating of the CART cars allowed for his increased size.

Despite all the effort in getting the car to fit him, Nigel just wasn't into Formula One any more; the new era of car design had left him behind. After two races it was patently obvious he wasn't going to get the car going at any really competitive speed so Mark Blundell (commonly known as Billy) stepped in.

The other MB, Martin Brundle, was a real good thinker — and still is, as he's an excellent TV commentator. When he was racing he could analyse what was going on with the best of them. Not only could he work things out quickly, he was also bloody good on the track. He beat Ayrton in Formula Three a few times when they raced together.

When Martin was driving, McLaren was using the Peugeot engine, which in the beginning was being touted as the next big thing. Billy, on the other hand, drove the McLaren when it was powered by a Mercedes for the first year.

The Peugeot turned out to be an unmitigated disaster and how Ron got out of a multi-year contract with the engine supplier and got Eddie Jordan to use the Peugeot power plant I'll never know. One of the great mysteries of modern Formula One, you'd have to say. Ron had managed to extricate McLaren from an airtight contract with one of the biggest motor manufacturers in the world and get Mercedes, whom he always wanted, to come on board. And their engine's been in the back of the car ever since.

Martin was forthright with his opinions and views of the car and while not a super fun guy to be around, he was OK.

Billy was a fill-in driver after the Mansell debacle and was never going to be a world champion, yet he was fast enough and exceptionally brave as a driver. He was in the same mould as Derek Warwick and other drivers who just seem to pass by. Impressive on their day but not consistently quick enough. They did very well in endurance racing and that's maybe where their forte lay instead of being behind the wheel of a super-fast Formula One car.

Billy Blundell is now involved in driver management and was in business with Martin for a while doing the same thing. Their company was called 2MB but Martin is no longer a part of this. Confused about the two MBs? So am I — and I was there. In a nutshell Billy Blundell drove the Mercedes-powered MP4/10 for one season after Nigel Mansell gave up in 1995. Martin Brundle drove the Peugeot-powered McLaren in 1994 and then the Ligier in 1995, raced against Ayrton Senna and is the one with the television career.

Patrick Tambay was another of those drivers who on his day could mix it at the front of the field but just couldn't string a race or a season together, despite winning two Grand Prix for Ferrari — yet he was still good enough to be on the grid. Shaune and I got to know him and his American wife quite well and one time Patrick took me around the old Nurburgring in a BMW three-litre CSL touring car; that was an amazing ride. He was way too nice to be a racing-car driver; Patrick was just an all-round lovely guy.

He was obviously a very talented driver but when he drove at McLaren I don't think we had the best car available in 1978/79. Patrick was much more even-tempered than some of the moody French drivers I'd come across.

Stefan Johansson, who later became Scott Dixon's manager, was another who was in the wrong car at the wrong time. He reminded me a little of Chris Amon's Formula One career — if only he'd been given the best at the time, he would have surely won at least one world title. Stefan was bloody quick. He'd already proved that in his Formula Three days.

It was a shame when he arrived at McLaren because everyone realized he was number two to Alain and was only going to be there for one year until Ron could get hold of Ayrton. Although a great driver, he didn't have that team-leader quality Ayrton, Alain or Niki had to galvanize a team and get them to play at the top of their game.

By no means am I inferring he was a wasted talent when he drove for McLaren; in my view that mantle goes to Jan Magnusson. He replaced Mika Hakkinen, who had had an appendix operation, for one race in Aida, Japan. He was a bit of a waif-like scruff and way too young for it all. He was hugely talented in the junior formulas but just couldn't make the step up. Jackie Stewart always said Jan was one of the best talents he'd ever seen and was the best prospect since Ayrton Senna. Unfortunately he turned out to just be another kid who didn't make it.

I don't know why, but thinking about Jan has made me remember Jochen Mass, as he was about as opposite to Jan as you could get. He was a bear of a man who was extremely powerful. There was a ladder bolted to the side of the motorhome giving access to a viewing area on the roof. One time Jochen grabbed two rungs and levered his body out parallel to the ground and held himself there — scary, really.

He had an inquisitive streak about him too. In Sweden one year we were all staying at a Western-themed hotel called the High Chaparral. This place was like a miniature town with a small Ferris wheel and all sorts of Wild West props. Not surprisingly, the mechanics did a good impression of the bad guys riding into town and wrecking the place overnight.

The sheriff who owned the complex (he dressed like a Wild West character, wandering around with a holster and a six-gun) turned up at the paddock the next day and demanded reparation from Teddy Mayer, who was running the team at the time. Teddy agreed with him and told every single McLaren employee involved to pay £50 towards the repairs and Jochen and James Hunt were told to schmooze with him to calm the waters.

Jochen started off by mentioning how impressed he was, with not only this guy's six-gun but also all the other weaponry he had back at his 'ranch'. He had sheds full of old army gear including AA guns, pistols, rifles, revolvers — in fact, almost anything that could fire a bullet or shell. As the sheriff warmed to the conversation, Jochen asked if he could hold the pistol the guy had in his holster. He removed the gun and handed it to Jochen, who promptly pointed it towards the ceiling and pulled the trigger. Luckily it only had blanks in it but it still blew a hole in the polystyrene ceiling squares.

Jochen had a chequered career but he was a good journeyman driver and just what McLaren needed at the time, because James Hunt was their resident superstar.

It wasn't just the McLaren drivers we got to know. McLaren and the Williams team had quite a close relationship back then and I got to know Alan Jones rather well. He went on to become world champion with Williams and was a real true-blue Aussie, much more so than Mark Webber. Jonesy could swear and drink beer with the best of them. He was very talented in the Nigel Mansell style, in that he'd muscle anything on the track. It was a shame from a Williams point of view that Clay Regazzoni won the first Grand Prix for Williams at Silverstone rather than Jonesy, because the Aussie deserved it more.

You could describe Clay as a typical man's man. He had a certain presence in the paddock and a big black moustache that was the envy of anyone who was a fan of facial hair. He had a dark side to him that would sometimes reveal itself. He was a driven racer who would give his best every time.

This was evident after his accident at the 1980 United States Grand Prix where he was left paralyzed from the waist down. After recovering from his injuries he competed in the Paris–Dakar rally and Sebring 12 Hours using hand controls. He competed through the late 1980s and into the early '90s.

Clay may have had moments on the dark side but Carlos Reutemann was the king of that realm, and at times a pain in the arse. He wouldn't say anything to anyone and came over as so superior to the rest of us he could have had his picture in the Collins dictionary under 'haughty'.

I was in the Williams' motorhome once with Tim and Maureen, who ran the place, when Carlos turned up. They asked him if he'd like a cup of tea and he said yes. He always sat up front in the driver's seat and they had a bowl of Twiglets sitting there on the dashboard.

He picked up one and started to scratch the inside of his ear with it, pulled it out, gave it a quick glance and then put it back in the bowl. The next person into the cab was a Williams' engineer, who later became a McLaren designer, and he grabbed a handful of the Twiglets just as Maureen and Tim were about to tell him not to. It was too late by then because the engineer had a handful of them; there was no knowing which was the dodgy one so they couldn't say a thing. In the meantime, Carlos just sat there brooding silently. Not the kind of man you warm to.

After he sold his F1 team, Jackie Stewart would from time to time turn up and have breakfast in our motorhome. He would always insist that the one thing the modern race-driver didn't have that would make him a great driver was a morning bowl of porridge. Without porridge he'd never be any good. Jackie would bring his own real porridge oats and sit in the motorhome and have his breakfast of champions. Shaune was the only one who was permitted to prepare and cook the great man's oats.

Ron didn't get on with Jackie at the best of times and hated it when the Scot would show up unannounced and have his breakfast in the McLaren motorhome. It didn't help any that Jackie would forever be telling anyone who'd listen what to do and how to go about it. All credit to Ron, though; he'd begrudgingly sit down with Jackie and nod occasionally while Jackie 'suggested' how Ron could improve the team while sharing his porridge. He was always very entertaining and I loved just sitting there listening to some of his great stories.

I'm pleased to be able to say that personally I never had a bad relationship with any of the drivers I came into contact with in the team, even though, as mentioned earlier, at times the camp would split down the middle in taking one driver's side over another's. Perhaps it was because I wasn't a threat to any of them as I ran the hospitality side of the business. In essence I was looking after their personal needs, therefore I had no input on the vital engineering, mechanical or race tactics aspects.

There were many drivers whose personalities polarized people to like them or hate them and Nelson Piquet was one of those. His mechanics at Brabham could not do enough for him and he was really one of the lads. The people at Benetton thought he was a great bloke, always up for a laugh and ready to joke. I didn't mind him but Shaune could never warm to him. I think he was, and probably still is, a classic chauvinist and he tended to give out that typical Brazilian trait, especially associated with the wealthy Brazilians, of total disdain, mixed with an air of indifferent superiority.

His wife at the time, a Dutch woman named Sylvia Tamsma, was in my view a high-maintenance handful, especially after the birth of their son Nelson Ângelo Tamsma Piquet Souto Maior, or just plain Nelsinho, in Germany in 1985. He's better known these days as the ex-Formula One driver Nelson Piquet Junior.

Nelson senior and Sylvia parted soon after Junior was born and she relocated to Monaco. Therefore every Monaco Grand Prix Sylvia and Junior paid us a visit, and they also called on all the other team motorhome managers. Most of us thought Junior was a spoilt child and it seemed to me that Sylvia liked to offload him on to others so she could prance and preen around the paddock.

Nelson seemed to be indifferent when he was around and the young Piquet was soon off to live in Brazil with his father. Nelson senior was a typical race-driver in that he had many lady friends.

Some of the best drivers to spend an hour or two with were the older ones who had retired because they had the best stories. There were times when I wondered how the heck they went racing at all. Innes Ireland is a fine example.

He was an almost larger-than-life character with a military bearing and a voice that would have been the pride of any warrant officer on a parade ground. To top it all off, he had a healthy capacity for good alcohol. Innes was a sort of 'Boys Own' hero figure.

Innes had at one time been an officer in the Parachute Regiment, a racing-driver in the late 1950s and 1960s, a trawlerman, an author and journalist, and a man who didn't suffer fools lightly. He was an absolute joy to listen to as he told stories of a bygone era.

Baron Emmanuel 'Toulo' de Graffenried is another who springs to mind. He was the winner of the British Grand Prix in 1949, the year before the official FIA World Championship began. The Baron had that old-school walk and deportment of the ruling elite — tall, elegant and slightly aloof, with a moustache and shock of white hair. Although French/Swiss by birth, he had one of those cut-crystal English accents that could only be acquired from the best public schools and he would have been right at home in any of the gentlemen's clubs that grace Pall Mall in London.

The stories of pre- and post-war racing made you understand why there were so few 'old' racing-drivers left to talk about their time in the sport. It wasn't a game for the faint-hearted back then.

I consider myself very fortunate these days to know the former Ferrari F1 driver Chris Amon and he is as enthralling as any of the colourful characters I have described in this chapter. I love to listen when he talks about his dealings with Enzo Ferrari, Colin Chapman, Jim Clark, Graham Hill, Bruce McLaren and all the rest of those wonderful names that have slipped into motor-racing legend and whose exploits are now a part of our sporting folklore.

Chapter 9

A1GP: a series of disappointments

At the time of going to print the A1GP World Cup of Motorsport is reportedly in liquidation and the website has been taken down. This chapter charts the beginning of the glory days and chronicles the ups and downs and how I got involved. Who knows whether this interesting concept will ever be revived?

New Zealand's round of the A1GP World Cup of Motorsport was held at Taupo in January 2009. It was great to see world-class race-cars and drivers battling it out on our shores again. Although it pains me a little to say it, I have a sneaking suspicion we may not see the likes of these cars back here again. More's the shame, as those cars were based on seven-time world champion Michael Schumacher's 2004 Ferrari, albeit with a V8 engine. It's the closest thing to Formula One racing we are likely to see here.

I think the A1GP was staged in Taupo in 2009 solely because of seat-holder Colin Giltrap's intervention. Colin knew that if he didn't provide the money he wasn't going to have a race in New Zealand. He found himself over a barrel; I think he felt personally responsible for making the race happen, because he's a huge fan and supporter of motorsport and the A1GP management knew that. My understanding is that Colin was advised that the cars were not going to be shipped out of Asia unless he picked up the bill.

In fact Colin did put up the money to release the cars, as they were allegedly being held for non-payment of freight costs. It's ironic he had to pay for all New Zealand's A1GP competitors to get their cars here, as Black Beauty was already in New Zealand. The car had been freighted over earlier as it was being used as part of an exhibition at the SkyCity Sky Tower to promote the Taupo race.

'A1 was a little short of capital, but they've had an injection of finance with a little bit from me,' Colin explained.

You could almost say A1GP, in New Zealand at least, was Colin's baby and I think he wanted to ensure the event took place. And if Colin says there's going to be an A1GP event in New Zealand, then by God there'll be one.

Without a few passionate patrons like Mr Giltrap, who have a few dollars to send the way of struggling talent with the gift to go fast, many would never get a shot at the big time.

Colin is someone whose passion for motorsport has not only allowed many youngsters to achieve their dream, but also brought a global single-seater racing series to our shores. I believe that 'the powers that be' knew how Colin felt about the series, and were able to capitalize on this. Further, I understand Colin is one of the few who actually paid a franchise fee. I don't know the exact number of teams that did so, but there would be only a handful that paid to go racing in the series. Most of the franchises were owned by Lyndhurst Racing, which was in fact linked to A1GP and Tony Teixeira, so Colin had a certain amount of influence in A1 and quite a bit of say in what went on.

At heart, though, Colin is inherently a racer who likes to go racing with his team working for New Zealand. He lives and pays his taxes in New Zealand, unlike a lot of his wealthy compatriots who relocate to Europe, for reasons of their own. Colin has businesses in New Zealand employing a lot of people. He supports motorsport from the lowest levels right up to the internationally contested A1GP events.

I think the A1GP management traded on what they knew was Colin's passion and patriotism for the sport to get the A1GP here. Whether they wanted it here is debatable; what is certain is that Colin did. The organizers may have made Colin pay for his insistence on having a round of the series in his own country. It's just a shame he had to bail out the New Zealand event. One of the problems was that Taupo failed to attract big crowds in the three years the race was held there (2007 to 2009). And without Colin, there would not have been grandstands at Taupo.

I have been a huge fan of A1GP since getting involved at its inception. I sincerely hoped it would be the future of international motorsport. Having been so closely connected with motor racing, and Formula One in particular, for 30-plus years, the only thing missing for me was not being able to race for your country.

Since all the cars in A1GP are the same, drivers were picked on talent and not the size of their chequebooks. Drivers are able to wear their country's flag on their racing suit, not just because of how proud they are of their birth nation, but because they've been picked to represent their country. A marvellous idea.

Another saving grace for A1GP is that the cars are genuinely fast, look like real open-wheel racers and do in fact pass one another — unlike another form of motorsport I can mention, where you have more chance of finding King Solomon's mines than seeing an over-taking manoeuvre.

The whole premise of the A1GP World Cup of Motorsport is that any country can mix it with any other. Each gets the same equipment, so it's all about which team has the best driver, and that driver must be a national of the country he's representing. A1 was the first opportunity, in any form of motorsport, for nations to compete on a level playing field. A1GP is a series where technology and innovation are deliberately equalised, making success dependent on bravery and pure driving skill.

This was an entirely new concept. Pitting driver against driver, it brought together more than 20 nations, representing 80 per cent of the world's population, to compete without financial or technological advantage. If you think we Kiwis were doing well against the might of such nations as China, India, the US or Great Britain, spare a thought for A1 Team Monaco. The principality is smaller than most New Zealand farms and has only 6500 passport holders, called Monégasque.

In normal New Zealand motorsport parlance, it's equivalent to Kerikeri fielding an international motor-racing team in a global series. But compete Monaco does, often punching above its weight, the same as we do. It's a matter of record New Zealand has finished outside the top five only once since the start of the first series and has been runner-up twice. Even Switzerland has won the championship.

Although the concept of a global motorsport series with countries racing one another was always an attractive idea, there was some scepticism when it came to actually making it work. From the very beginning of A1GP, I and a few others who were involved didn't think it would last more than a year. However, season two came and went, but the wheels started falling off during season three. Although A1GP is now in liquidation, I still think it was a good idea. The series travelled around the world as much as Formula One, if not more so, and although the crowds sometimes weren't as big as the organizers would have wished, it had an appeal unmatched by any other class of motorsport. A1GP did not have the same level of sponsorship of F1, so it was no surprise that many believed it was on probation in its first three years.

Australia has a Formula One event and there's no chance of that circus heading east across the Tasman, as we don't have a FIA grade one track. And that's its attraction. A1GP cars are big, powerful machines that are identical and it's up to the drivers to get the most out of them. The aero isn't as ramped up as for a F1 car, so passing is more likely and when you throw in the ability of being able to hit the boost button, that's where the excitement really takes off. Anybody from about 80 per cent of the teams could win a race and that's clearly not the case in Formula One and hasn't been in years.

Anyway, back to my involvement. Soon after leaving Formula One, I heard a rumour on the motor-racing grapevine about this series. Then I heard Colin Giltrap was considering getting involved and was about to buy a franchise. I had known Colin when I was at McLaren, and one of his companies — Coutts — would lend me a car when I was back in New Zealand on holiday.

Arriving back in New Zealand in 2002, I had heard that A1GP was a definite goer and wrote to Colin saying it was great he was getting involved and becoming a seat-holder and if he needed a hand, to let me know. Shortly afterwards I got a phone call from him advising he had got this Formula One team and perhaps I'd like to come in and talk about helping to run it.

Firstly I commented that he hadn't actually bought an F1 team, and then we arranged a time and place to meet. We talked about the A1GP franchise and what he was going to have to do to make it work. It all went according to plan and Colin duly ended up a seat-holder in the A1GP World Cup of Motorsport series in 2005.

Shortly afterwards, Colin mentioned he'd been chatting to some-one else — Hamish Miller, as it turned out — who had also been keen on getting his hands on a franchise. Consequently I met Hamish a short while later, and he mentioned it was a good thing for New

Zealand to participate but unfortunately he couldn't get the money to get it off the ground.

After Colin had completed all the paperwork with the A1GP people, he got back in touch with me and asked if I wanted to be CEO of the outfit. Meantime he'd asked Hamish to be the sponsorship director. Hamish and I had a chat and agreed we could work together, and the adventure began. Now we just had to find someone to run the team from the mechanical, engineering and purely logistical side of things.

It was my idea to get hold of Dick Bennetts' West Surrey Racing organization to run the sharp end of it and as Dick's company was full of Kiwis, it seemed a good fit. Dick and his co-director, Mike Ewan, are both New Zealanders and were very successful in running racing-cars, having been in charge of drivers like Ayrton Senna in Formula Three. They also had a very successful British Touring Car Championship team so I thought they would be the ideal people to run the show, at least as far as the car was concerned.

Colin had his doubts, as Dick and his company hadn't been involved in single-seaters for a while, but he signed up to the idea for the first year and I thought it was a good partnership.

Once West Surrey Racing had been agreed on, I left it all up to Dick to talk to Colin about what would be required. In hindsight, I realized that was the first brick in the wall to understanding that I could do as much CEOing as I liked, but I was never going to run this team as it was Colin's train set and always would be. And he was never going to relinquish control of it, despite the announcement at the launch in Auckland where he said, 'I'm 65 now. I'm handing over control of the Giltrap Group to the boys, Richard and Michael, and although I'll still be around and part of it, they'll be taking the reins.'

Hand over control he did, but nothing ever happens without Colin's say-so. When Colin does things he goes all the way. I can remember at the time the brothers laughing and saying 'good on us for keeping Colin's interest somewhere else'. But I think it was Richard who said Colin would never let go of things. And so he shouldn't — he made the business and bought the train set, so he should be allowed to play with it any time he wants.

In the meantime, Hamish was phoning around, getting in contact with various people to get some sponsors to come on board. We ended up going to see Fisher & Paykel together, which we thought was a bit of a long shot, but you never know. To our pleasant surprise they came through and put up some money for their name to appear on the car and they remained a sponsor until the series' demise. They thought the concept of going racing as a nation fitted with their ideals. Along with them, Hamish managed to convince a number of other companies, including the *New Zealand Herald*, that it was also a good fit for them to get involved.

Hamish turned out to have a gift for persuading people, doing deals and getting decision-makers to sign on the dotted line. Landing Fisher & Paykel as a sponsor is a story in itself. Hamish and I went to the South of France for the test at the Paul Ricard circuit and Colin had his boat in the nearby harbour town of Bandol, just along the coast from Monaco.

We had been trying to get Fisher & Paykel signed up for some time and the two men at the top, John Bongard and Malcolm Harris, were in the area on a business trip. They were there for a meeting in Italy, the purpose of which became clear a couple of years later when the company purchased a plant there. We convinced them that since they were nearby, they should come and see us at Paul Ricard and check out the car. Colin decided to pick them up from the airport in a Renault Espace so they could stay on the boat with us.

At the best of times Colin's driving could be described as interesting — it definitely makes you sit up and take notice — and by the time John and Malcolm arrived at the boat, all vestiges of a suntan had disappeared from their faces. The rest of us threatened them with a return trip with Colin to the airport if they didn't sign the contract, which they duly did.

Barely weeks after the various deals had been done, and even before the ink had dried on the papers, discussions were swirling around about what colour the car should be. As far as I was concerned it was a no-brainer: it had to be black. Although there are plenty of black cars around now, especially in New Zealand (just look at the Toyota Racing Series, where it seemed every second car was black), back then it was not so common. There were, however, many long and convoluted discussions with the Dick Bennetts people, who wanted to put lines all over it to delineate it, but I said black, and plain black at that, is what it'll be. So black it was and black it remains.

After more discussion we realized we had to somehow get a stylised fern on the car to ensure everyone knew it was New Zealand's car. We got a young student from the Wanganui School of Art, Kai Lim, who had done some work for me in the past, and he came up with a batch of stylised fern designs. We picked one of them and that was it.

So the car's identity was sorted, or so I thought. Emirates Team New Zealand, the America's Cup outfit, found out we were called A1 Team New Zealand and promptly raised the protest flag. They thought the name was exclusive to them. Shortly after the ensuing verbal spat, we started receiving letters from them threatening us with legal action. Tony Thomas, the guy who had helped me into Formula One, was now the commercial sponsorship head honcho of the sailing team.

I even got letters and phone calls from him advising what they would do if we didn't change the name immediately. Now, not only was Colin the franchise-holder of the New Zealand A1GP team, he was also a substantial financial supporter of the yachting boys through his car business. So he told them to fuck off in ways only Colin can, adding 'Nah, we're not changing the name.'

However, we finally came to an agreement after reporting the trouble we were having to A1GP, and decided to call the racing team A1 Team.NZL, which seemed to suit everyone. Quite what the similarity is between a 45-foot, God-knows-how-many-tonne, 15-man boat and a race-car, which hopefully never ends up in the drink, is beyond me. This is at a time when the yachties weren't racing anyway.

By now we had a New Zealand franchise, a team and a car. As with all the other franchises that signed up, there was supposed to be a lavish launch party in the country of the seat-holder and everyone else in the series was to come. The catch to all this, though, was that the country hosting the big bash had to fly every man and his dog into the host country at its own expense. Did they really think we were going to pay for either His Highness Sheikh Maktoum Hasher Maktoum Al Maktoum's private jet to fly out, a first-class ticket for Teixeira, or any of the hangers-on, to attend a launch in New Zealand?

We had a better idea — why not have it in London at New Zealand House? So we contacted the government and, through Colin, New Zealand House in Haymarket and asked if we could have the launch there, using the top floor that looks over Trafalgar Square. We had a few viewings of the place and there were a couple of Kiwis in London who had a little promotions company to help us do it. We had a kapa haka group and a few other iconic Kiwi examples and all the A1GP luminaries turned up. It was a damn good launch and everyone enjoyed the occasion. We had Jonathan Hunt, the former Speaker of the House and now the High Commissioner in London, as the master of ceremonies and we paid for the food and drink, as you do at New Zealand House, but hey, that was OK.

This was the start of a glorious adventure that began in Europe but was headquartered in a small office in the Giltrap Porsche dealership building on Auckland's Great North Road.

At that time, before the racing actually got going, A1GP was being led by the aforementioned Sheikh, who had unveiled the A1GP concept in the Emirate of Dubai on 30 March 2004.

By this time, Sheikh Maktoum and his business partner, Teixeira, had got all the right people together to make the series happen and British firms Lola International and Zytek Engineering had been appointed to develop the chassis and 3.4 litre V8 engine respectively, based, it is said, on the initial drawings of Sheikh Maktoum himself. US company Cooper Tyres was chosen as the original official tyre supplier and by July of 2004, the first generation of A1 cars was ready to be unveiled. They were shown to the public for the first time at the Farnborough International Air Show in the UK.

While Sheikh Maktoum focused on developing his initial vision, from the design of the cars to the look and feel of the website, tickets, branding and overall consumer experience, Teixeira set about attracting investors and potential team owners. Over the following year, 25 national teams were developed, representing countries as diverse in culture and economic prosperity as they were in their motorsport experience. Countries like China and Lebanon would compete against the likes of the US, Great Britain and France and with the launch of each team came the support of high-profile sports stars and successful business people alongside world leaders and politicians.

Those who put either their names or faces to the fledgling series included President Thabo Mbeki, who unveiled South Africa's national car at the team's official launch. A subsequent meeting between the A1GP directors and Nelson Mandela confirmed the level of support the series could aspire to. Others to get involved were General Emile Lahoud, who was the second president to unveil his country's A1 Grand Prix car, at the A1 Team Lebanon launch in Beirut, and President General Pervez Musharraf, who attended the official launch of A1 Team Pakistan at Lahore Fort. A1GP made history, being the first to run a single-seat race-car in Pakistan.

One of the world's most famous international sporting stars, Brazilian footballer Ronaldo, was named as seat-holder for A1 Team Brazil at the official launch of A1 Team Mexico.

Alan Jones, ex-F1 champion and seat-holder for A1 Team Australia, unveiled their entry into the series while 1.3 billion people were added to A1GP's potential fan base with the launch of A1 Team China. Co-seat-holders for A1 Team Portugal, Real Madrid and Portugal footballer Luis Figo and Manchester United assistant manager Carlos Queiroz, became the first team in continental Europe to unveil their racing livery.

Also during 2004, two-time F1 world champion Emerson Fittipaldi joined Ronaldo as co-seat-holder for A1 Team Brazil, and Indian Prime Minister Dr Manmohan Singh welcomed representatives of A1GP for the launch for A1 Team India. Teams from France, Switzerland and the US were also announced.

Finally, at 9.51 a.m. on 3 August 2005, Great Britain became the first A1GP team to get their car on track as part of a 15-team test session at the historic Silverstone circuit, and we joined with Black Beauty. Shortly after, A1GP teams from Germany, Russia and Indonesia were announced as the series embarked on its second team test session at the Paul Ricard circuit in the South of France.

Another ex-F1 driver, Jos Verstappen, confirmed his place in the 2005/06 season, driving the bright orange A1 Team Netherlands' car. Austria, Italy and Japan, three nations with a huge heritage in motorsport, completed the A1GP line-up as they joined the series in the week of its first race.

The young sheikh, who had all the toys in the world and was always surrounded by bodyguards of varying sizes, was in his element and had everything going for himself. In fairness, he had driven the car a lot and engineered the exhausts to sound exactly how he wanted — after all, he was the front man. But the real power behind the throne was Tony Teixeira; with CEO Bruce Holmes it was those two who were really running the show.

At the first test at Silverstone there were dozens of people wandering about in black trousers and white shirts and to this day I still have no idea who the hell they were. In the early days the series was so top-heavy with people who looked important, it was embarrassing. There were time-wasters and no-hopers along with refugees from Formula One. Everyone thought it was one big gravy train, albeit a short-lived one, and many of them wanted their snouts in the trough as they smelt money and by their actions looked like they wanted to get as much out of it as fast as possible before they buggered off to something else.

There were ex-Formula One people the length and breadth of pit lane and the pits. As always there are diamonds among the rough and there were some very good people in there with the best interests of the series at heart. People like John Wickham, whom I knew through F1 and F2.

The team was staying at a big manor house near the Silverstone circuit, along with the other seat-holders, for a meet and greet and to watch the cars running for the first time. Colin was also there and because he has car interests in the UK, he was driving a big Bentley in which he would chauffeur us to the circuit in the morning. The trouble was, though, Colin is one of those people who have a lot of things going on in their mind at any one time and driving doesn't always feature high on the list. So here we are, in a car the size of a tank, whistling along at about 100 kph on very narrow English country lanes barely the width of the Bentley. It was a fight every morning getting into the Bentley, as everyone wanted to get into the back seat and hunker down so they wouldn't have a view of the anticipated carnage.

A couple of times we came across a Transit van, or farmers on their way to work, and Colin would make them back up all the way to a layby so he could get past. There was no way on God's earth Colin was ever going to put his Bentley in reverse.

Things started to accelerate rather quickly from then onwards and it wasn't long after the launch at New Zealand House when the first race came around on 25 September 2005.

We lined up with the other teams for the first race of the new global series at Brands Hatch in the English countryside, just outside West Kingsdown, in the south of the country. We turned up not knowing how competitive we were going to be and people looked up and down pit lane and noticed the New Zealand team was being handled by West Surrey Racing, which hadn't been involved in single-seaters for some years.

We were right beside the likes of France, Italy, Germany and Great Britain and the general consensus was that little old New Zealand wasn't going to be much chop up against those big boys. They looked at the name on the car and thought Matt Halli*who*? Halliday had been a favourite driver of Colin's for a while and he'd been supporting him for some time. He had come from seat time in the now defunct Champcar series in America. No one expected us to do well, considering there were names like Nelson Piquet Junior sitting behind the wheel.

Trying to come up with something to make our team stand out and generate interest, rather than being the whipping-boy of the grid, I decided to get the kapa haka boys back and put them on the grid before the first race at Brands. They turned up and did the whole thing out front on the grid in front of everyone and it was fantastic. The organizers broadcast it all around the circuit to a capacity crowd who went absolutely silent.

Even better, we were on the front row for the sprint race, so by the end of the haka, the A1GP world knew exactly who we were; and just to rub the more so-called established teams' noses in it, we ended up third in the race and on the podium first time up. It was a marvellous feeling to taste success so soon.

Loads of people have asked over the years how we felt that day, and I still give the same answer — I don't know; we were as stunned as all the other teams. But right from the off, the Kiwi team and the black car gained instant respect. Not only did we have the best-looking car at the first race of the brand-new series, we were the only team to have any sponsors on the car and Matt put it on the podium straight out of the box.

Those haka boys earned their keep that day, because when Matt was on the podium receiving his medal, they performed another gig in front of cameras that were beaming the presentation all around the world. What a sight that was, a full-on haka with our driver, all in black, up on the podium, and boy, did it make all the Kiwis in the crowd happy. Everyone in our team was yelling. We were of course predominantly Kiwi, though we also had two Poms at that point, and it brought a tear to many an eye. I would happily say it was one of the proudest moments of my motorsport life. It certainly cemented our position in the A1GP scheme of things.

As an aside, A1 Team Brazil's Nelson Piquet Junior took the double, winning both the sprint and feature races.

Although Colin had said he wanted to take more of a reduced role in things, staying in his house in London for a few days after our first-up success, you could see he was getting keener about this A1GP thing. And as a result, he wanted to take back more and more control. In fact, it was Colin who managed to get Scott Dixon to test the car in Dubai, such was his growing passion for the series and his wanting only good, fast Kiwi drivers in the car. He had this idea he could get Scott to drive the car on a regular basis, but that was never going to fly with Scott's commitments in the States.

I had a lot of email correspondence with Mike Hull, the manager of Target Chip Ganassis Racing, and it soon became apparent they weren't going to release him to drive the A1 Team.NZL car — ever. Because there was so much speculation about things, I decided to put a release out stating how much help Mike Hull and Scott had been and thanking them for their time. Scott was bloody good in the car and extremely fast. I believe we learned more from Scott in 45 minutes than we did from Matt in all the seat-time he had had in the car up until then.

Scott has this ability to go out onto the circuit, not even do a complete lap, come back into the pits and tell the engineers if something had worked or hadn't. He could analyse things quickly. Whereas I saw Matt go out and do three, maybe four laps, come back in and say maybe it worked and maybe it didn't.

It seemed Matt never really got on with the engineer Brian and it could be a bit confusing when he was trying to explain what was going on with the car. Scott was completely different, a breath of fresh air. At the end of the season we had finished fourth in the championship and Colin was convinced it was Brian who was the problem, making mistakes, so it was on the cards West Surrey Racing's contract to engineer the car was not going to be renewed for season two.

Although Matt was a good, fast driver who had the ear of Colin, he didn't get on with Dick Bennetts. Dick didn't help matters much himself as he's a very hands-on sort of guy when it comes to setting up a car. He'll get out onto the circuit and watch the car go through corners, watch it closely through bumpy parts of the track and so on. He'll then come back to the pits and give his penny's worth and Matt didn't like that.

Poor old Brian was right in the middle of all this, getting his ear bent by one comment from Dick and another from Matt. Consequently he didn't have the most harmonious relationship with either of them. Brian was a good engineer and in my opinion could probably have made the car go faster with better input from Matt and less from Dick.

This was proven when he went to A1 Team Malaysia and coached them to two wins the next season. I thought Matt has talent but he wouldn't listen to anyone. In the end we had to sit down and have a head-to-head with him and his manager to try to work out what the problem was — Matt or the car or the engine.

Unfortunately, Matt took it personally and believed we were attacking him. This was untrue — we were simply trying to figure out why the car was so slow. In instances like this, all race teams have to go through every bit of data and analyse everything in order to get to the bottom of a problem. His manager at the time, Grant Baker from the vodka company 42 Below, wanted to come into the meeting so he could defend Matt but we said, 'No, you're not coming into the meeting defending anyone. It's about trying to establish what's wrong, not about apportioning blame.'

At the end of the meeting we decided it was probably an engine problem. This was an issue, as we were a one-car team that didn't have a relationship with any of the countries racing in the series. To Colin's credit, he went off to have a chat with a number of other teams to try to gain an insight as to what our problem might be.

It was Jean-Paul Driot of the French team who let Colin have some data from their engine mapping and we soon discovered we had been to at least two race meetings where our car was significantly down on power. This discovery vindicated Matt, as sometimes he was up to a second-and-a-half slower down the straight.

Colin had his tail-feathers up after discovering we had a slightly shonky engine and demanded a new one from Zytec, the engine builders. They said there was no problem with their engine and it must be us who couldn't get it working properly. As far as Colin was concerned that was like throwing petrol on a fire so he promptly threw down the gauntlet and said New Zealand was going to pull out of the series there and then. The argument went back and forward for a while until the Sheikh heard about it, pulled rank, and said we could have another engine.

The old engine was sent back to Zytec, who then begrudgingly admitted our engine was, in fact, a few hundred revs down on accelerative power. They fired off a new engine to us immediately and in the very next race we were back in the points. However, not gaining any points in two races is too big a deficit to make up, but at least we knew we were back in the game. All credit to Colin — while we were trying to figure what was wrong with the old engine, he'd gone out there with all his inimitable bluster, banged on a few tables, rattled a couple of cages and got the problem sorted.

More and more Colin wanted to run the operation and there wasn't a lot I could do about it. Try as I might to do my own thing, especially if Colin disagreed with it, all hell let loose. A good example of this was when I sent out the release stating Scott would not be driving the Kiwi A1GP car. Colin nearly blew a gasket, saying if it was only about money, we could get him over here and in the car and they'd sort out the dollars in good time.

He hadn't realized I had still kept in contact with Mike Hull at Target Chip Ganassi Racing for weeks about trying to get Scott on board and it was abundantly clear there was no way Scott was going to do it. At about this time I realized that although I was the CEO of the team, Colin was in effect doing my job. It was beginning to dawn on me that there wasn't much point being involved.

By the start of season two Jonny Reid had appeared on the team's radar and had become something of a favourite with everyone. Reid was being managed by Graham Watson, who had helped Colin get in touch with the people who were in charge of the franchises, so to return the favour, Colin allowed Jonny a chance in the car.

Colin is not one to make decisions on sentiment alone and he wouldn't allow any bunny in his car. Winning counts a lot in his eyes — as it should — and he had been impressed with Reid's speed when watching him win the Formula 3000 Euro race at Donington 18 months before. As soon as Jonny got in the car you could sense a completely different attitude within the team. The mechanics liked him, the engineers could work with him and there had been a few other changes. David Sears of Super Nova Racing had taken over from West Surrey Racing as the engineering and mechanical organizers for the team and that was another indicator that being CEO didn't mean much.

David only agreed to come on board if he had complete control over all engineering and mechanical decisions as well as driver selection. I'm pretty sure David offered Colin a cheaper deal to get his foot in the door. You can't argue with the facts, though — it wasn't long into the second season before we started getting the results. Super Nova had an engineer named Chris Gorne and Colin had insisted he join the team, as Chris had been with the French team the year before when they had won the championship. Colin really had the bit between his teeth and was determined to win the championship in his second attempt, so he had to have the best.

Now the team had a new technical provider, a new chief engineer and a new driver who was sharing duties with Matt. When Jonny was in the car things went very smoothly and there was a busy but calm air about the place. However, as soon as Matt got involved, the wheels started to fall off. In my view Matt was unable to gel with the team and he and Chris certainly didn't get along.

As the season wore on, Jonny became more and more embedded with the team and he was fast right from the beginning. He went a long way in helping us finish second in the 2006/07 season, albeit by one point. We approached the third season rubbing our hands in anticipation as we had a settled team, a fast car and Jonny had proved he had the goods to get us our first championship win. The entire team, including Sears, came to the conclusion it would be better if Jonny drove for the whole season to get most out of the team and car.

We had a stable set-up now; Chris knew what the car was about and we had settled into a good routine. But motorsport is a fickle thing and we hit a few speed wobbles. There was no one big drama, just a number of small errors by everyone that were really felt halfway through the season when we started to slip off the pace. Jonny made some mistakes, there were some tactical errors, some of the pit stops went wrong and we just couldn't get back into our early-season stride and struggled to another second-place finish in the series. We just gave too many points away, simple as that. Frankly, not everything was properly organized that year and it showed. We should have come first but instead we endeavoured to come third, tried really hard to come fourth but we managed to come second.

At the end of the third season Colin was even more involved; he wanted a series win big time and was calling nearly all the shots. It was becoming brutally obvious the situation couldn't continue, so at the end of the 2007/08 season I left. I really enjoyed my time with the team, especially being involved in something new in my sport. The idea that I could represent my country was something truly special.

However, unlike the song where 'the future's so bright I gotta wear shades', there appeared to be a hell of a lot of storm clouds on the horizon for A1GP. The A1GP seasons of late had been fraught with drama, rumour and innuendo that swirled around like confetti in a dust-devil. Rounds were cancelled, Indonesia pulled out of the series and would you believe it, a change of date was requested by Mexico because of a Radiohead concert.

The Chinese whispers were almost a shout by the time the season was at mid-point in 2008 and it took the seat-holder of New Zealand's team, Colin Giltrap, to pull out his wallet to get all the cars to New Zealand. No matter what anyone personally thinks of Ferrari and its parent company Fiat, they're not daft and wouldn't buy into something that was about to crash. It may even be possible that Ferrari were planning for the demise of Formula One with all its expensive paper darts, pretty boys earning millions and bizarre night races. Maybe they wanted to get the jump on the other manufacturers with a global series no one else was allowed to get involved in.

They might even have been using A1GP as a glorified test-bed for stuff they want to put into their road cars (the engine is based on their F430 car), gaining all the kudos of being the only manufacturer to sell cars to the public with a 'race heritage'. Who really knows? Only time will tell.

On 29 January 2006, A1 Grand Prix attracted its biggest crowd to date as over 100,000 people lined the streets of Durban for the series' and the city's first ever street race. By 12 November of that year, in a challenging weekend for all involved, A1GP overcame all the obstacles to become the first ever racing series to compete on the streets of China's capital city Beijing.

A1 Team New Zealand made the best ever finish of any home team at the series' first visit to Taupo in January 2007. The event was a huge success and the enthusiastic crowd made it clear that their favourite drivers Jonny Reid and Matt Halliday were well supported.

In October that year, Jonny won both races in Brno to move the team into the championship lead for the first time in its history. Along the way, Sky Sports, the UK's leading broadcaster of motorsport, signed an exclusive deal to televise the series and became the first of 30 broadcast networks to back A1GP around the globe.

Following three seasons of A1GP action, the series took a further step forward in 2008 by beginning a six-year partnership with Ferrari, which was to provide the engines and design ideas for the chassis. The car design is closely based on the model Michael Schumacher drove to win the 2004 world F1 title.

The new car underwent 7000 kilometres of testing before the first round in Zandvoort and bar a few minor glitches has proved to be a winner. It was designed to produce exciting racing and allow overtaking. During testing in 2008 at Donington Park in the UK, it broke the outright lap record, and did the same during racing at Zandvoort, where Kiwi driver Earl Bamber put the black car on the podium twice.

By 2009, though, things were looking decidedly shaky for the World Cup of Motorsport. In January fans were warned if they didn't get to Taupo to watch the New Zealand round of the series, it would probably be the last chance Kiwis would have to see scaled-down versions of F1 cars on their soil. I don't think anyone actually realized it was the beginning of the death knell for the global series.

The last few nails in its coffin were hammered home a week before the Australian V8 Supercar round on the Gold Coast in October 2009 when event general manager Greg Hooton made a statement from the pit lane of the street circuit along the lines that there were rumours surrounding the appearance of the A1GP World Cup of Motorsport at this time. He said he needed to make clear that A1GP had not breached any terms of contract with GCMEC (Gold Coast Motor Events Company). After that, you knew trouble was definitely brewing.

His announcement was akin to the manager of a sports club issuing a media release saying he and the board have confidence in the manager. And just as the manager is duly sacked a week later, the A1GP cars did not make the grid on race weekend.

'I want to personally apologize to the people affected by this regrettable but unavoidable decision,' A1GP series boss Tony Teixeira said in a statement. 'The Queensland government, Gold Coast Motor Events Co, the management and chairman of the event have been patient and supportive of us in the past weeks. We were proud to be part of what has become one of the world's most iconic motorsport events, and are devastated at the decision we have had to make. We also know the Australian motorsport fans are very protective of this event and had welcomed us with open arms. To them I also apologize and stress that we wanted to put on a show for them that they would never forget.'

A statement released from the series said that the knock-on effect of the closed-season problems meant it was impossible to prepare the cars in time.

'One effect of the UK operating arm of the series going into liquidation in June was that access to the cars and the ability to pay its suppliers has been impeded. What should have been a summer upgrading the machinery in time for the first race of the 2009/10 season has turned into a frustrating time for achieving this.'

I think that's a load of rubbish. It was never about a lack of time to prepare the cars; it was because the cars had been impounded because of unpaid bills. Shortly after the Aussie fiasco the three next rounds were also cancelled and the Queensland government contemplated suing the A1GP organizers.

And that, as they say, was that. Neither sight nor sound has been heard since from Teixeira, or the cars, in respect to the A1GP effort in Australia.

Chapter 10

Indy 500: commenting on Scott Dixon's triumph

Some of you sceptics reading this will not believe me, but I had a feeling that after five attempts at winning the Indianapolis 500, New Zealand's own Scott Dixon was in with a serious chance in 2008.

For a small country stuck on the arse end of the world, we have a rich and acclaimed history of producing some of the best motor-racing drivers in the world, including a Formula One champion. Not bad for a country that when I was a boy had a population of fewer than three million.

But not even some of our greats like Denny Hulme, Chris Amon or Bruce McLaren had managed to win Indy. It was the only one of the triple crown of motorsport that a Kiwi hadn't won, until that year when Dixon stood up and put all the rest to the sword. Thanks to that most satisfying of drives, all of us who have either participated in, worked in or been passionate fans of motor racing can now rest happy in the knowledge that we have competed against and defeated the best at the highest levels of the triple crown.

Amon and McLaren set the standard with their 24 Hour Le Mans victory in 1966, followed by Hulme, who won the Formula One championship in 1967. Dixon completed the triple crown with his Indy 500 triumph in 2008. Some would argue that winning a single race is far more difficult than a championship spread out over an entire season, but I have no interest in such comparisons. Suffice to say that Scott Dixon is the first Kiwi to have his likeness immortalised on the Borg-Warner Trophy and therefore can now be regarded as one of the greatest New Zealand drivers. And I was there to see it, and not as a Johnny-come-lately either. Five times I turned up to watch him finish 17th, 8th, 24th, 6th, and then 2nd.

It started back in November of 2007 when Dixon and his future wife Emma (they married in February 2008) decided to have a real tilt at winning the 500. Emma was an elite 800m runner who competed at world and Commonwealth level, so she knew a thing or two about how to get physically and mentally prepared for the big one. She changed Scott's fitness programme and psychological approach as well as his nutrition, with one goal in mind and that was to win. When you couple that with Dixon's Target Chip Ganassi Racing team's focused approach on gearing up to win the 92nd running of the 'World's Greatest Race', it presented a daunting challenge for their competitors.

We had discovered early on in the IRL season that Ganassi Racing had made a decision to prepare the cars during the off-season with the 500 in mind, rather than wait until the opening rounds. The team had been doing a lot of pre-season testing and work for the Indy 500, something the Ganassi outfit hadn't bothered with in the past. Clearly there had been a shift in management thinking and they'd set that one race as their focus for the year.

Hindsight is a wonderful thing but as the motoring fraternity and the world at large soon found out, Ganassi's strategy was cunning. When Dixon crossed that famous yard of bricks just short of 4:40 in the afternoon of Sunday, 25 May 2008, becoming the first New Zealander to do so in nearly 100 years of racing at the Brickyard, I felt I had seen something very special for the second time in my life.

For me it was a bit like déjà vu. Back at the dawn of time, I was involved with another Kiwi whose name became synonymous with racing. In fact his is only one of three family names still left in Formula One. His name of course was McLaren — the others being Ferrari and Williams. But more of that later.

Over the years I had been to Indy eight times and for the last five, bar one, with TVNZ, in the hope that Dixon would one day be immortalised on one of the most coveted trophies in the world alongside Emerson Fittipaldi, Mario Andretti, Jim Clark and Graham Hill, to name but a few, something no other New Zealander has managed to achieve.

Indy is always going to be Indy. Everyone wants to be there, race there and, God forbid, win. It's a circuit that places a lot of expectations on drivers and teams and we commentators and spectators are fortunate to be able to watch the drama unfold. Indy is a place that can make grown men cry and it may only be one race, but boy is it a big one. It is possible to build towards winning a championship over an entire season, even allowing for mechanical failures and crashes, but at Indy drivers and teams alike have only one chance to win. To make matters worse, the drivers have nearly a month to get the cars right for that one race so it's pressure, pressure, pressure. If you come up short on the day, you don't win, simple as that.

So, to be able to watch another Kiwi achieve something quite extraordinary in motor racing was worth the hassle of getting trackside. I could almost taste the bitterness and disappointment Dixon must have felt in 2007 when he lost the IRL championship to Dario Franchitti on the last corner of the last race at Chicagoland Speedway. This blow only compounded his woes that year, as he also finished second in the Indianapolis 500.

During May, in the four-week run-up to the 25 May race, it was easy to see that the speed Dixon and his team-mate Dan Wheldon had showed so far that season was on display at Indianapolis. The team's pre-season testing really started to pay off when a lot of track time was lost due to long rain delays. This resulted in a number of teams losing valuable set-up time, so our small TVNZ crew were rubbing our hands in anticipation as we got ready to fly out to America.

A bonus for us that year was that A1GP driver Jonny Reid had a rookie test organized to prove to the IRL folk that he was ready, willing and able to compete in the feeder series for the main IndyCar game, the Firestone Indy Lights. This is a series Kiwis have done well in with both Scott Dixon and Wade Cunningham having won the championship.

Reid was due to take the oval test on Tuesday, 13 May at the Kentucky Motor Speedway, just a little over two hours' drive from the Indianapolis airport. We (our group included Hamish Miller, Ron Dixon, Clayton Reid, and expat Kiwi and NZGP race driver Dave McMillan, who is based in Indy) had all been working on getting Jonny the drive, as his options in GP2 or World Series by Renault were limited due to finances. With the best will in the world it was becoming obvious that Jonny, despite being very talented and driving A1 Team New Zealand's Black Beauty to second place in the A1 championship, was not going to make F1.

His next best option was to try to make his mark in the States, build a reputation there and get his career on the road to actually making some money from racing cars, instead of spending what little he had on buying drives in other classes. It's still possible to get to the top in single-seat racing in the States on a budget, and there's potential for earning a decent wedge from prize money on the way to the top. It's a lot more likely to happen in the good old US of A than it is in Europe, where most rookie international drivers live from hand to mouth. Just look at Dixon — I doubt he'll be short of a dollar or two over the next few years.

After much gnashing of teeth and arm-twisting, David Turner (TVNZ producer and director of the Powerbuilt Tools Motorsport show) and I convinced everyone we had to be there to see how Jonny got on and that we should leave on 13 May.

A rather large bump in the road, and one I should pay more attention to as time marches on, was that the day we had chosen to fly out on was also my wife Shaune's birthday, and 2008 just happened to be a very significant one in her life. As any understanding (note I did not say 'long-suffering') wife would do, and as Shaune has always done throughout my career, she supported my 'request' to leave for Indy the day before her birthday. It probably helps that Shaune has been in, around and involved in motorsport almost as long as I have, and she knows that big events will occasionally clash.

After a journey of about 20 hours we got to the Indianapolis airport and as soon as I turned my phone back on, I got a text from Jonny telling me the rookie test had been cancelled due to the bad weather that had plagued the Midwest for weeks. I called him to find out where he was and discovered we were actually at the same airport, as he was on his way back to New Zealand to sort out his US visa. A bit of a schoolboy error in this day and age when everyone in authority thinks everyone else is up to no good, and not the best of starts to Jonny's big American adventure. He had to go straight to the States from an A1GP race at Brands and had not found time to sort visas and other paperwork.

After a quick chat we arranged to meet outside the arrivals building so I could catch up with what he was up to, what it was like being in America and how he felt about racing ovals in a car he'd never been in before, let alone seen. I also wanted to use him on the Indy 500 TV show to find out what his first take was on the Speedway. Soon Jonny said he had to go back inside to make sure he'd catch his flight back to New Zealand, which left me standing on the sidewalk wondering what the hell all the rush had been about to get here. I decided to use the extra time I now had to go and buy Shaune a cool present for her birthday, as I realized I could have been back at home celebrating it with her.

It was not long after the Reid rookie test fiasco that the Indy 500 started to loom very large indeed. The extra days' preparation came in handy and it wasn't long before we learned that the rest of the crew were about to arrive. David and I thanked our lucky stars we weren't on that flight, as the TVNZ film crew had what can only be described as a mini version of Dante's Inferno in getting to Indianapolis. Their trip started with a delayed flight, quickly followed by a number of unscheduled overnight stops culminating in cancelled flights. There were various other minor mishaps on the way to which, by this stage, the TVNZ management merely raised a troubled eyebrow.

Listening to the rest of our crew, who were ever so slightly strung-out from their travel adventures, tell us about their misfortunes only emphasised just how well organized the Indianapolis Motor Speedway is. I feel I'm well qualified to make comparisons when it comes to motor-racing events and series, having spent three decades heavily involved in Formula One — a category of motor racing filled with egos the size of small houses, infighting, backstabbing and pontificating self-importance you have to see to believe.

Coming to the 500 for five years as a spectator and fan — as well as a worker — has not only been a revelation, but pure joy for me. I don't know if it's because we're Kiwis and that the Americans still remember how good Bruce McLaren and his Can-Am cars were, or if they still don't actually know where New Zealand is, but the organizers and staff have taken us into their hearts and homes. We have developed a strong relationship with both the Speedway and IRL media departments that has grown into a genuine friendship and we now get invited to their homes for barbecues.

Each year it's the same feeling, though: as you drive up to the media centre you can't wait to get your hands on the much sought after and coveted metal badge, which allows its holder access to the greatest race on earth. With the all-important media pass around my neck, I head out to trackside to breathe in the smell of 92 years of motor-racing history that includes joy, disappointment, heartache, danger and even a whiff of the grim reaper.

Looking out over the famous yard of bricks, this time I had a different feeling from that of previous years. Call it a vibration in my bones or whatever, but I got the feeling and smell of victory. And victory for 'one of ours', for the first time in the history of the race. Scott had been in scintillating form all season and it seemed almost inevitable that he'd win this year after coming so close in 2007. Some will say it's easy to claim such things in hindsight but I'd been telling all and sundry this was Scott's year, even to the point of bending the ear of the motor-racing correspondent of *New Zealand Herald* on numerous occasions.

Scott had been fastest, or among the fastest, for the entire month of testing as well as for the season to date. In four races he had qualified on pole in two of them, second in one, and had finished with a first and two thirds. When he put his Target Chip Ganassi Racing number 9 car on pole, there was a lot of cheering and jubilation but it wasn't a huge surprise. There was a certain calm determination about him before, during and after qualifying that had rubbed off onto his crew. He waived his first qualifying time, which would have been good enough for the front row, to make a second attempt at being the outright fastest car on track. The rest is history.

A lot of folk were banging on about how in almost 100 years of the 500, only 18 drivers had won from pole position. I looked at it from the perspective that more people had won from pole than from any other grid position. At the time of writing, 19 people have won from pole, still more than from any other grid position (for example, 11 from p2, 10 from p3, 6 from p4, 7 from p5, 4 from p6, 5 from p7).

God bless America and its love of statistics, but there was one interesting nugget that caught my attention — did you know that out of the almost 1000 drivers to have raced in the Indianapolis 500, not one has been named Smith?

The crew and I had got to know Scott and his family quite well over the years we had been coming to Indy, but this year there was someone else close to him we needed to get acquainted with. When Scott tied the knot with Welsh middle-distance runner Emma Davies, she seemed to have brought a certain roundness to his whole demeanour. For a long time he had been known as the Iceman, due to his perceived aloofness when around others. Nothing could have been further from the truth. Scott didn't suffer fools lightly; rather, he just got on with the job sans pomp, preening or grandstanding. It was this trait, and his single-minded focus, that first registered him on team owner Chip Ganassi's radar.

Scott had always been very civil and professional towards us TVNZ guys and away from the camera, we all got on well. However, Emma had apparently awakened something deep in his character: he was now not only noticeably more relaxed around others, but even more focused. It was like there was a preordained belief that this time the Borg-Warner Trophy was his for the taking. Just another little indicator that 2008 was to be his year.

It was all well and good schmoozing with the star drivers but my co-presenter Robert Rakete, producer David Turner and I had to get the show on the road in the run-up to the big event.

With David cracking the whip, we had to concentrate on story ideas and we had to plan to fill the hours of television time we would be beaming back to New Zealand before the race. Quite a big ask, as it was going to be the longest show we had ever done.

After a few brainstorming sessions we decided to do an overview of the whole American motor-racing scene, especially those things particular to the US. These would include trips to dirt and pavement speedway events, a must-do visit to the NHRA drags and some of the teams involved and the guys who build and work on the engines for all manner of motor-racing styles, including karts.

Along the way we came across midget and sprint car teams, exhaust manufacturers, go-fast accessory fabricators and all manner of the good, the bad and the ugly that go to make up the amazing Indianapolis family that lives and breathes motor racing in that fabulous city. To top it all off, we were having a crash helmet specially painted by one of Indy's finest detail painters. This valuable piece of memorabilia would later be featured and presented on the show.

Jamie Ferrell of Jam Air Paint really seemed to enjoy his work, spending hours getting the minute details of the distinctly Kiwi-flavoured design just right. I thought he might have been just enjoying the lacquer fumes and after spending some time with him in and around the paint booth, I was beginning to see why.

The motor-racing scene in America was built on big fast cars, big tracks and big fearless men. In an odd sort of way the tradition carries on. Or rather, the big men are still in evidence. Although I've been to the States too many times to count, it never fails to amaze me just how much food the Yanks can fit on a plate and how the hell they manage to eat it all.

As race weekend approached, we interviewed anyone and everyone who would stand still long enough to answer a question and by race day the atmosphere and tension was almost palpable. From the moment we got up that morning, the hours were packed with pomp and ceremony, bands both marching and instrumental, fly-pasts, cheerleaders by the score accompanied by huge blokes playing even bigger tubas and enough saluting to keep any African despot happy for years.

The patriotic chest-thumping is nicely balanced by an odd marching band prerequisite that puts the fat kid with the enormous brass musical instrument, or big bass drum, on the outside of the bend. This then requires him to have to run to keep line formation. Not a pleasant sight, all that sweat running down his face while he holds up his pants to stop the crotch dragging on the road like some deranged gangster rapper.

The Indy 500 is always timed to take place on Memorial Day, when the country honours servicemen and women, past and present, with parades, ceremonies, fly-pasts of Stealth bombers and other aircraft in a show of military might. Consequently, the Indianapolis Motor Speedway is a moving sea of uniforms of every colour and description with five-star generals mixing it with National Guard motor mechanics. There are military helicopter static displays where you can climb all over the latest Black Hawk or Apache or climb aboard a simulator.

The sight would cause what's left of the RNZAF brass to hold their heads in shame and cry tears of frustration. There's more air power on display at this one motor-racing event than the entire New Zealand Air Force could put out. Say what you like, but the Yanks do parades better than anyone — with the possible exception of the Brazilians during carnival time in Rio.

The visual and aural assault continued with sports stars, daytime soap stars . . . good Lord, there were even porn stars mixed up with generals, Iraq veterans, past, present and future drivers, mechanics, engineers, team owners and men in plaid trousers purporting to be sponsors. And the comb-overs and wigs were another story. As for the women, Europe doesn't have much to worry about. Only in America could you find a bunch of women proudly strutting their stuff, and I do mean stuff. What they put in their bodies is truly amazing; botulism in their foreheads so their faces look like operatic masks, silicone in their boobs, implants in their butts and God knows what they do to get that weird orange look to their skin.

In the meantime, Robert Rakete found Scott's mother Glenys and tried to interview her, but to no avail. Understandably, she was a bundle of nerves as the clock ticked down towards the start. Glenys was torn between hiding away in some back room and wandering around soaking up the amazing atmosphere.

Scott's dad Ron was having a slightly better time as his main focus was on the job at hand — and it was not one with his son's team. Ron was on the far side of the track high in the stands acting as a spotter at Turn Three for Roth Racing's John Andretti. Naturally, though, part of his mind was on his son and his own preparation for the race.

John Andretti, nephew of the great Mario and cousin to Marco, was driving in the 500 as part of Marty Roth's team. The job of the spotter is to keep a close eye on his driver and warn of any cars that may be getting close, or any incident on track that may affect what their driver does. A spotter doing a good job may not be able to win the race for his driver but he sure can lose it for him by not paying attention and giving him the wrong, or no, information.

With 20 minutes to go, Scott had disappeared deep within the confines of his team on the grid as they all stood to attention next to their respective cars. The grid was cleared of all the hangers-on and eye-candy, leaving just the critical members of the team behind to listen to the invocation read out by the Indy Racing League's personal religious representative, Father Phil.

The Indianapolis 500 is the largest single-day sporting event in the world and the sight of over 300,000 people standing to attention along the mile-long straight is something that will never leave me. As *The Star-Spangled Banner* blasted out over the public-address system, the air shook and the boom of the US Air Force's B-2 Stealth bombers as they screamed overhead assaulted our ears. Some may call me a cynic, but even I felt a little patriotic among all this gung-ho chest-thumping and a-whoopin' and a-hollerin'. Criticize them if you will, but the Yanks sure know how to rouse a crowd and make a huge feel-good statement.

While contemplating how different the Americans are to us Kiwis, with our reticence to show emotion or enthusiasm, I was brought back to the here and now as Mary Hulman George (the daughter of Tony Hulman, the saviour of the Indianapolis Motor Speedway) uttered those iconic Indy 500 words that echoed around the Motor Speedway; 'Lady and Gentlemen — START YOUR ENGINES!' (The lady was Danica Patrick, who was fifth-fastest qualifier on Pole Day.)

As the 33 engines coughed and spluttered into life, a wall of sound created by the awaking of 21,000 bhp caused the ground to vibrate. It must have sent a shiver up the spine of everyone at the circuit and a roar of approval swept around the huge stadium as we all realized it was 'game on'. With race suits on and TV camera recording, standing on the grid as all those engines erupt into action shakes the very foundations of your being — it was an unforgettable moment for all of us.

A few warm-up laps later, at precisely 1.11 in the afternoon, the green flag was vigorously waved and it was time to go racing. At times at speeds in excess of 230 mph / 370 kph / 337 fps / 102.7 mps — you have to be there to really get an understanding just how fast these IndyCars go and just how close the racing is. I have to admit that television doesn't do it justice.

Right from the start it was clear Scott Dixon had the fastest car on the track. We watched with great excitement, tinged with a little fear and apprehension that he might get caught up in someone else's incident or be blind-sided by an errant driver. Scott serenely went about his business. He was never fazed by what was going on around him, even to the extent when, at one stage, he found himself outside the top 10. He kept his head as those around him fell by the wayside, and regained the lead.

The race seemed to go on forever, especially the last 30 laps, but as it unfolded we had to tear ourselves away from trackside, get organized, make plans and work out how as part of TVNZ we'd deal with his win and try to get close enough to get a few words. We decided Robert was going to take the lead with interviews and I would be a backup in case of emergency, or if he got stuck in the wrong place at the wrong time.

Robert did a great job of muscling, cajoling and begging his way into Scott's pit area, which was right at the other end of the pit lane far from the podium. He managed to have a chat with Glenys, before having to leg it all the way back to the podium to catch up with what was going on there. By the time Robert arrived back at the winner's enclosure, he was drenched in sweat, having had to lug a heavy microphone all the way back up pit lane. Not to mention our cameraman John Robertson, who had done at least five lengths of the pit lane with all his equipment during the race, to accommodate our whims and demands for various shots.

I had spent the time leaning against the fence of the winner's enclosure enjoying the atmosphere and vicariously accepting the congratulations of people around me who were shouting, 'Go, Kiwis . . . well done, guys.' It was bedlam, with Scott having to go through the rigmarole of drinking the milk and having hundreds of photographs taken wearing a myriad of different caps. It's the same the world over for winners of major sporting events. For a period of time the media, who in a way made them stars in the first place, owns them but it's hell for the family to try to be a part of the celebrations.

Ron Dixon had to fight his way back from Turn Three and could be seen trying to ride his scooter against a tide of humanity shouting, 'He's my son! Get out of the way!' He seemed to battle for an age until someone recognized who he was and made a narrow path for him to join Scott, Glenys, Emma, sister Adele, Chip Ganassi and the team that helped Scott become the 92nd winner of the Borg-Warner Trophy. There wasn't a dry eye in the place as Scott celebrated becoming the first New Zealander to win the coveted trophy. He would soon have his face immortalized alongside many of the greats of the sport. The trophy with his likeness on it was unveiled at the Speedway on 13 January 2009.

At one stage during the ensuing proceedings, Chip threw his Ganassi team hat in the air and one of the team's sponsors, who happened to be standing next to me, picked it up and gave it to me along with the words, 'For the Kiwis.'

Later Chip kindly signed the hat for me, and it now sits pride of place among the mountain of memorabilia at my home. The media people of the IRL and IMS are very strict about who is permitted from among the hundreds of journalists and camera crews into the inner sanctum of the winner's circle, and then on to the track to get the shots and interviews on the yard of bricks — pictures that are subsequently broadcast and published all around the world.

That yard of bricks, located at the start/finish line, is all that remains from the original bricks that the entire track was made of back in the 1900s — hence the circuit's nickname 'The Brickyard'. There is, however, a warehouse at a secret location that is reputed to hold most of the remaining original bricks.

All TV, photographers and assorted media were kept away from Scott, his family and extended members made up of the team crew and we were prepared to be shoved to the back with the rest of the great unwashed. But we weren't about to go down without a fight and we were quite ready to do a bit of good old-fashioned scrummaging to get to the front. Just as we were forming up the flying wedge, Charles Burns, the head of the IRL security, yelled out, 'Folks, you make way for those guys at the back.' Not too sure whom he was on about, we stopped in our preparation to barge our way towards the front and looked around to see whom he was referring to.

When Charles continued to insist, 'Make way for them folk from TV Noo Zeeelan', we realized he meant us. Without a moment's hesitation we announced, 'Yeah right, move it, we're from N'Zeelun and so is Scott.'

Within moments we were sharing one of the greatest achievements of a New Zealand motor-racing driver, standing arm in arm with his mum and dad and at the same time pumping handshakes with his manager Stefan Johansson. It was quite a sight for me, seeing Stefan in the winner's circle again, having worked on his car when he raced for Ron Dennis's Project Four Racing team back in 1980 when he won the British Formula Three championship. After much success in F3, Stefan went on to race Formula One with Ferrari among other teams, before moving to the States to race. He was the man who recognized Scott's talent and helped him in his early Indy Lights days.

Well after the race had ended and all the presentations and photo-ops were winding down, there were still a great number of New

Zealand flags being waved in the grandstand by Kiwis adorned in All Black shirts. Ron and Glenys acknowledged them, going over to the fence to share in their delight. Scott noticed them too, waving enthusiastically at seeing his compatriots who were relishing the moment with him.

We milled around, basking in the reflected glory of the first New Zealander not only to put the car on pole but to win the 500. We talked with Scott, on and off camera, and all the while my phone was ringing non-stop with calls from New Zealand as the radio and TV stations wanted to get as much information and reaction as possible.

It wasn't long before Scott had to deal with the responsibilities and the avalanche of duties now required of the winner of the race. A good part of his life was now public property and his every move would be precisely mapped and managed for the foreseeable future.

Most people would think that having just won, the winner would enjoy being feted, wined and dined until the small hours and then head to bed for a well-earned rest. Not so for Scott.

As soon as the race is finished, and the presentations completed, the race winner becomes the commercial property of the IRL and IMS while his family, friends and team are relegated to the backbenches.

We left the track late in the day to relay to New Zealand the news stories we had gathered after the race. However, it wasn't long before we were asked to return to the track to get some 'live' interviews with Scott for TVNZ and Mark Sainsbury's *Close Up* programme.

The live cross was scheduled for 10 p.m. on Sunday and we arrived back in the media centre to find Scott still there doing satellite interviews to various countries all around the world. He was sitting in the middle of a glass room with an earpiece seemingly permanently glued to his head, staring down the barrel of a camera and doing 10-minute takes.

My own phone was press-ganged into service with a microphone attached to the speaker, and then to Scott's ear as he spoke with Mark Sainsbury, who just happened to be in Australia at the time. Down by the side of Scott's chair sat a warm and half-empty bottle of beer. It was the only celebratory drink, other than the milk, most of which went over his head, that Scott had managed in the five or so hours since the race had ended.

He left that room at around midnight, totally exhausted but still elated and waiting for the whole experience to sink in. The next day he was up early and out of his motorhome to do the traditional photo-shoot back at the track with the team and his car. Monday evening was the posh, let's-get-dressed-to-the-nines, Indianapolis 500 Banquet where the prizes are officially handed out to the drivers and teams.

Robert once again had the honour of speaking with Scott as he arrived at the banquet, while we sat at a respectful distance on a garden flowerbed wall like a bunch of street urchins waiting and watching for scraps from the high table. Amazing what a tuxedo can do for a man and a sophisticated little black number can do for a woman.

That race was one of the highlights of my life and I regarded it as a privilege to have experienced the occasion. The sense of pride in Scott's achievement and the feeling of empathy with his family was immense and powerful for those of us around him. After four days of successive guest appearances, TV shows, interviews and with hardly a second to himself, he remained the consummate professional, gracious in victory and never once complaining about the demands on his time.

There was no time for him to rest on his Indy 500 laurels, as the next weekend he was back in his number 9 car to carry on with the title chase at the Milwaukee Mile. Back to trying to win the championship — which he duly did.

The following year did not quite reach the heights of 2008 for Scott. After a bad start to the season he came from 17th after two rounds to challenge for the title. However, he was pipped at the post by team-mate Dario Franchitti at the last race of the season to finish second in the series for the second time. Another Kiwi driver, former Indy Lights champion Wade Cunningham, won the Firestone Lights Indy race, so New Zealand did not come away from the Indy 500 weekend empty-handed.

Scott was also unable to repeat his Indy 500 feat of 2008 and finished sixth, to match his 2006 effort. On a brighter note, Scott signed for a further three years with Target Chip Ganassi Racing in December 2009. He had a smile on his face when I presented him with his Halberg Sportsman of the Year Award statue and the citation for being inducted to the MotorSport New Zealand Wall of Fame.

Chapter 11

From now on in

In May 2002 I had arrived back in New Zealand to start a whole new chapter of my life. My move at that time into television and radio is chronicled elsewhere in this book. Formula One and McLaren were now a part of my past and I had to contemplate my future without the constant travelling and the buzz of the F1 paddock. This was something I wasn't really looking forward to, despite being able to keep my hand in with the odd bit of colour commentary on New Zealand television.

I was pleased to be home of course, but I was concerned that my departure from the 'street' of pit lane, garage, race circuits and motor-homes and resultant adrenaline rushes would leave a huge void in my life that would be very difficult to fill.

My first few weeks and months back at home went by in a flash and were akin to a holiday of sorts. I enjoyed the physical work on the property and getting things done that I'd neglected in my absence. I was heaving chainsaws about, lopping off branches and felling trees with merry abandon. Once I'd had my fill of chopping things down I moved onto erecting fences, digging drains and a myriad of other things involved in getting the land and garden up to scratch.

I was managing to get to the odd race meeting, purely as a spectator, as I still enjoyed watching close contests on the track. It didn't take very long for the course announcer at one or two of these events to find out that I was present and to ask me to pass a few comments from the commentary booth during an event.

If I'm to be completely honest, being able to play even such a small part in motor racing back in New Zealand fed my ego and I found I quite enjoyed it. I wasn't the only ex-employee of McLaren who had moved back to New Zealand. I caught up with Peter Burns, the former marketing manager, and we decided it made perfect sense for us to start a promotional company. After the relevant paperwork was drawn up and registered, Springboard International was born.

It all started rather well and we had some success with a number of projects. One of the bigger ideas was to initiate an Australian V8 Supercar race around the streets of inner Auckland. However, as with many great entrepreneurial ideas that end up in the hands of local authorities, it all goes to pot when minor public officials get involved. To begin with, the council sounded interested in our concept. But when push came to shove they were all hindrance and no help.

At one stage we also put in a bid, backed by a couple of influential businessmen, to take over the running of the speedway track at Western Springs. Just as we thought the plan was coming together rather nicely, for some reason the deal fell over.

Not to be put off, we continued to look for new avenues for our respective talents and as time went on, memories of the F1 paddock began to fade into the background. The only times I felt a pang of loss was when fronting the odd motorsport show for TVNZ or doing a live show from the Melbourne Formula One Grand Prix.

By now I was getting into the swing of how motor racing worked in New Zealand and was relishing the more relaxed atmosphere compared with the full-on approach of F1. I hadn't been this active since the days of helping out friends on the Formula Ford and Formula Atlantic/Pacific series some years earlier. I was also enjoying watching some of our younger drivers start on their careers.

During my last couple of years with McLaren I'd been helping the trustees of the MotorSport New Zealand Scholarship Trust to arrange for the winners of the scholarship to visit various teams and workshops in the UK. I continued doing this until the discontinuation of the award in 2004, when the Elite Academy was formed. Although the overseas part of the scholarship was discontinued, I was surprised, very proud and honoured to have been asked by MSNZ, and the trustees, to become a Trustee of the Academy. This is a responsibility I enjoy greatly and one I take seriously.

Towards the end of 2004 I heard talk about the formation of a new series in New Zealand to be called The Toyota Racing Series. I thought this was a fantastic innovation for single-seater racing in our country. Proper wings-and-slicks race-cars had not raced on New Zealand circuits or held their own stand-alone championships since the days of Formula Atlantic/Pacific. We were in danger of losing an opportunity for our younger drivers to cut their teeth on this kind of event before heading overseas to compete with more experienced European or American drivers.

It occurred to me the potential new racing series was going to fill a gap that was desperately needed; and more importantly, with modern, safe, state-of-the-art, wings-and-slicks cars that were powerful, and above all, totally relevant when it came to gaining international racing experience in top-notch cars.

Having made up my mind this was a cracking idea, I soon found out who was looking after the practical side of things. It was Barrie Thomlinson, along with Steve Boyce, the Motorsport Manager of Toyota New Zealand. I offered them my congratulations on their efforts in trying to get such a series up and running.

Toyota New Zealand had made a major long-term commitment to initiate and support this series and I thought their actions were absolutely fantastic. And I told them so. It looked to me that the future of single-seater racing in New Zealand was bright and I couldn't be happier, as I was developing a keen interest in watching the careers of our young drivers and wondering just how I could contribute.

Soon after our first conversation, Barrie called me and asked if I wanted to be part of the Toyota Racing Series in a kind of ambassadorial role. Without hesitation I said I'd be delighted. To be part of the most exciting new development in New Zealand motorsport for decades was an opportunity I simply could not turn down.

Since the first season of TRS in 2005 it hasn't disappointed. It remains the premier single-seater series in New Zealand, if not in Australasia, and has helped the careers of so many of our up-and-coming talents. The winner of the first-ever TRS race, Brendon Hartley, is now a Formula One reserve driver for Red Bull Racing; Firestone Indy Lights series winner Wade Cunningham, European series driver Chris van der Drift, V8 Supercar and A1GP driver Daniel Gaunt, A1GP driver Earl Bamber and V8 Supercar driver Shane van Gisbergen are but a few to make the move to international racing.

The series now attracts overseas drivers on a regular basis and is the class for which most of New Zealand's most prestigious racing trophies are contested — the New Zealand Motor Cup, the New Zealand Grand Prix and the Chris Amon Trophy. The Toyota Racing Series has the biggest prize fund in the history of New Zealand motorsport and is capped with a test drive in Europe.

At the time of writing, tempting the young talent in 2010 to take part in the TRS is more than $100,000 in cash prizes, including $10,000 to the series champion, who also wins a test drive at the World Series by Renault post-season collective test, tentatively scheduled for October 2010. This new incentive will provide a unique opportunity for the 2010 TRS champion to test his skills against other talented rookies from around the world participating at this European Renault 2.0 test.

In the spirit of the 'Driver to Europe' prize of yesteryear, this latest TRS initiative includes return airfares and accommodation during the European test. Furthermore, as part of the package negotiated with Renault, the 2010 Toyota Racing Series is now exempt from the test ban that has previously restricted Renault Eurocup drivers from competing in New Zealand.

It's been a pleasure to be involved in the series. I was also honoured to be the recipient of the MotorSport New Zealand Personality of the Year award in 2006 and the Motor Industry Association Contribution to Industry award in 2007. I was truly at home.